How to Play Philosophy

How to Play Philosophy

Michael Picard

HAMILTON BOOKS
an imprint of
ROWMAN & LITTLEFIELD
Lanham • Boulder • New York • London

Published by Hamilton Books
An imprint of The Rowman & Littlefield Publishing Group, Inc.
4501 Forbes Boulevard, Suite 200, Lanham, Maryland 20706
www.rowman.com

86-90 Paul Street, London EC2A 4NE, United Kingdom

All figures provided by the author unless otherwise stated.

British Library Cataloguing in Publication Information Available

Library of Congress Cataloging-in-Publication Data

Names: Picard, Michael, 1963– author.
Title: How to play philosophy / Michael Picard.
Description: Lanham : Hamilton Books, an imprint of Rowman & Littlefield, [2022] | Includes bibliographical references and index. | Summary: "How to Play Philosophy is a series of lyrical, creative essays that explore timeless and timely ideas about who we are and how we live. MIT-trained philosopher Michael Picard shares ideas of numerous philosophers from conflicting traditions and builds an intellectual background to enable readers to draw their own conclusions"—Provided by publisher.
Identifiers: LCCN 2021056011 (print) | LCCN 2021056012 (ebook) | ISBN 9780761873068 (paperback) | ISBN 9780761873075 (epub)
Subjects: LCSH: Philosophy. | LCGFT: Essays.
Classification: LCC B21.P64 2022 (print) | LCC B21 (ebook) | DDC 100—dc23/eng/20220110
LC record available at https://lccn.loc.gov/2021056011
LC ebook record available at https://lccn.loc.gov/2021056012

™ The paper used in this publication meets the minimum requirements of American National Standard for Information Sciences—Permanence of Paper for Printed Library Materials, ANSI/NISO Z39.48-1992.

To
Joseph George John Robert Picard (1962–2016),
who called for it.

Contents

List of Illustrations

FIGURES

TABLE

Acknowledgments

Thanks are due to many. Above all, Douglas College has supported me over several years in writing this book, notably by providing a halftime education leave during 2019 and 2020 to complete the book, but also for awarding me with a Research and Scholarly Activity Travel Fund Grant to meet publication costs. Douglas also funded my travel to the Twenty-Third World Congress of Philosophy in Athens, Greece, in 2013, where I read the essay on Integrity, as well as to the Fifteenth International Conference on Philosophical Practice in Mexico City in 2018, where I first presented the background theory for Philosophy Sports.

For even longer, Yosef Wosk, has been a constant support in my scholarly endeavors; without him this book would not exist. Jesse Finkelstein of Page Two Strategies Inc. was a tremendous help in a wholesale rethinking of the book, which resulted in its present form. Zoe Grams of ZG Stories was also part of those fruitful discussions, and is a force behind the book. Lydia Amir played a crucial role in getting the manuscript to publication.

Gretchen Goertz, scholarly communications librarian at Douglas College, was very persistent help, and came through on innumerable occasions during final revisions.

I must also thank Brooke Bures and Julie E. Kirsch of Rowman & Littlefield for taking on this project. Thanks to Meguido Zola for meta-coaching, and for seeing something in me.

It is a pleasure to thank Gretchen Carlson, who was my first proofreader, back when these essays were first written for Café Philosophy audience, and also to Jan Rennie, who later proofread a large sample. Sam Brawand of Brawand Consulting, who proofread the manuscript, was a pleasure to work with.

Thank you to Mark W. Clarkson, whom I still think of as my first reader, to Lital Rosenfeld who also met with me several times to review drafts, and to Eve Norton who read some chapters and provided copious feedback.

Thanks to Philosophy Documentation Center for permission to reprint a revised version of my "Integrity: A Philosophical Exploration" (2018), and to Yosef Wosk and Simon Fraser University for permission to use parts of an early version of "Mythology," which appeared in an *SFU Philosophers' Café* circular.

This book was written in Canada on unceded land. Beyond reconciliation, we need restoration.

Introduction

The opening moves are an invitation, an explanation, and a justification of sorts for the book.

COME INTO PLAY

Philosophy can transform your life—not my philosophy, but yours. The only philosophy that can save you is your own. But when misinformation is the norm, and spin is the news of the day, where is the air needed to breathe the honest spirit of inquiry? How can one wrestle free of the mind-numbing blather, crossed purposes, and alienated silos that public discourse has become?

How to Play Philosophy is a joyful and somber collection of philosophical play written for the thinking public and for public thinking. Written for a lay audience, the book breaks down preconceptions and builds up an intellectual background, referencing numerous philosophers from conflicting traditions, with the aim of enabling deeper public conversations. The Introduction contains an account of the origins of Café Philosophy, the public participatory philosophy events for which these essays were originally written, and introduces its successor, Philosophy Sports, notably the board-game, "Tug of Logic."[1]

The author, who also wrote *This is Not a Book*, is an MIT-educated philosopher and philosopher practitioner living in Vancouver, Canada.

CAFÉ PHILOSOPHY AS PLAYGROUND: ON THE ORIGIN OF THESE ESSAYS

How to Play Philosophy is a collection of essays and other texts prepared for a common purpose: to prepare readers to participate in public dialogues in philosophy. The topics had all been chosen for discussion by participants at prior meetings; topics were, in short, crowd-sourced, and can perhaps not unreasonably be taken to be philosophical ideas of particular interest to the public. These are concepts people are curious about. No theme unites the topics, only this common purpose and the general preference it indicates.

That purpose, again, was to prepare members of the public to philosophize together. The public participatory philosophy events, known as Café Philosophy, took place in Victoria, British Columbia, Canada, and continued weekly for over twelve years, extending to over 540 sessions.[2] Participation presumed no formal background in philosophy, so the essays were written with the same presumption. Thus readers are assumed to be innocent of any philosophical tradition, nor was it my *primary* aim to advance my own considered opinions, steeped as they are in my long and ever incomplete philosophical education. I wanted nevertheless to take what knowledge and expertise I may have and make it useful to the public, which I could not sufficiently do during the dialogues themselves, being expected not to lecture but to facilitate and to animate the conversation. I will also say the need for such assistance was, at times, achingly manifest, as naive attempts at philosophy often are. The point of such gatherings ought, in part, to be the development of logical skill, but the first attempts to display it are seldom exemplary of that much needed yet very personal capacity. The point of the essays, then, was to anticipate possible confusions, to head off error, to counter one-sidedness, to elucidate ambiguity, and broadly, to correct and to inform the public mind before it opened its mouth and itself committed these faults of logic.

Far be it from me to complain about popular ignorance. I leave that to distinguished colleagues. But I cannot deny witnessing it up close. Indeed, colleagues questioned, silently and to my face, why any self-respecting philosopher would desire *for philosophical reasons* to engage the public in philosophy. How can you learn a high-wire intellectual act from a clutch of conceptual klutzes? Since the ignorant and untrained are incapable of being transported to the sublime heights of philosophical speculation, the only possible motive would be *for their sake*, to train and to improve them, to initiate the masses into philosophy. But this too seems like a futile effort. The naive can indeed be trained and made into philosophers, but for that a rigorous education of years is needed, not weekly fun-clubs discussing a hodgepodge of topics. Of the first 500 sessions of Café Philosophy, I can count on one hand the number of academic philosophers who attended even one time. I was philosophizing in the wilderness, and it might have been with wildebeests, as far as local academic colleagues were concerned. Fellow travelers the world over kept in touch regarding their own efforts to instigate street-level philosophy, which others had begun well before I started; I do not wish to portray myself as first out of the gates, or a sole pioneer. I had among philosophers some academic supporters, but they were few and far between, and almost never academic *philosophers*. By and large, the philosophy professors I spoke to thought the entire attempt to philosophize with an unprepared public was naive, futile, and boring, if not benighted.

I was undeterred. I persevered in the face of an unlearning mass. Others before me who had also peddled philosophy in a café wrote essays *after* the discussions, in order to record, report, capture, and praise the discussions, and to justify their irregular endeavor (originally Marc Sautet, in *Un Café pour Socrates*, but also Christopher Phillips in *Socrates Cafe*).[3] I took a different approach. I tried to stimulate participants' thinking by sending out provocative essays in advance. Now to do that without being didactic or pedantic, with the aim of encouraging people to attend, it was essential to leave main controversies open, to invite and to allow all sides into the debate, even highlighting those less likely, disadvantaged, unpopular perspectives that otherwise might get no airing in the event. Apparent sensibleness of ideas was therefore not the first criterion of inclusion in an essay, so that by my example diverse opinions would be emboldened to raise their voice in the moment. The essays were written, not to settle belief upon the presumed most rational conclusion, but to give readers options for belief, to leave room for thought. I wanted to provide (not final but) second thoughts on subjects, to push people beyond first impressions prior to the event, so that public reflection did not sink to superficial self-display.

It is crucial to appreciate the origins of these essays, certainly unusual as philosophy writing, to grasp their spirit. As noted, they were written in advance of participatory philosophy dialogues to prepare participants to get the most out of the sessions. It might help to know something more about the original audience, as in many ways readers of this book are that same audience writ large. But when one asks the question, *Who are the sort of people who came out in a café to philosophize with others?*, one is soon disturbed again by that critical question, dismissive of the entire enterprise, posed so often by my academic colleagues: *why would anyone who had climbed so high in the ivory tower bother to stoop so low to the street to philosophize?* In short, why would a philosopher even want to philosophize with those who know so little philosophy? This intellectual challenge to that public project is also a challenge to this book. It deserves an answer.

But lest critique crowds out thought, let us look first at the practical question more closely. How, after all, does one philosophize with a roomful of minds largely innocent of philosophy? Of course, academic philosophers know well how to introduce their subject to a roomful of fresh, young impressionable minds. But the typical crowd at Café Philosophy is not so fresh, young, or impressionable. By and large, participants are fully adult, and even trend senior. Chances are, there are zero professional philosophers beside myself in the house. Yet most present are not wholly innocent of philosophy either, but have perhaps years ago taken a course or two in philosophy, or sought out the texts of some particular philosopher or philosophy that has attracted them; or they have exposed themselves to the philosophical depths of their own profession. Backgrounds in philosophy comparable to these yield little in the way of what academic philosophers prize and praise in budding philosophical minds. Yet the audience is at once more sophisticated than the average first-year student, considerably bolder, but just about as lax in adhering to strict semantic distinctions, to rigorous forms of inference, or in balancing masses of contrary evidence.

It would seem to follow that a typical Café Philosophy audience should be at least as interesting to philosophize with as a first-year undergraduate class of comparable size usually is, and, however surprising, I found this to be the case overall. This puts the critical question in a different light, since that challenge has always been framed snidely, suggesting that it is a waste of time to philosophize thus with the unwashed masses. One would do well to reject the elitist assumption that hides behind this critique of Café Philosophy *as philosophy*, but that is not my concern here. In my experience, academic philosophers exhibited hostility to Café Philosophy, rather than embracing it as a form of outreach to the public. There is a doubt that philosophy is even what happens at these events. This is a question I have addressed elsewhere,[4] and I raise it here not to reply to it (let my book itself be the reply), but because these features of the original audience go a long way to explaining the unusual character of these essays as philosophy.

With little to no academic background in philosophy, and no will to acquire one, participants did not need a systematic history of philosophical treatments of our dialogue topic; still less did they need my own opinions (though they inevitably got that, since I was doing the writing). Nor was it vital that I always advance a thesis in the writing, as long as I left readers with a broader and deeper approach to the topic. Instead, it was more important in this context to present conflicting views from a seemingly impartial standpoint, so that participants could make up their own minds. What philosophers may see here as a curious reluctance to take a stand on issues under consideration, a refusal to take sides, and an insistence on hearing out different opinions even when matters seem settled, is really a response to the needs of the event. I dance over questions so as to reveal their depths, but rarely put my foot down. I play the teacher who prods and questions, not the one who deduces or dictates from on high. In effect, I here extend the impartial facilitator role into the authorial voice, to open up the possibilities of dialogue, not to close them by settling on the most rational position. Thus, some logical defects in the essays are deliberate attempts to provoke the reaction of independent thought, and reduce the perceived reliability of the author as authority.

That said, it was never my aim to shy away from provocative claims if I felt they were substantive and defensible, nor did I avoid conveying a decided attitude, sometimes only partly hidden behind a mask of neutrality, when doing so seemed more effective at provoking the search for truth in readers. This leads to another aspect of the present writing that is not typical of the sort of philosophy I was educated to produce. I play freely and frequently with authorial voice—I mask it, pluralize it, fictionalize it, and fake it, at times imitating the impostor to reveal the imposter's tricks. There is much play here, and much at play—some will say too much—but this again arises from the needs of the public reflection the essays are intended to stimulate. Those events too were fun, filled with jokes, puns, and play voices; and not only mine, but also those of many others who participated too. Once, in an early Café Philosophy session on humor, a participant flashed anger at the overly-intellectual sort of humor being discussed and left, only to pretend on the way out to slip on a banana peel. The person (a regular) actually left, but he had faked the anger, and made a nice point in exit. I extended such playfulness into the essays, which gradually became an entertainment unto themselves. Enjoy.

Although the essays or other writings sent out each week were meant to prepare readers to participate in public philosophy, I never had the luxury to assume that all or even most of the participants would actually read them. Too often I sent them out impossibly late. Frequently new people would show up at the event who had had no chance to read the essay. Some who attended regularly did not want to be on the email list, others on principle would not read the essays I sent out until later. Thus the essays were never presented as, nor ever became, the focus of the discussions, though a few regulars referred to them on occasion and had clearly used them as intended. The essays would no doubt read quite differently if I had written them to be the focal point of the dialogue. I might then have felt pressure to formulate straight up arguments for or against positions, that could then be evaluated in discussion. In most philosophy classes that I have ever attended, the unit of thought was the argument, and its construction, inspection, and ultimately acceptance or rejection was the name of the game. Exactly this is expected in all the leading journals of philosophy in the analytic tradition. To be sure, there is much argument going on in the following pages; but purists will be appalled at what else they find (the puns, the paradoxes, the personas). I take no joy in appalling those I admire, and fear I can expect little sympathy from that quarter. But for all the rest, including the many readers of my previous books,[5] they will, I hope, find here a fun-filled but ultimately serious and helpful plunge into the deeper meanings of contemporary life.

Other features of the writing flow from its original audience. While it was never the aim of participants or the events to teach people the history of philosophy, the ideas of, or similar to those of, the great philosophical traditions inevitably came up. Sometimes participants were unaware of the precedents of their words, and it seemed important to bring out the fact that long-hallowed traditions and eminent minds had trodden the terrain we now moved over. This insertion of historical precedent must be done gingerly, since participants can feel upstaged to discover that Aristotle had already said that. Thus, it fell to the essays to give a sense of such traditions, especially opposing traditions with alternate takes on the concept in question. I would have to write without relying on the familiarity of my readers with the great names of philosophy or the technical vocabularies associated with each. Yet I needed to give some sense of the depth and complexity of the philosophical traditions in regard to the chosen topic. While not all essays in this book attempt to do so, many do.

The theme of self-deception runs through many essays in the book. Other popular illusions, cognitive biases, and common philosophical confusions are exposed in passing, so that the reader is constantly warned away from common pitfalls and fallacious traps of reasoning. For instance, the insipid moral relativism on every pre-reflective tongue today is exposed and converted into a sensible pluralism and objective relativism. Crude forms of both theism and atheism come under attack, directly and indirectly, in several passages, but the aim is always to guide readers to richer and more interesting forms of either, as they see fit. Although sides are often taken, and the author's voice and story are evident on most pages, the aim is to deepen the reader's understanding of topics treated, not to maximize author-reader agreement. The façade of neutrality is often maintained with mask partly pulled down.

One minor stylistic point. The essays were occasional, in that they served the needs of the occasion, the Café Philosophy event. As such they were meant to stimulate the public to partake in philosophy. Many essays therefore end with an invitation to participate. I decided to modify but retain these to keep alive the spirit of participation, and to leave in closing the open questions with readers, to carry on, on their own or at a nearby café.

PHILOSOPHY AT PLAY: ORDINARY LANGUAGE AS HOLIDAY

This book strictly follows the advice of that illustrious enigma of a philosopher, Ludwig Wittgenstein (1889–1951): "Never stay up on the barren heights of cleverness, but come down into the green valleys of silliness."[6]

Despite the play that permeates *How to Play Philosophy*, a serious theoretical motivation lies behind its Socratic ambitions. Although expressed in passing in various essays, it might be useful here to briefly explain this motivation, which stems in part from the theory of linguistic meaning originated by Wittgenstein. Wittgenstein revolted from earlier theories of language (to some extent, even his own) by conceiving of "meaning as use."[7] The meaning of a word is not the image or other associations that arise in your mind when you hear it; that is not even what it means *to you*. Meaning is nothing so fleeting or subjective. Meaning is the use that words are put to, and use takes place in a social space and within a historical context. One implication of Wittgenstein's theory that linguistic meaning is use is that meaning is not in the head, not private and subjective, but social, shared, and objective. As a consequence, most words can be seen to be multiply ambiguous, objectively possessing multiple and possibly-inconsistent meanings (like numbered sub-entries in a dictionary definition, but not so ordered). At Café Philosophy, participants often heard people trying to summarize a controversy by saying, "for me the word means X, but for you the word means Y." This seemed to be very satisfying, but in many cases, both X and Y were objective meanings of the words that both parties shared. Their apparent difference came from unwarranted emphasis, not any objective feature denied by the other. One says, "for me zebras are black with white stripes"; another says, "but for me zebras are white with black stripes." If they leave it there, they both miss the objective duality that zebras are striped black and white. One cannot found a philosophy on a narrow reading of the dictionary, yet people do.

Wittgenstein famously wrote that "philosophical problems arise when language *goes on holiday*."[8] He meant that we befuddle ourselves when we stray in our use of words, insisting for example on using words in certain ways but not in others, or in imaginatively novel ways, or in old ways in novel contexts. We disrespect the rules of language games. I found that when people came out to Café Philosophy, it was as if their language went on holiday. They recreated and played with words, not always fairly or by the rules. Not the great historical philosophers only, but everyday people, today philosophize by using words in shockingly novel ways, or insisting that they always be used in certain recognized or innovative ways, despite other shared uses objectively existing. As if clarity could be won by turning a blind eye to ambiguity! Like the great philosophers Wittgenstein was criticizing, everyday people often let language run away with them. In response, I wrote essays in advance to expose all the tricks, to beat people to their flights of verbal fancy, revealing the unwitting ruse. To that end, my own language took flights into paradox, irony, satire, personification, and various other rhetorical devices that could be used to jolt people from the all-too-easy paths onto which they had strayed. Expect neural short-circuits and semantic culture-jamming Hijinx ensue.

Wittgenstein also called for a kind of therapy to clear up philosophical missteps. In effect, *How to Play Philosophy* takes on a therapeutic aim: to exorcise the semantic demons and misconceptions of ordinary people wanting to approach philosophy. But this has nothing to do with overcoming an illness. "Philosophy is a battle against the bewitchment of our intelligence by means of language."[9]

My aim in this book, underneath all the play, was to represent topic-relevant historical philosophers so that they too could have a say in our public thinking like those weekly confabs. But to clear the way for that, I often took away all the low-hanging fruit, exploiting and exploding all of the ready clichés that I knew people's minds would rush to, requiring them thereby to reach a little higher to grasp the fruit. For instance, writing on Beauty, I personify her. She never actually appears in the piece, which is instead narrated by her butler, who points out how hurtful clichés about beauty can be to her: in the eye of the beholder, skin-deep, and so on. Such clichés are typically cited to end a conversation, not to begin one; but thus inverted, they give a pleasant jolt to reconsider—or rather to consider for the first time—what common sense has long taken for granted. The lists of incompatible definitions in some entries are meant to have the same sort of result. Paradox has an enlivening effect, like an affectionate slap on the cheek. An earlier reviewer, Luisa de Paula, noted, "paradox is the real engine of Picard's philosophical writing."[10]

Ever the teacher, I want to provide readers with a taste of the diverse wealth of ideas that the various traditions of philosophy contain. Yet I do not want to induct them into this or that tradition, so I only reluctantly take sides or place my authorial authority behind any one theory. Instead, having cleared the ground, I lay out options for readers, and invite them to think for themselves. Many essays end with an injunction to philosophize beyond the essays, urging readers to seek out philosophy and think for themselves, together with other seekers.

PHILOSOPHY SPORTS: A NEW WAY TO PLAY CAFÉ PHILOSOPHY

After twelve years of Café Philosophy, and over 540 sessions, the old idea needed some new energy. I quit Café Philosophy under the fortunate pretext that I had a new job in a new city. Although I continued to facilitate public participatory philosophy under the aegis of Simon Fraser University's (SFU) award-winning Philosophers' Café Program,[11] I was looking for a new way.

I published a rather searing critique of my own practice, and of what little I had observed at SFU, and came up with a list of desirable changes, influenced by a social theory of reasoning worked out in charming detail by Anthony Simon Laden.[12] To go beyond critique, I also drew up a list of nine guidelines for facilitators, using Laden's theoretical language, in service of ensuring a reasoned conversation.

Here I would like to summarize—in the briefest possible way—the growing problems at the end of Café Philosophy, as well as the guidelines that I came up with much later to address those problems. But my aim in doing so is to motivate and introduce a new form of public participatory philosophy, embodying these guidelines, that I call *Philosophy Sports*.

First the problems. In the end, the problems at Café Philosophy in Victoria were many, but perhaps the main one was that friendliness had over-swamped critical thinking. It was a case of too much of a good thing. It was mission-critical to maintain warm hospitality at the events, to present a welcoming front. The community aspect of the event came to flourish in later years, and each week, when sessions ended, they would transform into after-parties (dubbed the *Après Café*), which took place nearby at a prominent participant's private residence. These confabs were fun, and lent to the public event an intimacy and vitality that it would not otherwise have had. But this essential positive element came to drown out the equally essential *negative* voice of critical thought. Without that voice, we could not even hear each other. Regulars knew what to expect of regulars the moment the microphone was handed to one of them to speak. Once their mouth opened, everybody else's ears closed. Those who came to hear themselves did not mind. At other times, people took up positions not earnestly, but merely for show or only to provoke. We indulged the problem speakers rather than confronting the logical or other problems in their thought. Newcomers could smell the stagnation. The fires I set under people's seats, and the reform projects I launched, produced no results. I was stuck.

Fast forward a few years, after I had time to reflect and frame a self-critique, I drew up guidelines that were eventually published.[13] In summary, the guidelines called for facilitated encounters among participants seeking to articulate positions they are prepared to stand behind, yet willing to place before others to be subject to their scrutiny, thus becoming vulnerable to their objections, with other participants who are doing the same. In Laden's terms, position statements need to be taken as invitations to others to accept (that is, they need to risk rejection), while the grounds for them, as well as any objections to them, need to be based upon "we-reasons," rather than idiosyncratic opinion. Such reasoned dialogues were to be explorations of this unknown "we" present in the room. Concern for that "we" was to be managed (by the facilitator, in my guidelines) through regular checking in with others regarding the intelligibility of each speaker's claims, and returning to each speaker to allow for explicit "attunement" and "adjustments." The facilitator is to explicitly aim at constructing a "shared space of reasons," but must manage participant vulnerability while maintaining a welcoming climate for the public.

Once my critique and guidelines were published, I promptly forgot about them. But with the help and encouragement of fellow facilitators (Randall MacKinnon and Charles M. Marxer), I developed a new idea. The basic idea behind Philosophy Sports is to exploit the immediately-recognizable framework of a game, joined in the spirit of fair play, to re-introduce into the casual café context the semblance of shared or objective logical standards. Fallacious arguments may be understood as unfair play, and ruled out. Those with similar opinions can collaborate, those with different opinions compete to build an argument satisfactory to all (most). In the inception, technology was key to displaying and to revising, in real time, the logical structure of the argument established so far in the game. People would initially take sides by voting on a controversial main claim, but then vote in real-time facilitated Bouts of Logical Scrimmage on proposed premises. A large shared monitor would show the argument under construction so that all could see; and it would be sent to participants phones as well, which they use to vote. In building an argument on common ground, nobody can rely on premises unless they are collectively established by vote. The technology allows for the exact wording of the premise under discussion (the Reason-in-Play) to be altered, and the resulting vote swings, fed back to all in real-time, can be dramatic. An html version of the first game now exists and is undergoing further development.

But as proof of concept, I created a technology-free version, the first Philosophy Sport, called Tug of Logic. Tug of Logic is a board-game in which players place their game-piece in different areas to reveal their opinions (votes) on premises put forward. The logical complexity of issues is spread out over the structure and the duration of an interactive game, which again consists in a series of Bouts of Logical Scrimmage. Only those premises that are established in these Bouts are elevated to a common ground, and both sides of the main issue (like shifting opposing teams on opposite sides of the board) try to garner sufficient all-around support for the best reasons (organized into logical arguments) that they can come up with to win support for their view. Players quickly learn whether their deepest value premises are or are not accepted by their opponents. Sometimes they discover that some of their most cherished reasons are easily endorsed by their opponents, who nevertheless do not see them as decisive, as sufficient reason to change sides on the main issue. This may be due to common values but divergent priorities, which the game soon reveals. Other reasons that they regard as conclusive may be rejected out of hand by opponents. Shifting alliances emerge and, to get anywhere, players learn to get inventive in the search to articulate common ground.

I presented the basic idea of Philosophy Sports at the Fifteenth International Conference on Philosophical Practice (ICPP) in Mexico City, in 2018. The fullest treatment so far is to be found in a chapter of *Cafe Conversations*.[14]

Tug of Logic was played by almost one hundred public high school students from across Canada at the Canadian Museum for Human Rights as part of the first national Canadian High School Ethics Bowl,[15] which took place April 24 to 25, 2019. The Ethics Bowl is organized annually by the Manitoba Association for Rights and Liberties,[16] along with numerous partners.

Tug of Logic is *do-it-yourselves* philosophy. Complete game instructions for Tug of Logic, along with a game-size board (pdf file) on which to play the game, are available at no cost at www.philosophy-sports.com.

Philosophy is a team sport. You do not need opposing teams, or more than one. But you need another person who is game to play. Even a solo one faces imaginary opponents, our very own interpretations of ancient and living philosophers, who seem to leap from their pages to extol, interact, or contradict us. The contest of ideas is the battlefield of truth, only this war of words has no victims, only victories and failures, houses of cards that stand and then do not stand. This book is not presented to the public as the one or only way to play philosophy, as if there were some fixed set of steps or rules to apply blindly. The emphasis in the title is not any narrow sense of how philosophy should and should not be conducted. The emphasis is on the playfulness, on the open interaction with others who do not share your view or your worldview, without striving for their overthrow and refutation. As part of a learning process, one may try on a philosophy as one fits oneself into a costume. Philosophy in its final stages, when it arrives at its conclusion, may run as gravely as one likes; but when it starts out, it needs to play with ideas, like trying on new shoes, pacing and play walking, before committing to a long journey wearing them.

NOTES

1. For more information on this game, see a description and event poster, Michael Picard, "Tug of Logic: A Competitive Board Game for Collaborative Reasoning," *University of British Columbia, Vancouver Campus*, May 31, 2019, https://ecps.educ.ubc.ca/tug-of-logic-a-competitive-board-game-for-collaborative-reasoning/ (accessed September 16, 2021).

2. An account of the long-running event, its problems, and some solutions is included in *Cafe Conversations: Democracy and Dialogue in Public Spaces*, ed.

Michael Picard (Vancouver, BC: Anvil, c. 2022), essay "Philosophy Sports as the Next Café Philosophy." The first book (in English) to take up the theoretical underpinnings of this public participatory philosophical practice, this edited collection of reports, critiques, and theoretical inquiries features the work of café philosophy animators from all over the world.

3. See Marc Sautet, *Un café pour Socrate: Comment la philosophie peut nous aider à comprendre le monde d'aujourdh'hui* [*A Cafe for Socrates: How Philosophy can help us understand today's world*] (Paris: Robert Laffont, 1995); Christopher Phillips, *Socrates Café: A Fresh Taste of Philosophy* (New York: W. W. Norton, 2001). The relevant portions of Sautet's book are translated in *Cafe Conversations: Democracy and Dialogue in Public Spaces*, edited by Michael Picard (Vancouver, BC: Anvil Press, forthcoming). See also a chapter in that book by Christopher Phillips, "What Happens at Socrates Café," where Phillips recounts some of the philosophical influences on his public participatory philosophical practice.

4. Michael Picard, "But Is It Philosophy? Café Philosophy and the Social Coordination of Inquiry," in *Practicing Philosophy*, ed. Aleksander Fatić and Lydia Amir (Newcastle upon Tyne, UK: Cambridge Scholars Publishing, 2015), 163–81. Presented at Thirteenth International Conference on Philosophical Practice, Belgrade, Serbia. August, 2014; repr. in *Café Conversations*, ed. Picard (2022).

5. Michael Picard, *Philosophy: Adventures in Thought and Reasoning* (New York: Metro, 2012). Revised edition of *This Is Not a Book: Adventures in Popular Philosophy* (London: Quid, 2007).

6. Ludwig Wittgenstein, *Culture and Value*, ed. G. H. von Wright and Heikki Nyman, trans. By Peter Winch (Chicago: University of Chicago Press), 76e.

7. Ludwig Wittgenstein, *Philosophical Investigations*, Trans. by G. E. M. Anscombe. (Oxford: Basil Blackwell, 1958), pt. 1, no. 58.

8. Wittgenstein, *Philosophical Investigations*, pt. 1, no. 38; emphasis in the original.

9. Wittgenstein, *Philosophical Investigations*, pt. 1, no. 109.

10. Luisa de Paula, Review of *Philosophy A-Z. Essays for Cafe Philosophy*, by Michael Picard, *Philosophical Practice: Journal of the APPA* 10, no. 2 (July 2015): 1611, https://appa.edu/product/philosophical-practice-volume-10-2-july-2015-printed-version/ (accessed September 11, 2021).

11. See Yosek Wosk, "Simon Fraser University's Philosophers' Café: A Synoptic History," in *Cafe Conversations: Democracy and Dialogue in Public Spaces*, ed. Michael Picard (Vancouver, BC: Anvil, 2022).

12. Anthony Simon Laden, *Reasoning: A Social Picture* (Oxford: Oxford University Press, 2012).

13. Picard, "But Is It Philosophy?" 163–81.

14. Picard, "Philosophy Sports as the Next Café Philosophy."

15. Visit Canadian High School Ethics Bowl (last updated 2021) online at https://www.ethicsbowl.ca/ (accessed September 12, 2021).

16. Visit Manitoba Association for Rights and Liberties (last updated 2021) online at http://www.marl.mb.ca/ (accessed September 12, 2021).

Chapter 1

Playtime

It is said philosophy was born in opposition to myth, reason from disbelief in story. The development of philosophy would then be the long overcoming of the *just so*, the vanquishing of myth by proof. But myth-killing and myth-telling also go together. Even Plato—who burned the poems of his youth and cast out the intemperate poets from his fabled *polis*—even that honest son of Apollo *told tall tales.* He went so far as to counsel us sometimes to break from contemplating eternal matters, and amuse ourselves with mythical discourse about the world of becoming in "measured and reasonable play."[1] For the noblest and best thing about us, he said, is that we are "a toy for God." And therefore: "All of us, . . . men and women alike, must fall in with our role and spend life in making our *play* as perfect as possible."[2]

Let the play begin!

MYTHOLOGY

Mythology. This dusty-closet discipline somehow grew flowers. Imagine collecting and cataloging false beliefs and dead religions from every age and culture, ancient or recent. One would have to master long silent tongues, learn the names of defunct deities, argue tediously over minutia, and endlessly bore loved ones. Still, emerging from such studies are clarion narratives that have taught the world. Emerging from such studies . . . are some good old yarns.[3]

To get some perspective on this exciting mess of a topic, and to begin to discern historical chaff from perennial wheat, I suggest that we examine some popular misconceptions about myths, in the form of a list of the top four myths about myth. Of course, I shall employ my signature method of scorning consistency, allying myself with opposites, fighting overstatement with overstatement, and defusing by wit. Do not try too closely to understand. Just take it in like a good story.

The first myth about myths is that myths are not facts. Are myths in their day not taken for fact? Much like so many *common-sense revolutions* that sweep electoral politics every so often, but which later dwindle into dithering and deficits, the solid fact of today is the bygone ideology of tomorrow. What is taken as fact today is liable to be rejected in the future in light of the evidence and interests then prevailing. In that sense, myth is on a par with fact; the only difference is that we here today believe in facts, and all those other types, times, and tribes believe in myths. Also, if I may conduct my conflation from the opposite end, today fact has become the prevailing myth. Obedience to fact is the preferred epistemic stance, a kind of calling card among the *cognoscenti* (the *well-to-know*, who are the *well-to-do* among the knowing). A perfunctory gesture toward truth, deference to fact is now on its way to becoming an empty formality, a rhetorical flourish.

A second myth: myths are false beliefs. It would be more correct to say that a believed myth is a false belief. The point, however, is that myths are not universally there for the believing. It is wrong to equate myth with primitive belief, as antiquated and inadequate science, as the first failed attempts to know what we today know for fact. Many myths are radically misunderstood by taking them as hypotheses tendered without an understanding of scientific control. For instance, there is a difference between explanation and entertainment. It is sometimes considered that primitive minds (say, the Greeks before philosophy) were too ignorant to understand a rational account (*logos*) of the world, and so relied in their understanding on hand-me-down stories (*mythos*). But it strains credulity to picture even these primitive minds (let alone the Greeks after two centuries of philosophy) nodding along to the hypothesis that, say, lightening is the thunderbolt of Zeus, or the sun rides a chariot across the sky, innocently lapping up such tales like wide-eyed toddlers at story-time. We don primitive blinders ourselves when we likewise think that those ancient Indian *rishis* [seers[4]], competing for immortality, individually praised dawn, dawn's first light, fire, and the sun, and personified each without ever realizing that personification is their own poetic artifice. If we further claim that this is a discovery that will require centuries, and even the very birth of Indian philosophy, before it is made, then we merely blindly transfer the blinders we are wearing to philosophy itself.[5]

If the false belief that myth is false belief is handed down to you, refuse to accept it. The past was not trying but failing to attain the objectivity we enjoy today. Without science, you do not automatically think any story being retold must be the science you are missing, or gospel and God's own truth. Having no science, people share with lovers of fact the power of entertainment.

Story is story. Song is song. And myth is not proto-science for the specially credulous.

Myths are lies. This third myth is only a half-truth. No doubt myths have often been created or relied upon to prop up the status quo and other dictators, to govern the masses religiously or politically, and to move product; for what else does raw power have to recommend it? Of course, the truths that swaddle the lie serve similar rude ends. At times, conversely, the lie swaddles the truth. Plato licensed a political lie,[6] and he censured the poets and myth-makers, excluding them from his imaginary ideal city unless they would all sing in his not-yet-well-tempered scale. The move stems from a concession that myth is indispensable to rule, since dialectical reason can not establish the moral truth, which may yet be grasped with a sort of mock-intellectual intuition. But if the moral truth he thought essential to good government could not be established dialectically or with logical rigor, certain purpose-built symbolic stories could rally society in place of the old and vulgar myths told by ancient poets and featuring the dishonorable antics of the gods. And if these new coded-truths were not Truth as intuitive reason or geometric demonstration provide, they were at least *probable* (in the old sense of "approvable") since they were consonant with, or like unto the truth: in a word, *verisimilar*. Thus Plato's adulation of truth contains a wink to the lie, to the approximate, to the *good* story. Is a lie with a wink still a lie? Such myths are told, not to be taken in whole, or not at least by those in the know, but with added layers of meaning beyond the word (*logos*) that yet serve the truth. Such myths, since they are not to be believed wholesale, are not simply lies, nor indeed myths of the hand-me-down sort. Self-consciously created, they yet reflect no selfish will to deceive, nor yet a mere will to entertain, but nurture and advance a will *to entertain the truth*. However, comparing them to an intimate relationship without sex, we may call them Platonic Lies.

Myths are dreams. This fourth myth is sacred. But I am weary of my old knowledge. This closet mythologist wants to bust an idol.

There is a theory out there that myth is equivalent to dream.[7] Both reflect the same sorts of mental processes, which include imagination, emotion, healing, and libidinal or archetypal eruptions. The principles of interpretation of both dream and myth are thus presumed to be the same, perhaps because one is reluctant to admit one's hard-won skills in one domain are not transferable. This fourth myth can be related to the earlier ones, in that dream and myth are both thought to be produced by the human mind at a disadvantage: in one case, by sleep; in the other, by ignorance, uncertainty, primitive conditions, spiritual struggle, or a personal history that has clouded the wondrous knowledge we are all heir to. Myth and dream are "from the same zone" (to quote Saint Joseph Campbell)[8]; they are alike because the same light is shining through them, and as media they are about equally muddy.

I question the equation. Myth and dream may both be emotional, but that does not make them the same, for emotions and the roles they play vary greatly. Myth and dream also both involve imagination, but to the same degree or to the same ends? If one's lenses are not clear, even the highly distinct can look alike. In a Jungian context,[9] the equation of myth and dream is one strategy to buttress the theory of archetypes, by extending its empirical base (somewhat dubiously, since we go from the mental life of the dreamer before us to the stories told of old recorded in the most various, distant, and fragmentary manners in unreconstitutable circumstances for widely-ranging purposes). Really, one is comparing dream to literature. Should we presume the same theory and apply the same tools to reading and interpreting Homer, Plato, Moses, or Vyasa as we do to analyzing and interpreting dream content?

Sigmund Freud too voraciously loved fiction; he was intellectually addicted to it. Thus we find in his formal psychology constitutive reference to the tragic myth of Oedipus.[10] His theory of the patriarchy (with its references to a sacred "band of brothers"[11] who overthrow a strong-man father and divvy the girls) is based on an analysis of Greek and Judaic myth, more than on dream analysis per se. But the two sources of evidence are accepted side by side. The child, the savage, the unconscious mind were all one: so one could look to dream, as much as to personal and cultural development (that is, shifting mythologies) to support one's theory of the psyche and its depths.

But surely the contrary is true, and the cases are worlds apart. The nightly neural agitation that is dreaming involves its own set of dissociations, its own cognitive, emotional, social, and immunological functions. It cannot be assumed to be the same set of constraints and needs that drives social and aesthetic narrative, that writes great literature, that entertains the waking, or that records the wisdom and dross of civilizations. The equation of dream and myth is really only a license for scientific posers to mine literary sources to lend credence to their pet theories. Vivid and great stories are worth the telling; but are they evidence for a theory of dreams or of the unconscious? I conclude this fourth myth is only a license to tell stories; and as such it is worthless, for the license had already been granted and issued. Rejecting the theory will not revoke the license. Read on, friends.

Diffuse the tension of ignorance: attend to the *logos*, but tell your story.

DREAMS

Are dreams the idle fancy of the sleeping mind, or are they the arduous work of the developing spirit? Is the stuff of dreams illusion or a reality higher than the waking world? Have you had what Carl G. Jung called "big dreams,"[12] dreams that take the whole of existence into their interpretive frame, and change the course of your life? Have you dreamed a future only to see it come true? Have you dreamed your past, perhaps past lives or forgotten traumatic experiences? Do you ignore your dreams and the messages of your dreams? Have you ever been harmed by your dreams? Why do we have nightmares? Is there something you are hiding, repressing, keeping in the dark like a skeleton or a ghost? Do dreams connect us with the upper world, the lower world, with god, with the dead, or even with other living spirits? Can you share your dream in an actual and literal sense with another co-equal dreamer? Can two dreamers dream one dream? Or are dreams merely chemical imbalances in our brains? Is a nightmare only a neurochemical? What do dreams mean? How are they to be interpreted? What is the key to their deciphering? How do you, after all, read a dream?

To define a thing, it can help to name its upper limit. Where does the study of dream lead? Where do we hope to get by understanding our dreams? Here we must be careful that our philosophy itself does not fall asleep. There is an old Hindu theory (in the *Māṇḍūkya Upaniṣad* that there are four states of consciousness: Daily Waking, Dream, Deep Sleep, and Self-Realization).[13] Only when clear consciousness is brought down into dream, so that dreams are lucid and at the command of our will, brought down past dream to the stillness of deep sleep like a waking night, and brought below even that lucid darkness, only then can consciousness begin to taste its own self-realization, a kind of *lucid waking*. So perhaps dreams can after all lead us to our selves, but not by being believed. Dreams are real, but false, as they are not what they seem, even if lucid. Where does the path of dream lead? Perhaps only to the door of reality, not in, not to what lies essentially beyond dream. And enlightenment is no dream, though it be the realization that waking life is but a dream.

Bad dreams can come from poor sleep and stress or some other organic cause. As such they may have no psychological or spiritual value except as a signal to change conditions, if you can, to attain fuller rest. But some dreams do have meanings that are important for us to recognize and know or, if that is impossible, at least to sit with and contemplate with an open mind. Regarding the mind, the most important aspect in dream interpretation is to exert emotional ownership of the images and events of the dream. Dreams seem like other (that is, not self), but they are our own creations. We are the dream-maker, even as God is the world-maker, for we make the world of our dream. Finding yourself or part of yourself in every image or character in the dream by emotionally identifying with it, is the first step. It is not your mother in the dream, but your image of your mother; same obviously for father, relatives, animals, plants, monsters, gods, and so on. By emotionally identifying with all aspects of the dream sequence (which can only be done by remaining open to them emotionally), we can become our dream, as if God became the world and then found himself present in every part of it. As dream-maker, we transcend the dream, just as the Creator transcends creation. By identifying with each dream element, we find ourselves manifest in our dream, much like god-as-immanent, god as one and the same in each element of his creation. Dreamland is the evidential basis of philosophical monism.

When dreams frighten us, our will scurries away to hide. To open the heart to what is fearful is very difficult, but begins with stabilizing the will in face of the remembered dream image. Try to "be okay with it" or accept the image, as disturbing as it is. Recall that it is only a dream, only an image. You are not "being okay with" or accepting evil, but only with the image of evil that has occurred in your dream. Mentally try to accept the dream as image; then let yourself patiently feel each part of the dream. Expect no answers, and sometimes in the silence of contemplation they will arise spontaneously. More likely they reveal themselves indirectly, not with a bright label or the clarion ring of truth, but in a lessening of the interpretive tension, and in a reduction in the wonder of what it all meant, without the dream thereby wholly losing interest or being forgotten.

These few gestures lie in the direction of a methodology in dream interpretation. But they do not amount to a method, even in suggestion, and they issue no interpretations at all. And if interpretation is taken to mean wrangling some lexical correspondence of dream-image to lived reality, then it is wisely given a wide berth.[14] The only dictionary to consult on your dreams is in your dreams. But there the writing on the pages is so unstable, that it no longer reads what it just did. If dreams do write the thoughts of our unconscious, their text remains illegibly unstable even after we waken.

FATE

Obligation is seldom a welcome guest. Nobody pays taxes with excited glee.[15] Even holding the door open an extra moment for the burdened body following you through it can feel like a nuisance and a chore. Duty is so unfashionable.

Yet no duty is more placidly embraced today than the need to create your own destiny. No one else will do it for you. We must each spin the yarn of our own fate, as there is no longer a goddess to weave our fortune for us. The self is plastic, and may be extended in any manner we like. Extreme makeover has become routine. *You can be anything you want to be.* Destiny is choice.

It is the inconvenience of the given world that first leads us to suspect that perhaps nature and circumstance have more of a say than such wishful individualism would allow. Chance and necessity randomly and regularly intervene in self-creation. Yet oddly, these two mutually contradictory concepts, *chance* and *necessity*, are workable namesakes for *fortune* and *fate*. So our blithe optimism crashes at once into a paradox of identical opposites. Yet if we patiently wade through this semantic morass, and take a short tour through the deep history of these words, we may emerge with new clarity on a very old, but very personal philosophical problem.

Fate and *fortune* are nearly synonymous in popular usage, but they differ in emotional tone. *Fortune* has a felicitous ring, and *fortunate* is a wholly positive adjective. *Fate*, by contrast, is ominous and suggests a *fatal* ending, meaning ruinous, disastrous, or with deadly outcome. Yet the two words are united in signifying necessity, particularly a predetermined necessity that somehow turns out to be morally appropriate. A kind of poetic justice in finalities, it distinguishes itself as *meaningful necessity* from the more prosaic scientific determinism, codified in impersonal value-free laws of nature. The reigning necessity today is shorn of all poetry, and the goddess has lost her popular authority.

Fortune, at its root, means *chance* or *luck* as a cause of events and changes in human affairs. As an ancient goddess, she represented "the power supposed to distribute lots of life according to her own humor."[16] Her humor, by all accounts, is more often cruel than funny; whim, rather than wit, is at work. Likewise *fate* derives from a Latin word, *fatum*—literally "that which is spoken," implying a divinely decreed dictum, and again suggesting an arbitrary, or at least unaccountable, will. Fortune is just playing. Life is her game of chance.

And yet, a statue of Fortuna in ancient Rome was kept always veiled, on account, it is said, of her shamefully partisan favors. If her results are consistently uneven, they cannot be due to chance alone. One suspects the chance theory is an early cover-up for a fixed game, a rigged roulette, of a stacked deck. Fortuna's image is a wheel, but she rides rough. She is not the same on all sides.

In ancient Greek,[17] fortune is the goddess *Tyche*, and the fates are the *Moiria*, the apportioners (three sisters who spin, measure, and cut the thread of life). Both are associated with *ananke*, which means "necessity" or "the sublime." By some accounts, however, *tyche* originally meant "chance," and the *Moiria* were originally "birth-spirits." But both notions evolved along with changing ethical thought, and took on moral functions, such as punishment and reward. In wayward times, when there is no avenger, it becomes necessary to invent one.

It was no little struggle to press Fate into the service of morality. She seems not to like the work. Even so notable an authority as Hesiod (c. 700 BCE) vacillates in assigning the Fates their parentage. His waffling is instructive. At first he says they are daughters of Night, herself a fatherless child of primordial Chaos. Besides the Fates, and without aid of a mate, Night also gave birth to Death, Sleep, Dreams, Blame, Misery, Deceit, and Strife. With such siblings, it is no wonder the three sisters turned out so unruly.

Elsewhere, Hesiod makes the *Moiria* the most honored daughters of Zeus by the Titan Themis. Despite being both Zeus' lover and his aunt, Themis represents righteousness. Whether in this mythic revision Hesiod is motivated more by cosmic optimism or by cosmic despair is a difficult matter to judge. The difference might be compared to a cabinet shuffle in the Olympian administration of justice. As a change, it not only affirms that the apportioning to humans of good and evil is born of righteousness; on appropriate patriarchal assumptions, it also transfers ultimate judicial authority to Zeus. It clarifies the chain of command and the issue of final command. Like the pure-chance theory, this tale is no doubt told with the main aim of legitimating the divine status quo. Unfortunately, rather than sanctifying the decisions of fate, the story inadvertently runs the risk of tainting Zeus with the same arbitrary morality. A cabinet shuffle cannot go to the root of the rot if that originates at the head.

Technically, as a child of Night, the Fates would instead be great aunts to Zeus and the other Olympian gods. That is, fate would be above the gods, not a daughter or a decree of them. Put differently, the Fates are *ananke*, the sublime and fearful necessity to which even the gods must bow. Of course, the Christian worldview would unambiguously resolve this division of powers. Thus John Milton (1608–1674): "what I will is fate. / —So spake the almighty."[18] But again it is the fear of God, not moral justification, that is augmented by thus subsuming dreadful *ananke* into the Godhead. There is a pretty line in Francis Bacon's (1561–1626) ingenious essay on *Fortune*: "a serpent must swallow a serpent before it can become a dragon."[19]

The dragon is Leviathan, the sublime and unaccountable power of God. It is precisely *meaningless necessity*, at least if meaning is to be measured in human or moral terms. We cannot easily make moral sense of our world or its necessities. The unfathomable and undeserved suffering occasioned by tsunamis, hurricanes, earthquakes, and pandemics (to speak only of recent events) presents us today with the same problem, newly clothed, as we find in these ancient embarrassments about the true father and author of fate. If we say such disasters are due to some divine plan, of which we in principle know nothing, we are really just consecrating our ignorance with the name of faith.

We are not privy to the ultimate secrets of destiny, but we can work to remove moral corruption in our personal worldview. Faith or belief is not the problem, but only smug faith, which, convinced of the righteousness of itself and God, explains all suffering as penalty for individual moral error. If the universe is fundamentally just, then those who suffer must deserve it. The comforters of Job live on. The same corruption reduces karma to blame, as when we explain someone's present misery by their moral failings in past lives—*as confidently as if we ourselves had been eyewitnesses to those lives!*

The identical danger lurks in the glib fantasy of pure self-creation. For it follows from that sanctimonious twaddle that those who amount to little in this life have only themselves to blame. Better far that we should warmly embrace our cosmic ignorance, than that we should save our morally tidy worldview by saddling the victims of circumstance and systemic rot with presumed but unknown sin. Believe in fate if you can, but avoid the wishful vengeance it has so often perpetuated.[20]

CHAOS

> out of where there is no movement
> it is possible to speak . . .
>
> —Picard[21]

In the Greek myth,[22] *Gaia*, or Earth, is a child of Chaos. It is natural to think that this birth was a replacement, so that once earth or nature appeared on the scene, chaos was no more. Like the mother octopus, who nurses her young till they are born—and then dies—this mother of mother earth succumbs immediately to her progeny, and order replaces chaos. Or so it seems.

Chaos, however, has never been a respecter of order or of logic. A little consistency never got in the way of an overarching inconsistency. Thus chaos lumbers along behind, with its fearsome grin.

Such was her original fecundity that, without the instrumentality of a mate, *Gaia* of herself gave birth to the first male, *Ouranos*, the heaven. That may have been her first mistake, since he, being tool-focused, immediately took the upper hand in a move that has ever since read like a mythic retelling of the rise of patriarchy. The need for the male was imposed, and the mandate of the new order is clearly the continued suppression of the *Urmutter* Chaos.

For contrast, we can look briefly to a quite different myth of origins, that in the book of Genesis. It too involves chaos, in the form of *tehom*, the primordial waters. Over this void, God hovered in the dark. But this formless void, contrary to the Greeks, is identified with earth. Only on the second day, after light has arrived, will it be separated into waters above and below. The vault of heaven is formed out of this formless earth. First day: light. Second day: the heavens or the waters above. Only on day three are the earthly waters made into landforms and the seas. Thus the world as we know it is made when (a presumptively male) spirit imposes an order on a formless female watery void called earth. In one sense, the heaven and the landforms replace the formless void; but both are made out of those primordial waters, which therefore remain with us. But I continue with the Greeks and their replacement project.

The original mists having not yet departed, the origin of philosophy is hidden in these stories. The *logos*, or rational order, was a story of origins that some came to regard as superior to the one we find in these wondrous myths. Now, even Aristotle (384–322 BCE) allows that the "lover of myth" is a lover of wisdom (*philo-sopher*), in that philosophy is born of wonder and myths are full of wonder.[23] But wonder betokens ignorance, and philosophy overcomes myth as order overcomes chaos. In short, *logos* replaces *mythos*, and knowledge replaces wonder. Wonder gives birth to philosophy, but reason kills wonder by achieving knowledge. Thus the mandate of reason is imposed on truth, and the muse of philosophy is oppressed even as grandmothers are, who suffer silently their futile Cassandra's wisdom.

Reason was rather full of itself in those glory days. Perfected and complete unto itself, it contained its own end, the human *telos*, or purpose. Reason had its own values, was bound to the good as supreme. Form (*logos*) determined function (*telos*), and a reduced nature became an ordered hierarchy. Essence was the instrument of this conceptual oppression. The conceit had its own charm, and soon became a myth unto itself. A cold knife was needed to slay this myth, this was the spare knife of instrumental reason. We call it science (read: technology), and it dealt a deathblow to the myth of the Ideal of the self-impregnated *logos*. Reason then lived on its own emptiness, on its value-neutrality, self-disemboweled. The firmament of its world was the order and regularity of nature it craved. If nature had earlier abhorred the chaos of a vacuum, now reason despised its own void, its own inner chaos. What it did not deal with inside naturally came out, and technology fashioned to yield to us power over nature began to degrade her. Instrumental reason grew its metal head and internal combustion stomach, and under the aegis of order, generated chaos. The war was taken to the maternal enemy's camp, and the patriarchy rallied on, extending its impersonal value-free dominion.

Lately kicked in the knees (by itself), reason has begun to come around, to rehabilitate chaos and to enshrine it as a scientific idea. What's that? Is it perhaps true that chaos never died, was never replaced, therefore, was always all along the nature science has sought to understand? *Ouranos* greeted his mutant offspring with horror and tried to swallow them. Was this perhaps a family tradition? Did Chaos not swallow *Gaia* after she gave birth to her, so that even now natural order swims in the jaws of chaos? But how can the monster of irregularity fit the presumptive regularity of scientific causation or natural law? Can science swallow chaos?[24]

Chaos, scientifically, is not the demon of yore, nor the annihilation of order. It is only a kind of complexity, not reducible to the pretty or symmetrical equations complacency had become accustomed to since Isaac Newton

(1642–1726/27). Sometimes what seems random actually contains a hidden source of order, as when randomness is constrained within a certain range or bound. Turbulence, the irregularity of a coastline, the meander of rivers, the rising column of cigarette smoke that suddenly curls and buckles in on itself, cloud formation, the shapes of mountains, leaves and trees—all these are phenomena of tremendous complexity, yet not complete or utter randomness. They are recognizably what they are and yet susceptible to incredible variation. This constrained but wild variation is natural chaos. And it makes up most of the world. Turbulence alone is found in a dripping tap, a stream, the economy, the ocean, in the atmosphere, and in the cosmos. The monster is reality.

There are in mathematics certain simple, calculable functions that, mapped out, yield shapes not unlike these phenomena. That they are calculable, and not beyond the means of a computer, shows there is some order. That they are nevertheless bafflingly complex, bafflingly beautiful, shows they are chaotic. What these functions have in common is called extreme sensitivity to initial conditions. The slightest seemingly insignificant variations in initial inputs yields in short order extraordinarily different outcomes, which nevertheless conform to the same general character. One obtains a different coastline, but still a coastline; a different mountain range, but still a mountain range; a different river, but yet a river. It is never the same cloud but it is another cloud. This is nature. This is orderly chaos.

When the sensitivity to initial conditions is so great that any attempt to measure the initial conditions changes them, then the resulting phenomenon is physically unpredictable. The inability to predict is not the result of our ignorance, but is grounded in nature, and the physical nature of our knowledge. Strangely, the functions themselves may be calculable, computable, and even deterministic. But measurement is a physical action that has a disturbing effect. It is observation that changes the world rather than merely observes it. Divine intuition may see it all and smile knowingly. But we need to observe, and to observe by our clumsy senses is to interfere. Thus may chaos escape us, even as it fled *Ouranos*.

Flee the private randomness of your thought and seek the shared chaos of philosophy. Bring your hungry sensitivity to inspiring conditions.

THE SUBLIME

In daily speech, something is sublime when it is heavenly or delicious beyond compare. "This ice cream is sublime," we say, when we are thrilled to ecstasy with each tiny spoonful, over which we would linger endlessly if we but could. Sublime sex is sex that pleases beyond all expectation, beyond even our wildest dreams of bliss. As we casually encounter it, therefore, the sublime promises that peace and final satisfaction that more than justifies the panting struggle or excruciating wait to get there.

Heaven, however, has its secrets, and our wildest dreams are not only of pleasures. The sublime has its darker side. But before we get there, let us take a tour of some of the curious possibilities of meaning that this word, its cognates and associates, afford us. For though we may call two opposite extremes *sublime*, its other meanings are not arrayed between these two as if on a continuum. Rather our word's history is spotted, is scattered, and has its highs in the finest poetry and its lows in bad science and worse religion. More recently, it passes its days as a mental case. But let me explain.

The sublime is twinned with beauty as the two great objects of aesthetics, the branch of philosophy that contemplates those finest and most transforming human feelings (which are not specifically ethical in character). What is sublime fills us with awe; what is beautiful fills us with joy. Awe is a kind of wondrous fear—precisely the fear that is the biblical beginning of wisdom.[25] It is an aesthetic experience, equipotent yet distinct from the easier comfort that beauty delivers.

To further contrast these terms (*sublime* and *beautiful*), I quote (with great reluctance) from Immanuel Kant's (1724–1804) famous little treatise on the subject, his 1764 book, *Observations on the Feeling of the Beautiful and Sublime*.[26] I will not spoil the effect of his prose by explaining my repugnance in advance.

> Tall oaks and lonely shadows in a sacred grove are sublime;
> flowerbeds, low hedges and trees rimmed in figures are beautiful.
> Night is sublime; day is beautiful. . . .
> The sublime moves, the beautiful charms.[27]
>
> . . .
>
> The sublime must always be great; the beautiful can also be small.[28]
>
> . . .
>
> Understanding is sublime, wit is beautiful.
> Courage is sublime and great, artfulness is little but beautiful.[29]
>
> . . .
>
> Sublime attributes stimulate esteem, but beautiful ones, love.[30]

Elsewhere in the same work Kant gives the following examples to illustrate the subjective feeling of the sublime.

> Deep loneliness is sublime, but in a way that stirs terror. . . .
> A great height is as sublime as a great depth, except that the latter is accompanied by the sensation of shuddering, the former with one of wonder.[31]
>
> . . .

> A long duration is sublime. If it is of time past, it is noble [that is, a "quiet wonder"]. If it is projected into the incalculable future, then it has something of the fearsome in it.[32]

These quotations lay out for us the emotional terrain of the sublime, and surely suffice to show the great interest of our subject. But there is more, much of a wholly different order, which I shall yet come to. Before I do, some reckoning with Kant is in order. As charming and stirring as these quotations are, they are difficult to quote. They come from the first two sections of his book, which are safe and fine, quotable and insightful. In the final two sections, lamentably, Kant moves smoothly from the sublime to the sexist and the racist. Unquotable and ignorant, disgusting and ugly, yet to pass them over in silence would be complaisant, even complicit. So I will pass by those chapters, pinching my nose with this comment only, that in time even philosophy can take on a fecal odor.

Now, in order to wrest something of relevance to our topic, I will pause to elaborate the central moral theory in Kant's little book, which theory (whatever its other faults) is not tainted by the rank prejudice masquerading as wisdom that spoils his final two chapters. Although the beautiful and the sublime are aesthetic categories, Kant's primary concern is moral theory, in particular virtue theory. Reasonably enough, he regards the *feeling* of the beautiful and the *feeling* of the sublime as essential elements of moral character. Both are important, and they must compensate for each other for best effect; but, from a moral point of view, he thinks, they are by no means *equally* important.

To see why, consider Kant's distinction between genuine or true virtues, on the one hand, and what he calls adoptive virtues on the other hand. Adoptive virtues are "beautiful and charming," but genuine or true virtue alone is "sublime and venerable."[33] Adoptive virtues arise from the feeling of the beautiful, and include sympathy, the universal affection, and complaisance, which I used above in Kant's sense of "an inclination to be agreeable to others by friendliness."[34] Adam Smith (1723–1790) and David Hume (1711–1776) had sought to base a new moral science on sympathy, fellow feeling, and thus to ground ethics, not on our capacity to reason, but on appropriate feeling and emotion.[35] Kant was having none of it.

The adoptive virtues, rooted in the feeling of the beautiful, are at least a step above the sense of honor, which Kant snubs by dubbing the "gloss of virtue."[36] The sense of honor is neither guided by that beautiful feeling nor grounded in moral principles and valid moral rules. Though allied to beauty, adoptive virtues are only incidentally moral, and thus remain liable to err:

> "As amiable as the compassionate quality might be, it still does not have the dignity of a virtue."[37]

For instance, complaisance, "this ground of a delightful sociability,"[38]

> is beautiful, and the pliancy of such a heart good-natured. But it is not at all a virtue; for where higher principles do not set bounds for it and weaken it, all the depravities can spring from it."[39]

The dangers are grave indeed: "Out of kind-hearted fellowship he will be a liar, an idler, a drunkard, or the like, for he does not act by the rules directed to good conduct in general, but rather by an inclination that in itself is beautiful but becomes trifling when it is without support and without principles."[40]

On the contrary, to avoid becoming an effeminate, "tenderhearted idler,"[41] or a Scottish ethicist, there is really only one manly course: "Subduing one's passions through principles is sublime. . . . Among moral attributes true virtue alone is sublime."[42]

True virtue requires a subduing of passions; it cannot just be happy talk. Behind virtue there stands an awe-ful fear. A shivering anticipation of divine retribution backs up the claim of reason to ground morality. As William James (1842–1910) has observed in a quite different context,[43] the stance of emotionless reason is a sublimated fear *of error*.

The role for the sublime in morality will survive the death of morality, as we shall see. But for now let me put aside both Kant and philosophical morality, step away, and look farther back in the checkered philosophical history of the word.

The sublime is a fringe concept, a topic that resides mostly at the borders of our consciousness, and transforms us and itself as we come to look more closely at it. It is a liminal concept, with an alchemical history. To sublimate is to transmute to a higher form, to rarefy or to elevate. It is to reach up to, or almost to, a limit, as when purifying something, such as poison or gold. Thus there gathers around the sublime images of life and death and power.

In the borderlands of Greek mythology, the sublime is *Ananke*, dreadful Necessity, under which even the gods must bend. We still recognize today the same hard necessity as the mother of invention. *Ananke* is responsible for fate, death, work, cruel chance, and all meaningless but (yet) unpreventable suffering—everything invention seeks to subvert. In biblical terms, it is Leviathan, the whale or sea-dragon, who symbolizes the power of creation and our slim chances of ever making moral sense of it. In the book of Job, Leviathan is an object lesson in the mystery of God, cited to chagrin the human mind, which wants to understand the suffering of Job, who was just. It is implied that, were we able to grok Leviathan, then only would we have a chance of insight into the reason Satan was let to interfere with the earned reward of virtue, which was due to him, namely Job's original wealth, health, happiness, and family. Meaningless suffering is the image of the sublime—meaningless *necessity*. Again the sublime holds power over life and death.

But we moderns know how to handle these old mythological disputes. We psychologize everything. At first the sublime enters psychological science as the indefinite bottom boundary of consciousness, as the *subliminal*—what is mental (an idea or feeling) yet just below the threshold of consciousness, what Gottfried Wilhelm Leibniz (1646–1716) had called a "petite perception."[44] We cannot hear the drop for the wave; but the sound of the wave is made up of the little sounds of each drop, just as the wave itself is composed of so many droplets come together.

But it was in the realm of moral psychology that the sublime, in the form of *sublimation*, came into its modern own. Here we are instructed above all by Freud, who both sublimates, and was sublimated in turn by his admirers. Freud, having read his Darwin, considered us to have only a few innate and instinctual drives (hunger, sex, and aggression, being the principal ones). Left to express themselves unhindered, these instincts would render society wholly impossible. Necessity thus requires the individual to self-police by subduing or *transmuting* their instinctual energies and choosing only socially approved objects. Thus meals, marriage, and an orderly military have their origins in a kind of social alchemy. This inner diversion is politely known as sublimation. It is the redirecting of socially unhealthy drives toward ends that are deemed collectively beneficial. Since such sublimation makes the normal possible, we may ironically say that the sublime has become normal. (Alternatively, we psychologize everything.)

Accordingly, the abnormal has lately been theorized as dysfunctional sublimation. Atrophied sublimation leaves us with a sociopath, who understands the code of moral discourse but lacks approved moral feeling. For, sublimation (especially of the aggressive death instinct) is Freud's psychoanalytic account of the moral conscience. Ultimately, Freud's "beloved *Ananke*"[45] accounts even for moral necessity. It is uncannily Kantian, but for the death of morality as a universal moral law.

If you ever scold yourself for having done wrong, you are experiencing inner aggression for a socially approved cause. If you never let up on yourself, then you may have the pathology of a guilty conscience, otherwise known as existential anxiety. You may become depressed. You may become an existentialist. Thus we see that too much sublimation produces a hemmed-in animal, what Friedrich Wilhelm Nietzsche (1844–1900) (whose views were astonishingly similar to Freud's on many of these matters) called "self-vivisection: cruelty to the animal within."[46]

For Freud, sublimation is an adaptive defense mechanism. It reconciles dreadful *Ananke* with social order, with normality. But normality is not thereby vindicated; much worse, it is *accounted for*, relativized, and exposed as contingent. Too little sublimation makes Johnny a very bad boy—but just enough makes him fit right in.

For Kant, moral necessity is necessarily shrouded in sublimity; duty finds its proper ground in the sublime. For Freud, by contrast, we find moral necessity in the same shroud, only now morality is un-grounded, not based in anything eternal or transcendent, merely a transmutation of baser instincts. Whereas Kant sublimated cultural fear of eternal damnation into a love of the Right, Freud sublimated the biological fear of death into a love of scientific Truth. Thus the dangers of too much sublimation is also a problem: Kant's ethics cover for his prejudice, Freud's science is bogus.

Do not be bad. Revert to philosophy. Enjoy the sublimest fruits of mind, the ridiculous antics of inquiry.

HOPE

> And no birds sing.
>
> —Keats, "La Belle Dame sans merci."[47]

Hope is a life-saver, like an orange floating ring flung out on a rope to catch ourselves, lest we drown in the sea of despair. And the seas are rising, literally and figuratively—never has so impossibly bleak a future been held up with greater authority before humankind. Calamity is at hand, yet a message of no hope has no legs. You need to give people the feeling that they can help; you need to explain the grounds of hope, smile knowingly to make the sale, or get the donation. *Your money gives hope*—if only you can persuade them of that, they will pay. They will pay for a life-preserver, if the need is known. But if the truth is worse than we fear, then will our despair act with any more urgency? Will our spending become profligate? Indeed, is hope worth it?

This question is like a secret dagger in the heart of all hope.

To question hope is to interrupt the good-news agenda. It is to rip apart life-vests, puncture the rescue-boats, and cast spare provisions overboard. To raise philosophical scruples regarding hope is like profaning the altar with reason. To doubt hope is as if to step on the fingertips of one who is hanging by them alone. It is to offer the counsel of despair, which is no counsel at all. (The despairing need not be advised to despair). Think of the deathbed doctor, who may know there is no hope of recovery. Still hope is not lost when it becomes futile. Rather, it is kept alive by switching its concern from longer life to a better death. Hope hangs on by its fingertips.

The so-called enlightenment arose when the great engine of human hope was hooked to the cart (*des Cartes*?) of reason, and unleashed from the stone of dogmatic faith. Progress has since been the way, and the technological juggernaut that has swept us (all) along gives us (few) the hope of a new, amazing even more convenient future, perhaps even a virtual substitute for the world it is also destroying. We are in a race against time to build a spaceship where we can live without a world. And yet, if you say hope is diseased, you are peeing on everyone's parade. (Or rather, not everyone's: only a few benefit from development; the spaceship cannot accommodate all).

Opposing hope is like devaluing currency; it is bad economics. To oppose hope is like slapping on a heavy ideological tax that dampens initiative and penalizes the spirit of venture. So which is it? Is necessity the mother of invention? Or is it a tax on entrepreneurs? Or is it the gleam in a profiteer's eye? Anyone who sets up shop hopes customers come by, and then leave some of their money before they go. Hope is just wanting to get ahead. That is, it is a gentler name for ambition. To be anti-hope is to be against people wanting to do well and better for themselves. It is only mildly more polite than overtly wishing ill upon people, or it is hoping they do worse or just go to hell. To oppose hope is to oppose heaven, and the free world. It is unpatriotic and irreligious.

Hope is a last resort, but that only means you find it everywhere, except in the end. Hope is the first inkling, the bold entry, the entrepreneur, or the visionary who sees things before they happen. Hope is a virtue of beginnings. It is said that hope makes a good breakfast, but a bad supper. Hope is a good in itself, so we want it for ourselves, and it becomes a primary end for mortals. But it is not the end. In the end, there is no hope. Finally it becomes unnecessary. What need has God of hope, or those who have arrived in the Promised Land? Hope is also a virtue of transitions, valid throughout the world of beginnings. It implies a contented waiting, a mindful endurance, like an optimistic work song. Hope is like whistling while you work. But the end leaves no place for hope. In heaven there is nothing left to hope for; it has all come true. No one hopes for what already is. We hope for what we want to be, even if it is more of the same endlessly. But heaven guarantees just this for its denizens.

Hope is one of two things: either it is a virtue, or it is an illusion (and if the latter, then an enemy of truth and of the virtue of truth-seeking). I have evoked the virtue tradition throughout, but not yet given it its due space.

Before I do, I will tackle the second disjunct, the view that hope is an evil. It seems so strange, but that strange philosopher of the foreign, Nietzsche, helps make it plain by his admiration for the heroic in the Greek imagination. He reveals a cultural relativity from which the view makes sense, by reference to the myth of Pandora's Box (one of the earliest surviving versions of which is in Hesiod).[48] And there is something very strange about that myth! To recall, Pandora is the "gift of all gods" to men. Indeed she is the first woman: beautiful, charming, eloquent, but deceitful as well. All the good she represents is only the packaging, for according to the story, Pandora is herself given in a spirit of retribution, to punish Prometheus (Forethought) for stealing fire from heaven to benefit human beings. That is the story those patriarchal Greeks told, but I suspect that, having acquired fire, they probably insisted someone else do the cooking.

Prometheus' brother, Epimetheus (Afterthought) accepted Pandora, and then (either he or) she opened a forbidden jar containing all the evils (such as Old Age, Sickness, Insanity, Spite, Passion, Vice, Plague, and Famine), which only then came to be known to mortals. Hope alone stayed in the jar, which Hesiod says then slammed shut. Where this jar, or box, as it is often known, came from is uncertain; in Hesiod, it is part of her god-given dowry, a part of the divine curse. In any case, the gods counted on Pandora's mischievousness, and they knew she would open it.

But why is hope in the jar of evils? In an age prior to the other miseries, there would have been no use or need for hope. In a different version of the story, Prometheus himself had collected the evils and sealed them in the jar, as he had no use for them in arranging the world for the benefit of human beings. Hope in such a commodious world would indeed be useless, but that does not explain why it would need to be hidden at the very bottom of a sealed jar. It seems, more cynically, that the gods put hope in the jar only to prolong the suffering caused by the other evils, thus conceding that hope allows us to put up with more misery than we could otherwise bear. Seen thus, hope was meant to escape along with the other evils, the better to satisfy Zeus' revenge. In any case, it is hard to deny that hope eventually did get out, for there is much of it in the world (if we include, as we may, all idle hope, all faint and trembling hope, all forlorn hope, even lost hope). Hope abounds, even if its validity is sparing.

There is a present-day irony in the version of the story that has Prometheus seal hope in the jar along with the other evils, seeing that they were of no use to him in his task of making earth habitable for human beings. For consider how today the merchants of hope are now making the planet inhospitable! It may be that hope causes damage, and having none is a blessing.

All the above, apart from this last comment on what is recent, I have based loosely on Nietzsche, especially what I gathered from the following quotation from his *Daybreak*, which I now provide:

> The Greeks likewise differed from us in their evaluation of hope: they felt it to be blind and deceitful; Hesiod gave the strongest expression to this attitude in a fable whose sense is so strange no more recent commentator has understood it—for it runs counter to the modern spirit, which has learned from Christianity to believe in hope as a virtue. With the Greeks, on the other hand, to whom the

> gateway to knowledge of the future seemed not to be entirely closed and (in countless cases where we content ourselves with hope) elevated inquiry into the future into a religious duty, hope would, thanks to all these oracles and soothsayers, no doubt become somewhat degraded and sink to something evil and dangerous.[49]

In short, why hope when you can read the future in the entrails of birds? Hope is only for those who do not know the future. But if hope was a weakness for those archaic Greeks, certainly envy was not, and even their gods displayed it. Envy played the role of the competitive goad, which commercial hope plays for us. Their world was a contest: ours is a market. And we too can read the future from the entrails of the present, as when we witness ice fields fracture and polar caps wither as they give up the past; forests give up their carbons sinks as the thick pith rings of ancient trees burn. In the soaring extinction rates of birds[50] we may discern, as from their entrails, a dire forecast for our anthropocene. Our scientist soothsayers prognosticate in their own way, and again hope is increasingly degraded.

Finally, as so many do in the end, I turn to spiritual hope, the religious virtue. Spiritual hope is defined in part by its exceptional object: it does not expect anything worldly. It is not ambition. Even where the acquisitive instinct is sanctified (as, say, in the work ethic), it is derivative and not comparable to spiritual hope. Spiritual hope is for things eternal, against which all worldly success rightly pales. It is too easy, and too crude, to say, this hope is for an afterlife. We hope we live forever after we die, and we want to think there is some place reserved for us in a blessed communion outside of time. But below this mythic rendition, there is a deeper hope. These symbols should not be robbed of significance by petty literalism, whether due to stupid fundamentalism or sanctimonious positivism.

Beyond the difference in object, spiritual hope has a different character. Hope is belief in the promise of god, which is based on things invisible, and therefore does not depend on the conditions in which one is living. Spiritual hope is hope against hope. As a hero of faith believes despite paradox and contradiction, so the beacons of spiritual hope have no evidence to go on but their faith. It implies waiting, patient endurance for a promised future that may or may not come at any time. But it is not mere stoical indifference, which is devoid of the sense of any such promise. Paul says the pagans had no hope; it applies as much to Hesiod as to the Stoics.[51] Spiritual hope implies a confidence, a joyful participation in the sufferings of the world, in calm anticipation of blessings yet to be. And these blessings are not one's own, but communal and to be shared; this hope shines with charity, and contains a bodhisattvic moment. It is a perception of radical certainty that scatters all fear and despair. Hope is strength, thus virtue or power, a spiritual excellence.

Virtue or evil? The least we can say is that hope is riddled with paradox. Hope is priceless, but it costs nothing. Only hell and the inhuman are without hope. Hope is a spiritual jewel, but it is not rare, as it is a ready coin, in every pocket. It is a goad, a bridge, a refuge, but also a feint, a lure, *un leger-de-main*. It springs eternal in every breast, yet catalyzes known evils. To take away a person's last hope is tyranny, but to feed them an upbeat line is to follow the playbook of scoundrels. Hope sells. Is hope the sell out of those too weak to bear their despair? Hope is a brazen warrior, but also the happiness of fools. We all know the lessons of false hope, forlorn hope, dashed hopes, but this includes many of our most fond illusions. If hope is a lie that works, or makes not-working more bearable, then let those have it who want it. One who lives without hope is not condemned to smash the hopeful idols of others.

I hope you have reached the end of my bah-humbug essay on hope. Do not despair for me.

SYNCHRONICITY

Synchronicity is not mere synchrony, or the happening of two events along the same time-line, but, in the philosophy of Jung, an a-causal connecting principle that explains otherwise inexplicable coincidence.[52] The term has come down in popular usage to mean the uncanny coincidences themselves, but it is important to see that, at least as far as Jung's theory of synchronicity is concerned, at stake is *what counts as an explanation* of such mysteries.

Notice, foremost, that to appeal to synchronicity to explain a curious coincidence is to rule out a causal connection. Explanatory appeals to synchronicity embrace a metaphysics that transcends cause and effect. Ruling out causation is in practice often neglected, or rather assumed, with a mysterian's shrug. But strictly, if synchronicity is invoked, causality is presumed inoperative. One is involved in quite a different explanatory game than local mechanistic pushes and pulls.

In causal analysis of phenomena, we want to identify causes, or factors that contributed to bringing the phenomena about. There may be competing theories as to causes, which will all have to be ruled out but one. In general, to defend any one causal explanation, one has to refute the alternative causal explanations. The situation is complex, because phenomena are complex, and because it is a fallacy to suppose events and existents have a unique or single cause. My point is that causal explanation is more like a style of explanation than like an actual concrete particular explanation. Competing theories must be ruled out as part of the process of causal explanation.

So the causal style of explanation is quite used to competition. But in synchronicity it finds an unwillingness to fight. Synchronicity politely waits upon *all* causal explanations to be ruled out, and only then it presents its new style.[53]

In strict parallel, one might expect synchronicity would be an a-causal explanatory *style*, rather than an actual particular concrete explanation on its own. One might expect to have a suite of competing synchronistic explanations, each jockeying for confirmation. But one almost invariably finds instead that the mere invocation of synchronicity as a possible explanation is greeted with good cheer and a wink, and perhaps a shared feeling of profound mystery. No actual explanation takes place, just the relief experienced when one abandons hope of rational understanding. Synchronicity is more of a thrill than a theory. It is more like rejoicing that meaning can spontaneously arise from the world, than like knowing why things have happened.

Astrology is an instructive example. I define it carefully as the influence of astronomical events in and beyond the solar system on our day-to-day lives. Astrology is more than that, but I will comment only on it as I have now (somewhat arbitrarily) defined it. Note that this definition leaves open whether it is causal or acausal (perhaps synchronistic) influence. Even critics of astrology can agree with this definition of it; for, admitting that astrology is that influence, they can simply say that such influence is null or non-extant.

Detailed causal chains from specific astrological events, such as alignments and oppositions, processions and retrogressions, etc., accounting for definite particulars of daily life, are hard to come by, to say the least, and speculation has all but ceased on the question. We might as well concede here that causal explanations have been ruled out. So synchronicity is well-suited (by its definition) for the job. And indeed one finds in charts and horoscopes that the influences reported are generally based upon semantic resonance, symbolic affinity, or at least some meaningful chain of associations. *Synchronicity is thus a metaphysical glue that connects events by meaning rather than by causal necessity.* But it comforts those who (like Jung) first construe causality in narrow mechanical terms. Thus meaning is restored to the foundation of the phenomenal world, and hermeneutics takes its place alongside ontology.

If there is to be no general contest to see which particular synchronistic explanatory stories are to be accepted for each meaningful coincidence that occurs (and surely there are many that may be offered), then at least one alternative non-causal explanation ought be considered, to make it seem like a contest. Chance is a fierce competitor, but those who like their meaning lathered thick will reject it. Causal arguments must compete against chance and win; synchronistic explanations safely shunt chance aside, or (more often) celebrate it as proof.

There is also, I propose, an explanation of why we appeal to synchronicity based on the well-known and widely documented tendency of fallacious thought known as the confirmation bias. We seek out and notice information that confirms our beliefs (such as our desire for meaningful lives) rather than information that would disconfirm them. We are content to see what we expected; but we should rather be checking that what we do not expect is not there. Not confirmation, but repeated failure to disconfirm lends logical and evidentiary strength to our beliefs, and shores up epistemic confidence. But if we only seek to confirm what we think we know, we may simply be cementing in our illusions.

Therefore, all of you, since I want you to be firm in your convictions, test your theories. Test synchronicity. Try to disconfirm it. If you fail, your belief in it will be strengthened. If you do not fail, the disproof will also add to your knowledge, by removing an illusion. Before we accept synchronistic explanations, we should at least ensure that alternatives, such as our irrational propensity to preserve our beliefs, are not at work.

The alternative, which will no doubt remain more popular, will be to accept those explanations of things that most fit our preconceptions, and to dispense with truth in the search for knowledge. If I am wrong, it will not be a coincidence.

Put simply, my point against synchronicity concerns its failure as an explanation, not its occurrence as a phenomenon. One may cite case after case of genuinely uncanny circumstances. That shows uncanny things can happen, and explanations are in order (we wonder, we scratch our heads, our preconceptions are shaken). To explain is to relieve that wonder, but synchronicity provides no explanatory relief. It has become a code word for the wonder of it, for the existence of the uncanny, and an affirmation of the actuality of mysterious phenomena in the face of a boringly rational world. In that latter capacity, the word is irreproachable. It only names an itch. But as an explanatory principle, non-causal influence is a non-starter. Jung's synchronicity is an acausal *explanatory* principle, not an assertion of wholeness or interdependency per se. The problem is that, in use, it typically explains nothing at all (therefore failing on its own terms), but instead celebrates the unexplainable. In practice, it is an influence without influence, an account beyond all accounting, an itch that will not be scratched. But the itch of being begs to be scratched.

INFINITY

The subject is too big for me. I admit I am dwarfed by it. Like a puny grain of sand pitted against the approaching sea, I am done for. But the finite numbers following along are expecting something from me. Expectation. Is infinity anything other?

Many people find infinity boring, and in truth it does go on and on. Indeed the technical mathematical side can become hairy, to say the least, infinitely hairy to say the worst. Like an infinite and non-undoable knot, it is easy to lose interest. So I shall stick to fun, and you will see how infinity provides no end of fun.

Walk with me. One step after another. Keep going. That's it! You have the principle.

Keep going, and I won't have to. But I see you are expecting more. So try this.

Climb. Step above step. Imagine a staircase with this peculiar attribute: *for every step, there is a higher step*. These few words together manifest a countably infinite staircase, a stairway to heaven. There is no need to purchase one, as a popular song suggests.[54] If, however high you go, there is yet a higher step, then there is no top step in this staircase.

I could go on, but I fear you will get weary. I bet you would also get weary if you had to truck your mortal frame up all those stairs before you could get to heaven. Most people would tucker out. The most adventuresome would pass by many skeletons before they left their own.

But it is easy to do if you are a deity.[55] They are so much smarter than we are. Why, once they do anything, the next time they do it they are twice as fast. And this learning pattern does not taper off, like a mortal's learning curve. It keeps going. Now suppose such a deity took half a second to arrive upon the first step of this stairway to heaven. If he continued without pause, he would only require an additional one quarter second to arrive on the second step, only an eighth to get to the third, and so on. If you keep adding these smaller and smaller fractions to one half, the most you will ever get is one second—$1/2+1/4+1/8+1/16+1/32+ \ldots =1$. This equation is about time, but it is nicely illustrated in a certain division of the circle (see figure 1.1): take a full circle, and cut away the bottom half; now strike out the top left quarter circle, so that only the upper right quadrant remains. Proceed to divide this too in half; taking away an eighth, still an eighth will remain. If you always only subtract half of what remains, some positive amount will be left over, though an ever-dwindling quantity. The division may become harder and harder, requiring greater and greater skill,[56] but for the Master Carver, no slice is too fine.[57]

So, to return to the division of time, we see that already after one second that that god has stepped on every step in that infinite staircase.

Now you have a right to wonder about the existence of my accelerating god. You will argue, I am sure, that this god's velocity would very soon surpass that of light, which we take, not only on Albert Einstein's authority, to be a physical impossibility. But these gods are of a luminous substance unknown

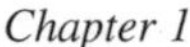

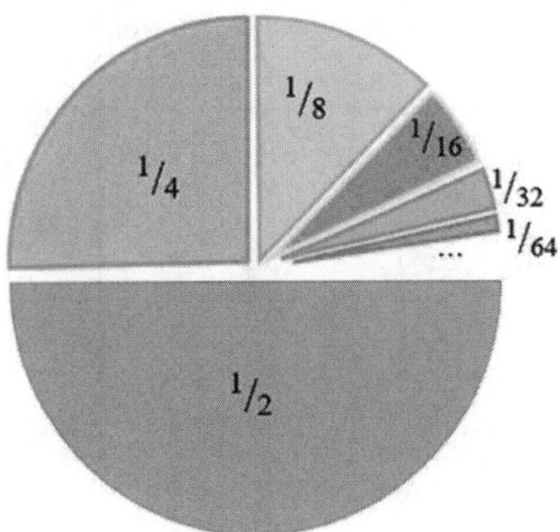

Figure 1.1 Infinity Pie Chart. The whole is equal to the sum of infinitely many diminishing parts.

to physics and contemptuous of its laws. Anyway, contrary to Einstein, his friend, Kurt Gödel,[58] that famous lover of infinity, showed remarkably enough that speeds faster than that of light are indeed physically possible, if only time be allowed to go backward. Conceivably, my god would arrive earlier than he had left. It would still take one second on our watches, but the god's watch would show a savings.

Now some of you will be displeased that I have assumed this god is male. But really gender has nothing to do with it. For these gods may alter gender. Suppose on the first step, the God is male, but that, by the send step, a goddess arrives. On the third, it is again male, and so likewise on every odd-numbered step. On every even-numbered step, we shall say with the Pythagoreans that she was female. That is all fine and good. But tell me: what gender is the god after one second (our time) has passed? Male? Female? Androgynous? Hermaphrodite? None can tell. If the god's gender were male after it all, it would have had to have last stepped on an odd-numbered step. If after ascending the god's gender were female, it would have had to have stepped last on an even-numbered step. But there is no last odd number, nor any last even number. For every odd number, there is a higher even number, and vice versa. Post-climb, then, the god's gender is therefore indeterminate. (They say that turns them on.)

People have trouble grappling with infinity because they do not realize that certain laws pertaining to the finite no longer apply. Thus, a virtual law of thought in Western philosophy has been that the whole is larger than the part. But it turns out that any infinite set of things is equal in size to a proper part of itself. Let the gods illustrate.

Suppose the god is in a hurry. If it were thinking like a human, it would mount two steps at one go. That way (that is, assuming that going up two steps at once takes the same unit of time as going up one did in the last illustration) we would again double our average speed getting up. And surely, on these assumptions, we would get up a *finite* staircase in half the time as we would if we touched each step along the way. But if the god went up an infinite staircase at their usual rate of acceleration (as indicated in the above formula), only now by twos, it would still require only one second to get all the way up. When you travel like a god, it does not pay to think like a human. In the infinite case, there is no overall savings in the time needed to go up (even though there is an advantage in every finite case!). With an infinite staircase, even going twice as high with each step in the same diminishing units of time, you do not get to the top any sooner. Indeed, the same argument applies if the god were to pass over three steps each successive time unit, or leap over ten or a million at a go, assuming all along it is twice as fast with each next foot, and took only a half-second on the first step (however long). In traversing an infinite staircase, one does not gain by skipping steps.

Ask yourself: how many even numbers are there? You could count them in order of size, so that the n-th one would be $2n$. You would never run out of counting numbers, nor would you have any left over after having counted all the evens. From this one-to-one correspondence, it follows that there are the same number of even numbers as there are counting numbers as a whole—odd and even combined (see table 1.1). The whole includes the part, but the part is of the same size (countably infinite). The staircase has infinitely many steps, only half of which are even numbered ones. But the number of even steps is the same as the number of steps in total. The whole includes a part as big as itself.

Indeed, it contains infinitely many parts as big as itself. For the part need not be half, but any fraction. (The bottom row of the table could be $3n$, $10n$, 10^n, and there would still be a one-to-one correspondence, showing sameness of size.) We can say, then, that any finite fraction of the infinite is infinite. That is, the infinite divided by the finite is always infinite. Finite fractions, you can see, are powerless against infinity, and meaningless in its terms.

After one second, when the god has arrived in his heaven on high, it is only fitting that he or she should ascend to his or her throne. Those first steps after infinity are the privilege of a regal mind. Like the day after eternity, they require some imagination to enjoy. And should we not have forever . . . forever? Should we not have it again and again? How many heavens upon heaven might there be?

Table 1.1 Infinity Essay

$n=$	1	2	3	4	5	. . .
$2n=$	2	4	6	8	10	. . .

There are just as many even numbers as there are counting numbers.

I said just now that skipping steps gained no (further) time savings for the accelerating god. But wait! Imagine that each step is a light and a light switch, so that stepping on it either lights it up or turns it off. Now skipping steps leaves a unique pattern, a particular way that this god might dance to heaven. It may go up by twos, or by threes, or by any rule, or by no rule. (Can every way up have a rule?) Each way up leaves a particular infinite pattern of ons and offs. Each pattern represents one way this god might dance to heaven. The question is: are there more ways to skip up an infinite staircase than there are steps in the staircase? In other words, are there countably many patterns, given that there are countably infinite steps?

In the finite case, a set of stairs with n steps may be mounted in 2^n ways. (2^n =2x2x . . . x2, *n* times). A simple staircase of 3 steps has $2^3=8$ ways up, if you take the time to count them all. So our question becomes: is infinity equal to $2^{infinity}$? In a finite staircase, the ways up always exceed the number of steps. Well, it turns out that *this* law of the finite does extend to the infinite. One can definitely say that there are more *ways* up an infinite staircase than there are steps in that staircase. There are a countless infinity of ways (stairways, if you will) up a single countably infinite staircase. From such arguments it follows, not only that there are distinct sizes of infinity, but indeed that, *for every infinite size, there is a higher infinite size.*[59] Among the infinite, as it turns out, one size does not fit all.

And since a rule that generates a pattern must be finitely state-able (or who could follow it?) there are more possible patterns on an infinite staircase than there are *rules.*

In parting, I offer you a bouquet of flowers, each flower in it a distinct species. As I know you have your preferences, but I do not know what they are, I allow you your choice of flowers. Take as many or as few flowers as you please, even all or none. How many choices have I offered you? Now if my bouquet were finite, and had only *n* flowers in it to chose from, then my offer would be limited, and though your choices would outnumber the flowers, they too would be finite, and in fact would max out at 2^n. But my love is unlimited, so, boundless is my gift. Your bouquet has a *countable* infinity of flowers in it, but *countless* are your choices, as many as there are "stairways" you can dance to heaven.

In the end, the infinite is bigger than you expect. For the endless is not all; after all, there is more. But here end these my anticipations of the absolute.

NOTES

1. *Timeaus*, 59D, as quoted in Paul Friedländer, *Plato: An Introduction* (Princeton, NJ: Princeton University Press/Bollingen, 1973), 123.

2. *Laws*, 803E. A. E. Taylor translation, in Plato, *Collected Dialogues of Plato*, ed. Edith Hamilton and Huntington Cairns (New York: Pantheon Books, 1961), 1374–75, 804B. Compare *Republic* (604B).

3. An early version of my essay titled "Mythology," *Philosophers' Café* (SFU Continuing Studies) (Spring 2008): 2–3. It is reprised and revised here with permission.

4. The *rishis* were the performance poets who composed the *Vedas*. See *The Rigveda: The Earliest Religious Poetry of India*, trans. Stephanie W. Jamison and Joel P. Brereton (Oxford: Oxford University Press, 2014).

5. The approach to early Indian philosophy that is criticized here may be taken as having started above all with William Jones (1746–1794), and continued most notably with Friedrich Max Mueller (1823–1900), an early translator of Hindu scriptures, who regarded early *Vedic* deities as nature worship (erroneously personified forces of nature). Scholarship, of course, has moved on; but errors die hard. Meanwhile older misconceptions have become widespread in more or less allied disciplines and trickled down to the popular mind. For Jones' views "On the Hindus," see his "The Third Anniversary Discourse" of the Asiatic Society of Bengal, from 1786. Mueller's views on India religion can be sampled in *Lectures on the Origin and Growth of Religion as Illustrated by the Religions of India* (London: Longmans, Green, 1878); and his *India: What Can It Teach Us? A Course of Lectures Delivered before the University of Cambridge* (London: Longmans, Green, 1883), especially chaps. 5–7.

6. References to Plato (428–348 BCE) throughout this paragraph are to his *Republic*, included in the *Complete Works*, ed. John M. Cooper (Indianapolis: Hackett, 1997). The first passage introducing and justifying a grand and noble lie begins in bk. 3 at 414b–c (in the standard Stephanus pagination).

7. The targets of my fourth critique of myth are Sigmund Freud (1856–1939), Carl Gustave Jung (1875–1961), and Joseph Campbell (1904–1987). The latter two especially were relatively beloved by certain stalwarts of Café Philosophy in Victoria, Canada, and so get mentioned elsewhere in this book.

8. The Joseph Campbell quotation comes from his televised video lectures, *Transformations of Myth Through Time*, dir. Stuart Brown, in assoc. Public Affairs Television and Alvin H. Perlmutter of Apostrophe S. Video, 14 episodes, (1989); and *The Power of Myth*, PBS (1988); Mystic Fire Video/Wellspring, DVD, 6 hours (2001). In the book version, *The Power of Myth*, with Bill Moyers (New York: Doubleday, 1988), Campbell says that myths "are the world's dreams" (15) and that "myth is the society's dream. The myth is the public dream and the dream is the private myth" (40). Also see Campbell, *The Hero With a Thousand Faces*, 2nd ed. (Princeton, NJ: Princeton University Press, 1968).

9. For Carl G. Jung's theory of archetypes, see for example his *Archetypes and the Collective Unconscious*, in *The Collected Works of C. G. Jung*, 2nd ed., ed. Gerhard Adler and R. F. C. Hull (Princeton, NJ: Princeton University Press, 1968), vol. 9, pt. 1, 3–41. This volume includes key papers written between 1934 to 1955 on the theory of the archetypes. On myth, see also Carl G. Jung and C. Kerényi, *Essays on a Science of Mythology: The Myth of the Divine Child and the Mysteries of Eleusis*, trans. R. F. C. Hull (Princeton, NJ: Princeton University Press, 1969).

10. Related Sigmund Freud writings include *The Interpretation of Dreams* (1900), trans. James Strachey (New York: Avon, 1965); *Three Essays on the Theory of Sexuality* (1899), trans. and ed. James Strachey (New York: Avon, 1962); *Totem and Taboo* (1913), trans. James Strachey (London: Routledge, 2002); and *Civilization and Its Discontents* (1930), trans. Joan Riviere (New York: Dover, 1994). Note that, though I cite English translations, I use parenthetical dates in notes and the Bibliography to indicate original dates of publication in cases where the dating of ideas is relevant.

11. Freud, *Totem and Taboo*, esp. chap. 4; and Freud, *Civilization and its Discontents*, 30.

12. Carl G. Jung, *Dreams*, trans. R. F. C. Hull (Princeton: Princeton University Press, 1974), 76–77. Crediting the distinction to "even primitive" peoples (by which he meant the Elgoni of Kenya, whom he had visited in 1925), Jung distinguishes between big and little dreams, which he prefers to call *significance* and *insignificant* dreams.

13. See *Upaniṣads*, trans. Patrick Olivelle (Oxford: Oxford University Press, 1996). For similar ideas in story form, see the *Chāndogya Upaniṣad* 8.7–12. The notion of lucid waking coined here represents, in my view, a key to Upaniṣad metaphysics. Its importance is less evident in Olivelle than in the English version of Swami Lokeswarananda; see his *Chāndogya Upaniṣad* (Calcutta: Ramakrishna Mission Institute of Culture, 1998).

14. The interpretive tips that, with so many qualifications, I offer about dreaming are confirmed in personal experience, but derived largely from Jung. I decline to list by title the scorned dictionaries of dream. But the dream-dictionary I imagine is an allusion to a book René Descartes fatefully dreamed in November 1619, but which he was unable to examine or make use of. See Stephen Gaukroger, *Descartes: An Intellectual Biography* (Oxford: Clarendon Press, 1995), 68–103.

15. This truism may not be true. Noam Chomsky says "If you had a free functioning democratic society, April 15, when you pay your taxes, that would be a day of celebration," in Noam Chomsky, "Noam Chomsky on Taxes," *Chomsky's Philosophy*, October 25, 2015, https://www.youtube.com/watch?v=oYuQRjLcGjY (accessed Accessed July 15, 2021).

16. *Oxford English Dictionary* (*OED*), compact ed., 22nd printing (Oxford: Oxford University Press, 1982), s.v. "fortune."

17. Hesiod, *The Poems of Hesiod*, trans. R. M. Frazer. (Norman: University of Oklahoma Press, 1983), lines 217–22, 900–906.

18. John Milton, *Paradise Lost*, in *Complete Poems*, ed. Charles W. Eliot (New York: P. F. Collier, 1909–1914), bk. 7, lines 173–74, available online at https://www.bartleby.com/4/407.html (accessed September 12, 2021).

19. Francis Bacon, *Of Fortune*, in *Essays* (1625) (Amherst, NY: Prometheus Books, 1995), 105. Bacon quotes it in Latin. I use my own translation.

20. In this essay, and in several others in this book, I make thorough use of the *OED*, s.vv. "fate," "fortune."

21. These are the opening lines of an unpublished poem, "Songroot" which is available online at https://philosophical-coaching.com/songroot.

22. Here again, I rely largely on Hesiod, *Poems* (1983), and, of course, Genesis.

23. Aristotle, *Metaphysics*, trans. W. D. Ross, 982b17–20, in *Complete Works of Aristotle. The Revised Oxford Translation*, ed. Jonathan Barnes (Princeton, NJ: Princeton University Press, 1984), 1554.

24. On contemporary chaos theory, a popular source is James Gleick, *Chaos: Making a New Science* (New York: Penguin, 2008).

25. Proverb 9:10, "The fear of the Lord is the beginning of wisdom" (*Holy Bible*, Authorized King James Version [hereafter cited KJV], Collins World. N.d.).

26. Immanuel Kant, *Observations on the Feeling of the Beautiful and Sublime* (1764), trans. John T. Goldthwait (Berkeley: University of California Press, 1960).

27. Kant, *Observations*, 47.

28. Kant, *Observations*, 48.

29. Kant, *Observations*, 51.

30. Kant, *Observations*, 48.

31. Kant, *Observations*, 48–49.

32. Kant, *Observations*, 49–50; "quiet wonder" 47–48.

33. Kant, *Observations*, 61.

34. Kant, *Observations*, 59.

35. I make passing reference to Adam Smith, I have in mind his *The Theory of Moral Sentiments* (1759), ed. D. D. Raphael and A. L. Macfie (Indianapolis: Liberty Classics, 1982); and to David Hume, who introduced an "experimental method" into moral questions in his books, *A Treatise of Human Nature* (1739–1740), ed. L. A. Selby-Bigge, 2nd ed., ed. P. H. Nidditch (Oxford: Clarendon Press, 1978); and Hume, *An Enquiry Concerning the Principles of Morals* (1751)*: A Critical Edition*, ed. Tom L. Beauchamp (Oxford: Oxford University Press, 1998).

36. Kant, *Observations*, 62.

37. Kant, *Observations*, 59 footnote.

38. Kant, *Observations*, 59.

39. Kant, *Observations*, 59.

40. Kant, *Observations*, 59–60.

41. Kant, *Observations*, 59.

42. Kant, *Observations*, 57.

43. William James, "The Will to Believe," in *The Writings of William James: A Comprehensive Edition* (1904), ed. John J. McDermott (Chicago: University of Chicago Press, 1977), 717–35. In this delightful 1896 lecture, James argues that "tough-minded" philosophers who rely on reason alone to determine truth, merely prioritize fear of error over the desire for truth, and are thus taking an emotional stance despite themselves. To not be objective, on the tough-minded view, is simply to have the wrong emotional priorities, which can hardly be construed as a principled stand against the baneful influences of emotional subjectivity.

44. The idea, due to Gottfried Wilhelm Leibniz, of subliminal or "petite perceptions" comes up in various places: see his *Discourse on Metaphysics* (1686), Reprint ed., trans. George R. Montgomery (La Salla, IL: Open Court, 1973), para. 33; and "Letter to Arnauld, April 30, 1687," in *Philosophical Writings*, ed. G. H. R. Parkinson, trans. Mary Morris and G. H. R. Parkinson (London: J. M. Dent, 1973), 65–71; and in his *New Essays on Human Understanding* (c. 1704), trans. and ed. Peter

Remnant and Jonathan Bennett (Cambridge University Press, 1981), 51, 134 (marginal pagination), a reply to *An Essay Concerning Human Understanding* (1690), by John Locke (1632–1704), ed. Peter H. Nidditch (Oxford: Clarendon Press, 1975).

45. For Sigmund Freud on *ananke* and sublimation, see esp. *Beyond the Pleasure Principle* (1920), trans. James Strachey (New York: Bantam, 1959). For a larger study, see Volney P. Gay, *Freud on Sublimation: Reconsiderations* (Albany: State University of New York Press, 1992).

46. Friedrich Wilhelm Nietzsche, *On the Genealogy of Morals* (1887), ed. Keith Ansell-Pearson, trans. Carol Diethe (Cambridge: Cambridge University Press, 2007), esp. sect. 24 of the Second Essay. Nietzsche elaborates on his theory of the moral conscience as self-vivisection.

47. John Keats, "La Belle Dame sans merci," in *Poetical Works*, ed. H. W. Garrod (Oxford University Press, 1987), 351.

48. Hesiod, "Works and Days," lines 44–105; in *The Poems of Hesiod*, trans. R. M. Frazer (Norman: University of Oklahoma Press, 1983), 97–100.

49. Friedrich Wilhelm Nietzsche, *Daybreak: Thoughts on the Prejudices of Morality* (1881), trans. R. J. Hollingdale (Cambridge University Press, 1982), 38.

50. In editor Tris Allinson's *State of the World's Birds: Taking the Pulse of the Planet.* (Cambridge, UK: BirdLife International, 2018) reports that "40 percent of the world's 11,000 bird species are in decline" and "1,469 species—13% of extant species (10,966) or roughly one in eight—are globally threatened with extinction" (22). The report estimates that "Since the year 1500, we have lost over 161 species [and possibly as many as 183 species]—an extinction rate far higher than the natural background rate" (20). According to the U.S. North American Bird Conservation Initiative (NABCI), *The State of the Birds 2019 Report* (Washington, DC: U.S. Department of Interior, 2019), https://www.stateofthebirds.org/2019/wp-content/uploads/2019/09/2019-State-of-the-Birds.pdf (accessed September 12, 2021), there are 1.2 billion fewer forest birds in North America than there were in 1970, a decline of 22%. In the same period, 700 million grassland birds were lost, down 53%. Since 1974, North American shorebirds, including many migratory species, are down 37%.

51. In Ephesians 2:12, Paul speaks of those "having no hope and without God in the world." The Greek goddess Artemis was then predominant in the city of Ephesius. See also 1 Thessalonians 4:13: "But I would not have you to be ignorant, brethren, concerning them which are asleep, that ye sorrow not, even as others which have no hope" (KJV).

52. Carl G. Jung, *Synchronicity: An Acausal Connecting Principle* (1952), trans. R. F. C. Hull (London: Routledge and Kegan Paul, 1972).

53. Lou Marinoff, *Essays on Philosophy, Praxis, and Culture: An Eclectic, Provocative, and Prescient Collection* (New York: Anthem Books, 2022), defends a synchronistic explanation in a case involving the sudden and seemingly-inexplicable appearance of snakes. Marinoff is unusual in upholding the explanatory strictures insisted upon here, in that he takes pains to rule out alternative causal explanations before embracing a synchronistic account. If I am not yet convinced of his success, my point here is the necessity of the general sort of argument he deploys.

54. Jimmy Page and Robert Plant, "Stairway to Heaven," *Led Zeppelin IV* (album) (Los Angeles: Atlantic, 1971).

55. The originator of such stair-climbing deities is James F. Thomson, "Tasks and Super-Tasks," *Analysis*, 15 no. 1 (1984): 1–13, https://doi.org/10.1093/analys/15.1.1; repr. *Zeno's Paradoxes*, ed. Wesley C. Salmon (Indianapolis: Hackett, 2001), 89–102.

56. "There are spaces between the joints, and the blade of the knife has no thickness. If you insert what has no thickness into such spaces, then there's plenty of room—more than enough for the blade to play about in." Chuang Tzu [Zhuangzi], *Basic Writings*, trans. Burton Watson (New York: Columbia University Press, 1964), iii, 2.

57. "He who tries to do the master-carpenter's chipping for him is lucky if it does not cut his hand" Lao Tzu, *Tao Te Ching*, trans. Arthur Waley (Hertfordshire, UK: Wordsworth, 1997), chap. 74.

58. Kurt Gödel, "An Example of a New Type of Cosmological Solutions of Einstein's Field Equations of Gravitation," *Reviews of Modern Physics*, 21 no. 3 (1949): 447–50, https://doi.org/10.1103/RevModPhys.21.447.

59. The italicized sentence is the mathematical law known as Cantor's Theorem; for a fuller account, see Picard, *Philosophy*, 165. The theorem was discovered by Georg Cantor (1845–1918), mathematician of the infinite, who overcame a lowly divine sentry and gained entry for us all into the paradise now named for him. We set sail soon for Omega Island.

Chapter 2

Playing Me

Must we not at times play ourselves badly to come at last into our own? Self-referential topics were ever among the most popular at Café Philosophy, so much so that one was tempted at times to call out in exasperation: "It's not all about you!" But we played with idea of self again and again, and under many guises, as the topics in this chapter show. The chapter ends in Play, with the idea that we play our way into being, and into being our best selves.

SOUL

Is there hoarfrost on this idea, this name, the Soul? Is it not a little white, a little wispy, a ghost in the night? Or is it the palpitating present, the dark ever-present well within, that passion that sweeps us, whose soul it is, off our feet? Is it a funky beat with feeling? Is it your stake in the real estate of the next world? Is it your final thought as you transmigrate to the next life, the proximate cause responsible for your future estate? Is your soul a blue flame the size of your thumb in the center of your heart? Or is your soul simply the highest bidder? Or is it the highest ladder? Are you an epiphenomenon of your body and its thriving brain? Are you simply the screen-dump of your computing hardware, a loose wheel for appearances' sake? Is your soul a twinkling in God's eye, a single beam in the infinite refulgence? Have you wings? Was your soul already you before you were born? Do you have a best-before date, an expiry date, stamped upon your soul, as its final day, or will you be enfolded into the arms of eternity when the dross of body drops? Do you cling to your soul as to the bedpost of a dream-frightened child? Are you your limbic system, do you gush with its secretions? Are you your glands and your rushing heart? Is the soul the fall guy for your every action, the one responsible, the knowing agent who may have winked? Do you depend on the soul showing up on the last day to be held accountable; for without this what amoral world are we in anyway? Is your soul the seat of your uncomfortable desires, your unconscious self, hidden from your sight by the nose on your face? Are your eyes the doorway to your soul or more like the vestibule, the dark entry chamber? Where do you put your galoshes? Is your soul a refuge from the rain, a home away from the storm? Or are you the thundercloud and the lightening? Is soul more than a metaphor?

Descend, appear, take flight, and join the hungry souls for a meal of philosophy.

SELF

Why are there so many good jokes about the self? This is a philosophical question of the first order, but one rarely ever seriously addressed. The truth in humor: is the self itself not a joke?

I am suspicious I am.

Your first memory. Can you tell among the early ones which is earliest? Or does the time line not fracture as it fades, events unclustering in a shadowy cloud, rather than stringing neatly along a single originary thread? And does that first memory include you? Are you already there? Or is your self not built up out of your experiences? If so, there was a time in your experiences when you were not yet built up. The time before your first memory: were you there? Or did you arise with that first remembered experience? Or was even that experience only a fleeting reference to a self yet to be?

And now? Is your self not still . . . yet to be? Is it not just the tattered assemblage of experiences, a heap of remembered and occurring moments, bound by the gossamer twine of association, and still open to the future? Are you merely the amalgam of your experiences, or are you the witness in virtue of whom they are all your own? But this witness—where is it in your experience? You rummage through your thoughts, like a miser through his storehouses; you note each passing intuition and emotion; you inventory your deeds and your intentions—but where in all these mental events is the witness that has them? Can the self as subject ever be object to itself? Or do you, dear witness, not transcend the very world your brain concocts?

Memories of self. Is that not a misnomer? Is the self the possessor of memories, or is memory not the mother of the self? We may think: the self is one thing, its memories are another. Or we may wonder whether memory does not subsume the self, contain it like a scrapbook or dusty photo album. The self may be the product of memory, rather than memory a capacity of a self. O forgetful ones! When you look into your memory to find yourself, who will find and who will be found?

What will you give me for this very fine self? They do not make them like this anymore. And right now you can take advantage of a once-in-a-life-time offer which will put you in the driver's seat of this sporty little self for a fraction of its resale value. Sure, it sounds like a lot; maybe its an arm and a leg; but sometimes you have got to sacrifice the part for the sake of the whole. I mean, this baby is pristine, hardly a dent in it, and a record of certifiably clean living. Okay, just for you, I will knock off a further 10% and forego the dealer's surcharge. Plus, if you pay in cash, no taxes. But that is my final offer. You will take it? Good. Let's shake on it. When this deal goes through, you will feel like a whole new person. And technically, you will not end as the same person who entered into it.

Thus we negotiate the self. We pay through the nose for the self. We bargain, we strike, we climb down, we settle for less. We battle over the self as over the remote control. But we do not remotely have control.

EGO

Do I exist? Assuredly. Does *the I* exist? No. It is a grammatical mistake. On this basis, I deny the existence of the ego. *The ego* is no less a grammatical mistake, only it has become ubiquitous, the ineradicable bogey of the mind. Yet this ghost of a grammatical error does not exist.

"The ego," as an expression in English, became commonplace as a consequence of the success of Sigmund Freud's books in translation. His famous, little and late-written book, *The Ego and the Id*, is in German titled *Das Ich and das Id*[1]—literally: "The I and the It." It was decided to use the Latin words in the English translation, and the result has been a sense of abstraction, even distance, compared with the almost intimate term *das Ich.* We speak about the existence of the ego as a theoretical postulate, as if this were somehow distinct from me. Do I need a hypothesis to intervene between myself and myself? Thus I question the need of the postulate (though I shamelessly persist in exploiting the grammar).

It is unwise, of course, to rely in metaphysics on grammatical arguments, even if they are negative. For the grammatical habits of one generation are often the principles of the next. Besides, the metaphysical victory is slim. If the ego does not exist, certainly egotism and selfishness do. One cannot remove a problem by renaming it or, as in this case, unnaming it.

So, at last literally, the Ego = the I, or I = the ego. I am saying: do not be persuaded by a name. Questions about the one are questions about the other. The theory of the ego is a theory about me.

The ego needs a name because it needs to be demarcated from the inner unknown, the inner It, to import Freud's term. The ego denotes that part of us that remains consciously accessible to us at all times. It is the inner part of us that is transparent, which is to say, surface only. For much of what goes on inside of us we have no access to. How we remember, where words come from, the origin of the imagery that unaccountably springs to mind, the maker of our dreams—over these questions we sit in silence, at the mercy of our unknown mind. The ego crouches and waits for input. Its obsequious waiting, its desire to be entertained, its cap in hand; what is there to like about the ego?

When we think about the ego, we usually think about the *me*, not the *I*. The *me* is the self as object; the *I* is the self as subject.[2] As an object, we are known; as a subject, we know. Again we are skating on the thin ice of grammar here, yet so be it. The "I" has its privacy. The "me" is social; it is the object of your knowledge as well as mine. If we have a conversation about ego, we enter into a conflict of interest. The ego we are prepared to discuss is the "me," the already shared object. The "I" hides, even in crowds. We talk about how we are seen, or how we want to be seen, or complain that we are never seen. Nearly all of our self-referential talk is directed at precisely bolstering the image of the "me" in the eyes of others. And when we are alone, we rehearse that bolstering, like practicing lines in front of a mirror. The "me" is the shiny self-reflecting surface. "As a thing is cut and filed, / As a thing is carved and polished"—an ancient Chinese epigram.[3]

The "self" (or ego + plus) is real, in the same way that a dream is real. It is real in our imagination, which is a real faculty. The ego becomes real by our ritual recognition of it each day upon waking. The dream is real, but what it is *of* is not real. Dreams are not what they seem. So with the ego. It is not what it seems. It is the name for the stomach of the mind, which wants to be fed, demands to be fed, cries until it is fed. The stomach is real. The need is real. If the ego only means a gaping wound, it is very real. But it is not to be believed in, like a bad dream from which one had best simply turn away. The ego is an illusion like success is an illusion. Not that one should not succeed. Only that one invests too much credence and deliverance in it. And when one gets it, one wonders whether it was worth it all.

PERSONALITY

Contrast personality with character, then with identity. All three can be meant as answers to the question: *who are you?* Yet they can also be teased apart by their respective semantic colorings: personality is psychological; character is ethical; identity is social (and/or metaphysical).

Personality traits and characteristics are cited in explanation of behavior; their stability is predictability, the glimmering hope of science. Character also has its traits, namely virtues and vices; their stability is trustworthiness, the shining hope of ethics. But ethical stabilities are measured over a lifetime, at least a track record, not once-off behavior. Trust is made possible by character, and while this has implications for personality psychology, it is the stuff of fate and in the political realm of prosperity. Here see the glimmer not of science but of greatness.

At last, identity, silent answer to the purest "who?" We jostle in packs and jockey like loners for our identities to be established. There is, no doubt, a political economy of identity formation. But is that the only grounds of being same? Suppose we turn our backs on the great race through life, and beckon to the inner beyond for some solace or truth. Is it out there, in the painful unknown, that we will find our ultimate identity? And if ego is the sacrificial cost, the fare for boarding this ferry, is not personality offered up too?

When the Buddha realized that there was no self, did personality and character also lose status? If we are allowed still to be individuals under the Buddhist regime of selflessness, why are so many Buddha statues identical? If everything has Buddha nature, must there not be rogue Buddhas? If we are to kill the Buddha on the road if we see him, is it not due to some character or behavioral flaw he retains?[4] Or perhaps character can survive the death of the self, as ethics survived the death of god (assuming, of course, that it preexisted it . . .).

Do we clamor for personality as if for the spotlight? Or do we want to blend in through personality, through conformation to the norms as we find them? If I know your personality, is there anything more of you to know? Do I need to know you to know your personality (or vice versa)? Must I identify your personality type before I can truly encounter you? (And how infinite is the taxonomy of personality?) Perhaps the schema of personality is a skewed concept, a slanted picture of who we are, only a biased slice of a larger life-view.

I do not know if you have a personality, or if you would be improved by having one. If you have one, I do not know which one it is. If I had one, I might know what I was looking for. Only I am not looking.

Open your closets and bear all your personalities to Philosophy.

IDENTITY

If the self is *what* you are, identity is *who* you are. But the word "identity" easily covers both, and thus *identity* is ambiguous. We may be considered either as an ineffable subject, a private experiencer, or as a type or a kind, as one among a many, as part of a group. A similar bifurcation (subjective and objective) arises in the notion of community: a shared belonging versus a bustle of interacting bodies. I might say: identity is a community of one.

Identity is not one but a community of notions. We do well to start at the very beginning, at the metaphysical foundation of identity, if only to set it aside. For it is not the topic most will have come to discuss. The law of identity states that $A = A$. And who could disagree? Yet our concern here is not with this abstract identity, a sort of timeless relation met in mathematics; so put aside the bare self-relation of each thing, or id-entity. The opposite of abstract identity is bare otherness, numerical difference, or, as it is sometimes called in maths, inequality ($\neq$). Of certain more pertinent senses of *identity*, difference is not opposite, but constitutive. Of those senses, however, in due time; first, consider identity *over* time (*A* at one time is selfsame as *A* at another time).

As the question before us bears most concretely on ourselves, we may further specify identity as the perdurance of self. The mystery of our identity is revealed by reflective memory. I think back to my earliest memories, and now ask: how do I know they are mine? Forget the question of truth of memory (was it really the same as I remember it?); shift the question to who remembers, and who is remembered, to the continuance of self across time. Ask: what makes me *me* through all my experiences? Who am I that I still am I? This identity is *mysterious* since it is not given in or mediated through experience, but claims to be known immediately, as a kind of transcending unity of experience. Metaphysics wants to know about this self, which perpetually seems to leap out of itself just to stay what it is. I say: jump right in.[5]

Of course, that kind of talk does not pass methodological muster, at least if one takes one's scientific reason with a helping of dismissive rigor. Freud imagined himself into such a straight-jacket in calling himself a scientist. He laid the groundwork of a science of identity by robbing myth. Myth One: the infant is primordially unable to identify itself, and mistakes itself for the once-subsuming mother. The oceanic womb[6] experience outlasts the womb and, once born, the infant experiences itself as non-different from its world. Moral: our adult sense of self is a fiction, born of correcting/managing the ignorance of the child. Next, through learning we identify objects, and then identify with them. This secondary identification is connected with the rise of the ego through the Freud's "reality principle".[7] But it too is an illusion, since it permits the psychological denial of separation, effecting an assuagement of the primordial separation anxiety which surrounds the false primary identity with the mother. Moral: ego development, proceeding through successive mis-identification, is a negation of a negation. The subsequent steps away from ignorance are . . . ignorance.[8]

Note: much of the illusion of scientific rigor in Freud's approach comes from denying ambiguity, from the easy assumption of external id-entity, a material reality of discrete objects, which the subject learns to discover and to distinguish itself from. The metaphysical identities are assumed (that is called "being scientific"); then (not identity but) identification becomes the object of investigation, and it turns out to be the psychological process by which a self is created. The irony is that (despite Freud's hydraulic metaphor of pressure dynamics to model repression and neurotic eruptions) the process of standing up an ego is more or less magic, and science only the wry, know-it-all smile that clinically characterizes the process in material metaphor.

In contrast to this approach, which is hardly dead, consider the yet more thoroughly social approach to identity, that selves emerge from self-to-self relations, not self-to-object relations. Contra Freud, the first significant other is the mother, not the breast. Put differently, we become ourselves in a world of others, a social world, not the natural world (which anyway is only given to us via cultural representation). The starting point of psychology (and self-creation) are I-thou relations, not I-it relations.[9] On the earlier view, the mother is first an object, and even the self starts with id, which we adults experience as a cavity in the subject, as unconscious; but it is the *It within*, an objective will which acts from within and is independent of our conscious control. Yet if the starting point of self is others (rather than a material other), we may have the free play of interaction, the collaborative creation of each other through interaction. Rather than the determinative metaphors of hydraulics or thermodynamics, we have choice, *play*, the reciprocity of selves constructing identities socially.

How free such play really is becomes a major question of identity politics. Our cultures also interpret mothers, and natures, and hold out to us available roles and positions for us to take up. The role of others is not merely interpersonal, or social, but *societal*, and mediated by social institutions. We become who we are only through the institutional frameworks of family, school, work, and/or the market. At best, these objective structures are free structures, which give us latitude of choice, a framework of action, rather than a prescription of ends. At worst, they limit us, define us, assign our identities to us and supply us with obligatory ready-made labels. Notice in this approach the issue is not illusion; the self is not born of a history of errors; instead the issue is power, the self being born, named and made without its own consent.

We need societal institutions, for they frame the essential dimensions of difference for us. That is, who we are is very much about how we differ from others. Identity and difference are not opposites but spatting siblings. Yet not everything that differentiates me adds to my identity. I am unique in countless meaningless ways, but also in a very few highly significant ones. As Charles Taylor argues,[10] you cannot found an identity on the unique number of hairs on your head; or rather you can only do so by investing that number with a cosmical or spiritual significance that it does not have by itself. The dimensions of identity are few, we have genuine "horizons of significance" we need to recognize and work within. Many of the things that make us "unique" are actually things that make us similar to others we identify with (for example, philosophers, Canadians, feminists, conservatives, co-religionists, sports enthusiasts, and so on). Our identity is constituted of significant differences that are more often shared than unique. Institutions facilitate these identities, but they can also impose them, as it does objectively in the institutions of global patriarchy, white supremacy, and hyperbolic law and order. Power must be opposed by freedom. But freedom must constrain its own preferences.

Moral: our identity is constituted of significant differences that are more often shared than unique. Perhaps our identities consist in the uniqueness of the totality of our differences from so many others. Me and we are closer than you think.

Come let us think together. Leap into dialogue. Come discover who you are.

SELFLESSNESS

There are few areas where ethics and metaphysics more clearly overlap than in the subject of selflessness. You can take it as a quality of moral action; or you can take it literally, that is, metaphysically: there is no such thing as the self. Often you find the curious view (based on an inter-disciplinary pun) that if you but once could glimpse the metaphysical truth of selflessness, your behavior patterns would be transformed, and you would become saintly overnight. That is not how most of us spend the dark hours.

It is wise, I suggest, if only from precaution, to keep some distance between the two meanings, to resolutely resist the pun. Certainly there have been many selfless persons who maintained a metaphysical belief in individual eternal existence. Any Christian this side of heresy, at least in so far as they believe all that talk of the enforcement in the final days of individual moral accountability, would seem to be bound to the metaphysical existence of a personal self. To believe that there exists (in a literal, that is, a true sense) a Self behind our actions surely does not render impossible a life of unselfish concern and service. I say, trust the deed, not the word.

We tend to overvalue the philosophical positions people take, as if every stance adopted expressed a considered opinion, a willful judgment, a final perspective. Put aside the issue that often a philosophical stance is adopted more or less for show, for purposes of public view, to be seen to believe. In point of fact, some truths about the world are more or less forced on us, at least for any earnest thinking person. Even if it is not really, it still feels that way. Nobody need wait upon the authority of some spiritual master to believe that the world is full of suffering. One's own eyes testify to it, if only one will open them. Of course to see all that suffering, to stare it in the distraught face, is to know a painful truth, and it is often more polite simply to look away. To the incurably suffering, that can help to distract their attention, and bring it to more pleasant matters. But the hard truths force themselves on us, and we are entitled to the occasional vacation of an illusion as a break from the perpetual grind that is our dysfunctional reality. And yet, if we love the truth, we also have to make the effort to observe the mess we find here, however disagreeable the task. We think people are expressing themselves when they express their philosophy. And perhaps they are, when they are not simply doing so to appear in a certain way. But otherwise they are often found to be merely reporting what they have been driven to.

This brings me to a different kind of defense of the above pun, or play on the two meanings of selflessness. For it can after all happen that the truth transforms our thoughts and behavior. But simple facts suffice, a whole new worldview is not necessary. As an example, I was once planning to meet a friend at a certain place and time, and I begged them not to be late, as I had a highly time-dependent task to do after our brief meeting. Unlike that person, I am not one to nitpick about punctuality, and I tolerate as much tardiness in others as I do in myself, which is rather a lot. Since this friend was well aware of my laxity in such matters, and took reciprocal liberties in my case, I felt it was important to stress that, in this instance, no such dilly-dallying was tolerable. My friend happily agreed to my condition, so I was justly annoyed when, fifteen minutes after the appointed time, they had still not shown up. My waiting showed no sign of patience, and I angrily swore at my friend in my mind: "Did I not stress to you how important this was to me? Did you not expressly acknowledge and accept my insistence? Why would you so selfishly disregard my needs?" My friend did arrive, and reported having just been involved in a bicycle accident and, but for a split second, almost killed. Once this single additional fact became known to me, though all the other facts of my case retained the same urgency, I felt all my anger immediately evaporate in concern for the safety of my friend. The truth can set you free.

In like fashion, I do not doubt that a fresh insight into the depth of the human condition might well totally reorient our self in regard to our moral relations with others. But when we fish for ethical insights in the pond of metaphysics, we are liable to catch what lives there, which is to say entire schools of impotent abstractions. Instead of a meal, we may reel in a rubber boot. All praise to the intellect, but when did its tinkering ever untie let alone tune the heartstrings? I do not wish to be dualist about thought and feeling, but much thought is thoughtless thought, and utterly fails even to seek to unbind or to make whole the miserable heart. Facts make a difference in morality; but morality makes no difference to fact.

There is one metaphysical belief which is often trotted out as a great goad to ethical or enlightened behavior. All is one. We are all kin. Everything is interrelated. All things are interdependent. Nothing is itself except through its relations to other things. All determination is negation. The forms of this belief are many, as colorful as its names: the jewel-net of Indra; the web of mother Maya; the flower-wreath doctrine; the identity of opposites; the pre-established harmony; the doctrine of mutually dependent co-arising; or *te*, which is the virtue and power of the *Tao*, nurturing each after its own kind. Or the Grateful Dead will sing it to you, inviting you to awaken and discover that it is through your eyes that the world sees.[11] In its extreme form, the belief entails a denial of all boundaries and all centers. This vision of Identity relegates all difference to illusion, but a softer vision of Harmony retains real differentness while affirming all the more the mutuality of all beings. Mystics trip over themselves to articulate this view, not knowing how to begin to say a truth that is without a beginning. Stuttering, yet they are voluminous, mostly in condemning every attempt at formulating truth as impartial and incomplete. Finally the great Oneness is expressed only by silence and a smile, presuming general agreement. Nothing is ever fully true, except the truth which cannot be said. What more can be said than that?

The question is whether a profound conviction in the commingling of all essential natures will make you a better person, say a better parent or a better citizen, more of a humanitarian, nobler, or more enlightened. Who benefits from your conversions? When you realize your existence is only superficially separate, that you are part of something greater (be it ecological or divine or both), do you then love your friends and family more? Does the plight of strangers weigh any more heavily on your conscience? Are you more compassionate to the evil or the needy now that you realize you are one with them? What is the moral payoff of your metaphysical realization? At what point does the acquired knowledge that there is no self yield the selflessness of action? Is it not just so many words until it does?

There is a curious dilemma of selflessness lurking in this widely-touted metaphysical basis of ethics. Is self-interest to be overcome, defeated, utterly vanquished? Or is the basis of its self-regarding rather to be expanded, and simply made less narrow? Neither option seems acceptable. Let us examine. Grant the objective is to arrive at selfless behavior, selfless action, the mark of compassion which, if true, is never idle. In this war against selfishness, one may either destroy the enemy or deceive them into supporting one's goals. The destructive approach involves a complete dismantling of the reflexively self-regarding behavior that pits self against self, and divides the eater from the eaten. This is the royal road to victory, and the problem is amassing enough firepower for the job without becoming corrupted and drunk on that power. Deceit may seem the better course, but it can only promise a cunning co-opting of the selfish response for a higher purpose. This it seems to me is the approach of the "all is one" strategy of metaphysical ethics. It invites us to go on in our usual selfish ways, except that now the self we are to privilege and to defend is not this mortal coil but the infinite web. I have not understood interconnectedness until I love each of the world's children as my own. I may (indeed I must) continue fiercely to protect my own, as much as any defensive or maternal instinct ever did, but now it is not me, or even my own child, that I defend, but my world, the great Mother ecosystem I have so wholly submerged myself in. When I am one with the Mother, my reflexive defenses will protect her, even at the cost of my own puny life, a drop in her ocean. I may continue to lash out in greed, only now my greed is for the greater good, and all my private concerns are as if in a blind trust. How can I harm another when that other is myself? But how will I protect it if it is not myself?

So here is my dilemma: either my metaphysics destroys my self without pity, in which case it loses compassion on the way to compassion; or it deceives self-interest, thus dispensing with truth on the way to truth. Either way, I see nothing here but pious hopes and a will to do better. And that is fine, but it is not a case of metaphysics improving your character.

There is a famous teaching story[12] from the time of the Buddha. Some wrangler had wandered in and was badgering the quiet ambiance with metaphysical questions. The Buddha would not answer. Instead, he asked how unwise it would be for one who was shot by a poisoned arrow to resist all treatment until it should be explained to him: the exact nature of the poison, who had shot the arrow, what kind of bow had been used, from which precise position, and so on. Such a quibbler would surely perish by the poison before their questions could all even be posed. Some metaphysical questions are profitless, and plenty of these pertain to selflessness. Is it any better than this to wait upon some all-consuming insight before loving the neighbor you do not know? The loving hand is quicker than the knowing mind.

You will have noticed that my essay may be suffering a little from the effects of such poison. My whole theme is the autonomy, as it were, of the ethical question of selflessness, in relation to the metaphysical issues. Knowing the truth of metaphysics is probably impossible. But thinking one knows is common enough. The question is whether adopting such philosophies will have any bearing on one's motivational structure. But I have spent my space warning you off the one, rather than directly approaching the other. Have I done more than name some poisons?

Pull out the arrow. Save yourself and your selflessness for philosophy. If philosophy is the poison, let more philosophy be the antidote.

SPIRIT

Breathe! That's it. Slowly. In and out. Here is spirit.

Quietly now, we must whisper if we would speak of spirit. It is soft as the air. Even a whisper scares away this ghost. Silence alone preserves its presence. Silence and breathing.

Life has long been regarded as the breath of spirit, and at death the breath goes out of us. When we exhale for the last time, we *expire*, which, etymologically, is the exiting of spirit. "Breath, which was ever the original of 'spirit'" (to cop a line from William James).[13] Here he is wresting a quasi-materialist theory of consciousness from the stuff of myth and a whiff:

> Let the case be what it may in others, I am as confident as I am of anything that, in myself, the stream of thinking (which I recognize emphatically as a phenomenon) is only a careless name for what, when scrutinized, reveals itself to consist chiefly of the stream of my breathing. The "I think" which Kant said must be able to accompany all my objects, is the "I breathe" which actually does accompany them. There are other internal facts besides breathing (intracephalic muscular adjustments, etc., of which I have said a word in my larger Psychology), and these increase the assets of "consciousness," so far as the latter is subject to immediate perception; but breath, which was ever the original of "spirit," breath moving outwards, between the glottis and the nostrils, is, I am persuaded, the essence out of which philosophers have constructed the entity known to them as consciousness. That entity is fictitious, while thoughts in the concrete are fully real. But thoughts in the concrete are made of the same stuff as things are.[14]

Here, James rejects positing consciousness as an entity in the intent to explain. If not as an entity or thing per se, it nevertheless exists as a process, flow, or stream, that needs to be explained. In technical parlance, consciousness is the *explanandum* that demands an explanation, not the *explanans* that supplies one. James here set his post-Darwinian position over against that of Immanuel Kant, himself salvaging the pieces of René Descartes' failing *cogito*[15] The self, soul, or spirit (*l'esprit*), whose substantial existence Descartes sought to establish, proved hard to find, impossible to locate, and too intangible to be presented. The substance claim fell through the bottom, leaving only a premise dangling over a void, the premise "I think." Already David Hume had pointed out that "there is a thinker" does not follow logically from "there are thoughts." The I is nowhere to be found in experience, and yet all of our experience and all of our thoughts, are, after all, our own. Immanuel Kant postulated the transcendental ego precisely to *explain* the unity of experience despite the absence in experience of the subject itself, the I. The transcendental ego is the missing I.[16]

The explanatory power of spirit is lost to James, who is far more impressed with the variety of its mysteries. The "original of 'spirit'" is breath, bare breath, along with the "muscular sensations" accompanying breath and other subtle but physical motions within the head and throat. The very thoughts in our heads are "made of the same stuff as things are," that is, as external physical objects. This is a realism about thought and consciousness, which takes their existence as a given, as something demanding explanation. However subtle it may be, spirit is not missing, not without location in space, like the essential consciousness of the Cartesian ego. Though James denies consciousness the status of a substance or thing with unique explanatory advantages, he embraces it all the more emphatically as a phenomenon, as a fact to be accounted for, as *explanandum*. Consciousness certainly exists, and even has a purpose, or a least a function or role to play in our everyday and not-so-everyday knowing. That function needs now, however, to be accounted for in an evolutionary context, as it is understood as an adaptation conferring survival value. Of course, an explanation or account based on "mechanisms" like natural selection will make no appeal to the metaphysics of essence, with its allusions to changeless being and eternal identity. Nor is it strictly mechanistic in the way that the machine universe of Descartes is mechanistic.

Aristotle had equated *psyche* and *eidos*, spirit and essence, soul and form. Spirit, taken as soul (*psyche*), is the form of the body, its essential activity, inscribing order and purposes on the body's dynamism (potential), hence the dominant explanatory factor. As form or *eidos*, spirit carries the bulk of the explanatory weight.[17] In Descartes, the soul (*l'esprit*) is a distinct and separable substance (reality) from the wholly mechanical body, which operates according to discoverable and quantifiable laws. Yet complex human behavior, as shown in even a dull wit's commentary, can only be explained by appeal to mind, which has its own essence, an essence that evades but can ascertain physical law. The ghost in the machine explains what the machine cannot explain, so again, in early modernity spirit, plays a major explanatory role and is postulated to clarify what is opaque, to resolve what is troubling. Though Kant could not follow along with Descartes substance metaphysics, nor could he shake the ever-present "I think," which thus evaporated into such *diaphaneity* as to earn the honorific, *transcendental*. Otherwise we are allegedly without any account of the unity of the self, the mineness of all my experiences. Spirit is the explanation we cannot speak.

So James' anti-dualism is hardly the usual perspective on spirit, which is *prima facie* a dualist notion. Spirit hovers, matter settles. A breath moves over the face of the deep. Thus in the beginning there was a whisper. The silence was disturbed, and spirit was no longer alone.

Still breathing? Shall I go on?

Spirit is what is left of the divine after consciousness came to be regarded as just another physiological phenomenon. Spirit retains a transcendence even while soul is particularized to this or that individual and their life story. Spirit is unconstrained by space or time and steps like mighty Vishnu across all worlds. Coincidence is the idiosyncrasy of spirit.

Ask of spirit, "Who?", and it will recede. You must wrestle your angels before you may name them—and even then you have a pang and maybe no answer. And if we may ask "who?" must we not ask "he or she?" Has spirit a gender? Or has spirit the ambivalence of *Siva Ardhanarishvara*?

In the West, for so long, spirit has seemed male. In Aristotle, for example, spirit is form (*eidos*), and form is male. Formless matter (*hyle*), which is passive and indefinite, was coded female. While matter differentiates individuals one from another, it is itself wholly lifeless; for form alone generates beings after their own kind. Likewise the Bible reads: "And the earth was without form, and void; and darkness was upon the face of the deep. And the Spirit of God moved upon the face of the waters."[18] Again the male creator of matter moves his hand over the waters (*tehom*, the deep; the abyss; allegedly cognate with the Babylonian *Tiamat*, the originating goddess or creatrix). Thus "the deep" has a feminine connotation, and the hovering spirit completes the usual male on top scene. Again the male is the active, the creator.

In ancient India you had the reverse. Spirit as *Purusha* is a male person, but he is inactive. He is the witness, doing nothing but suffering everything. Spirit is the true experiencer of your experience; your eyes are the eyes of the world. No doubt you think you do stuff too, but even your action you must surrender, for it is in the hands of the creatrix, *Prakriti*, Nature. The executive function of the divine is transferred wholly over to this female counterpart of *Purusha*, while *Purusha* lies around all day like a lazy man doing nothing, absorbed in his own experience. Meanwhile the she-spirit does all the work, which is to say, creates all the mischief. *Abandon the fruits of your action and consecrate all you accomplish to the one for the sake of whom all is done.* That is called right relation with spirit.[19]

This implies that living selflessly is living for spirit. But how can that be unless spirit is without a self? But without a self, can spirit retain an identity? Spirit without identity is just a plain old entity, an inert thing. Spirit is just not itself without a self. Thus the Buddha never became a god.

To be spiritual is presumably to be like spirit. Yet can you be like god—invisible, silent, deadly, sure, but unknown? How can you be like god without knowing yourself? But how can you know yourself without being yourself, and thus being a self, which disqualifies you from selflessness, unlike god? It seems the more you are like god the less you are like yourself and the more you are like yourself the less you are like god. How far then are we yet from spirit?

I will stop there. Enough going round in circles. Bring your mortal coil and your eternal ghost to philosophy. Let us whisper together about higher things.

PLAY

Play is nearly an embarrassment to philosophy, which prefers to don heavy robes and heavier faces, to grimace and to scowl, to think and to be serious, to play for keeps rather than to play at all. Philosophy is no child's play. While it may be fun, fun does not get you tenure. The academic tones of philosophy are a wet blanket thrown over the free spirit that loves to leap and clap hands. Philosophy prefers to lumber rather than to leap, to wave its hand in silent dismissal rather than to applaud, make a playful noise, or cast funny hand shadows with no better intent than to amuse. Philosophy knows few hurrahs.

Yet play is a deeply serious concept, stretching across many boundaries of thought. For instance, play has been evoked by social psychologists (who often pretend, in their professional capacity, not to be philosophers) in the very rise and creation of the self. It is a beautiful story. The infant is born without a self, having only an organism, sensory channels to the external world, delicately complex reflexes and fixed action patterns, and only a spastic control over its responses. But it knows mommy, and mommy becomes the one great significant other, at first separated from the infant only by the frustrations of its desires. Otherwise a happy oneness, self-absorbed, subsumed unknowingly in other.

But as it grows it plays, and mother is the first playmate. After babbling, it imagines others and acts out their role. The child in play takes on the role of other, plays at mother and scolds itself as child, then forgives itself. It plays at fireman, truck driver, tea, house, taking on all the roles and imaginatively representing itself or playmates in related roles. It plays at being adult before it becomes adult. Thus it learns self. Play is the infant's entertainment; whereas adult entertainment is a different business altogether.

This taking on of roles is playing other, taking an *other* into oneself. The other is internalized and introjected, and self only begins to arise as this happens. First self is itself only in relation to the significant other, primary caregiver. Then through the expansion of play and through play with actual others, rules are learned and created, and organized games become possible. Here all the roles are known to each, and each move or play in the game is a call for a response or a response to a call. The child learns the rules, loves to make up new rules for advantage (to stack the deck) or to smooth out differences, and knows a game when it knows all the positions, all the parts to play, all the rules that govern each part. Holding all of this in mind is internalizing a generalized other, not merely a single significant other. And the independent self arises when the generalized other is taken into itself, introjected. Play therefore is the very serious learning act that manufactures self, or rather generates it as a byproduct to fun and games. In play, we become who we are.

This brings up sport, organized games, and team play. Sport is a pasttime, an individual means of physical fitness, a diversion perhaps, but at times deadly serious. Sport professionalized is still best when joy and love drive it; but it is also a career, a daily grind of great sacrifice, the total commitment of individuals to excel, to compete, to triumph. It is as well an industry, play become business, and the clash of competitive interests and titanic egos. Besides the players, of course, and the contest on the ice or field, there is the competition of owners, the staked reputations of coaches, the servile loyalty of the water boy, and the thankless dedication of team managers and auxiliaries, who are the inner circle of die-hard fans, hangers-on of the game. Stalking the celebrity athletes are the omnipresent paparazzi Harpies. All these people mean business. Play is professional, serious, and disloyalty may mean shame, loss of employment, even humiliation in the media. When the stakes are high, play is not frivolous and may not be fun.

There is also an ethics of sport. Sportsmanship (as it used to be called)[20] is a noble ideal, where competition is fair and subordinated to common human decency. You may want to win but you need not try to win by humiliating or abusing your opponent. Sporting excellence can be sought without lording it over the less excellent. A synonym of *excellence* is *virtue*, and sport is one of the few domains of contemporary life where the ethical concept of virtue is still at play. Today we have few common ideals that we are consciously aware of, that identify us to ourselves. Also relevant under this heading of ethics in sport are the ongoing scandals in Olympic judging and the widespread problem of doping in professional, amateur, and varsity sports, which will only grow with the inventiveness of the pharmaceutical industry.

The politics of sport are worth mentioning, if only briefly. Noam Chomsky has claimed that professional sports, especially team and regional rivalries, are a great distraction of the masses, so that our political masters can carry on with their exploitation without making us too unhappy.[21] Give the people bread and circuses, and they will be pacified. Let them work out their aggressions on each other in play, in senseless team rivalries. We are played off against each other, while the real winners sneak off with the prize.

From sport we move to war. War is no game, but it is the ultimate competition. It is not fun but hell. Still, some like hell and practice for it. That hell can make meaning, so that veterans, though terrorized by their experience, can long for it again; at least there one felt alive, was in touch with ultimate things, and had real human contact. What we call war games are training for the real thing. Let us pretend to kill until we are good at it. For we may not have more than one chance, and if they are better at it than we are, we die before we kill. Military strategy is standardly likened to the game of chess, and warriors in their down-time have in all ages entered competitive games (is the javelin not the relic of a spear? is fencing not mock fight? are wrestling and boxing not ancient arts of war?).

The martial arts are pursued as sports. In correct jargon, one "plays" tai chi. One plays with the energy, or indeed it plays with itself through you, its instrument. Thus tai chi, though a martial art, has a spiritual side as well. It is both spiritual and military, if not a holy war, at least a sacred game.

We move now from the theater of war to the theater of the stage, to the dramatic play. This too is serious, an art and an industry. It is not mere imitation but convincing imitation. The illusion of reality is created, thus it is play. But pretending must be believable, it must be convincing, it must not look like play. The imitation fakes reality in a credible way. It is make-believe that must make itself believable. But this is an old idea of acting as imitation. Theater today may play it down, play on the expectations of the spectator, blur the illusory line between player and audience. The curtain may have fallen on this old idea of the dramatic play.

Socrates himself was something of a tragic hero, but not one without a certain capacity for comedy. He was very playful, a philosopher who knew how not to be serious. His use of dramatic irony transformed philosophy. Irony is the use of falsehoods to express truth. "I am ignorant," he said, meaning he was wise. "You are very wise," he said to his show-off interlocutors, meaning they were fools. This play proved deadly for him. In his trial, he could have saved himself, had he but played to the gallery, that is, the jury of some 500. But they did not take kindly to his jokes. And his own examined life came to an end.[22]

Second last and not least, we have Ludwig Wittgenstein, whose doctrine that "meaning is use" took meaning out of the mind and placed it in social space, among us rather than within us.[23] Meaning was not in the head and but in the loosely organized verbal interactions that constitute so much of our shared world and our reality. His concept of the language game revealed meaning, not as an inner fact in the psyche, but as something at play in our social life. We all know what games are, but no one can define the essence of game. We recognize games when we see them, but who can say what the nature of game is? We know by doing; we understand meaning by joining the game, playing within the rules (which do not determine what we play, not even wholly how, but only set up constraints of in/convenience, known to all players). Game (read: meaning) cannot be defined, but it does not need to be. There is nothing common to all games, no necessary and sufficient conditions to be a game. Yet this impossibility of a definition does not hamper your understanding or mine. Meaning is likewise. Meaning, therefore, is a social construct of real people, not the logical construction of a theorist or philosopher. Let us, therefore, play, and not be philosophers bent out of shape on semantic problems. Play, but do not be confused when language goes on holiday. Only take a ride.

Can I end without mention of sexual play, foreplay and all post-coital games? In the lingo, a player is a non-monogamous exploiter, always on the look-out for easy game, a liar and a user, a home and heart breaker, playing on the needs and desires of others. This play is serious but also fun, superficial but deadly. This is playing with fire, setting crotch or heart aflame.

Come out and play. Make me believe you. It is your move.

NOTES

1. See Sigmund Freud, *The Ego and the Id* (1923), Standard ed., trans. Joan Riviere, rev. and ed. James Strachey (New York: W. W. Norton, 1960).

2. Here I pick up the elucidating usage of William James, *The Principles of Psychology* (1890), authorized ed. (New York: Dover. 1950), vol. 1, chap. 10, 291–401. It is noteworthy that Freud reifies "I" and "It" to achieve a "scientifish" theory, whereas James only speaks of "I" and "me" after swaddling himself in emphatic and protective caveats meant to underscore that these are grammatical devices for rhetorical convenience, not theoretical terms. In this, James is a better exemplar than Freud, or even Martin Buber's theologizing in *I and Thou* (1923), trans. Walter Kaufmann (New York: Charles Scribner's, 1970), for how to safely play philosophy with pronouns.

3. From the *Book of Odes* (#55), quoted by Confucius in *Analects* 1.15. The Wing-tsit Chan translation is given; see Chan, *A Source Book in Chinese Philosophy*, trans. and compiled Chan (Princeton, NJ: Princeton University Press. 1963), 21–22.

4. The Buddhist doctrine of no-self (*annata*) needs to be understood metaphysically here, since personality (individual differences) and character traits (virtues or *paramitas* of Buddha-mind) clearly do survive enlightenment (*nirvana*, or extinguishing). That many Buddha statues are "identical" hints symbolically at the doctrine that there is Buddha-nature in everyone. Killing the Buddha on the road is a reference to Sheldon B. Kopp, *If you Meet the Buddha on the Road, Kill Him!* (New York: Bantam Books, 1972).

5. Through this paragraph there are allusion to John Locke, David Hume, and Immanuel Kant, whose ideas on related issue are discussed more expressly in this chapter heading "Spirit." Briefly, Locke clearly frames the question of personal identity *over time* and tries to solve it with a notion of conscious continuity, which Hume declines to accord any ontological significance; for the allegedly substantial self is not anywhere an object of experience, and, for Hume, that implies that we have no knowledge of it. Unsettled by the seeming undeniability of Hume's premises, Kant is led to "deduce" a transcendental ego, which is nowhere to be met in experience yet confers upon all our experience an immediate personal unity (all my experiences are *mine*). This is the significance of James, who prefers "thought goes on" or even

the zen-like "it thinks" to the Cartesian "I think," characterizing thought as having a "personal nature." See James, *Principles* (1950), vol. 1, 225.

6. I use the phrase "oceanic womb," but in Sigmund Freud's *Civilization and Its Discontents* (1930), trans. Joan Riviere (New York: Dover, 1994), he speaks of "oceanic feeling," the *womb* part representing his analysis. The feeling in question, reported personally by his friend, pacifist playwright, Indiaphile and Noble Laureate, Romain Rolland (1866–1944), according to whom the view is widespread and nothing less than the very foundation of the world's religions. Freud professed a sensible scientific inability to experience it: "I cannot discover this 'oceanic' feeling in myself" (2). But this does not stop him from interpreting it as a veiled expression of nostalgia for the womb, which more or less reduces those Indian mystics to primitive spiritual minds unconsciously hankering to return to the primordial unity they knew already *in utero*. And it is this regressive spirit, we are to suppose, which wrote the *Upanishads*. Note how Eurocentrism is partially constitutive of Freud's scientific virtue-signaling. See *The Upanishads*, trans. J. Mascaro (London: Penguin Books, 1965).

7. For a careful discussion of Freud's "reality principle," see Paul Ricoeur, *Freud and Philosophy: An Essay of Interpretation* (New Haven, CT: Yale University Press, 1970), 261–80. According to Ricoeur, reality for Freud is at first merely the opposite of fantasy, and not problematic, whereas loss of contact with reality indicates mental disorder. Later, Freud distinguishes two forms of mental process. One, governed by the pleasure principle (an innate tendency to avoid pain and attain pleasure), came to be associated with the unconscious Id, a part of the mind incapable of distinguishing reality and fantasy. The infant at first is all Id, and the Id never learns; but the child does, and the Ego arises with the gradual recognition of reality (utility, delayed satisfaction). Reality thus becomes an achievement, albeit an unstable one, correlated with everyday consciousness. Only the (romanticized) figure of the scientist, putting aside all fantasy, acquiesces in *ananke,* sees reality as it is. Thus, the reality principle eventually became "the cypher of a possible wisdom." Ricoeur, *Freud and Philosophy*, 262.

8. For "Myth One," see Freud, *Civilization and its Discontents* (1930): "Originally the ego included everything, later it detaches itself from the external world" (4). On the second illusion, Freud writes that the ego "seems to us an independent unitary thing, sharply outlined against everything else. That this is a deceptive appearance . . . was first discovered by psychoanalytic research" (2).

9. The *locus classicus* here is Buber's 1923 book, *Ich und Du* (literally, "I and You"), which was translated under the title, *I and Thou* (1970). Buber contrast I-it relations with I-you relations, in other words relations with things vs. relations with persons (ultimately, for Buber, God). But I go on in this paragraph to channel the social theory as in George H. Mead, *Mind, Self, and Society*, ed. C. W. Morris (Chicago: University of Chicago Press, 1934); and, in the next paragraph, that of Peter L. Berger and Thomas Luckmann, *The Social Construction of Reality: A Treatise in the Sociology of Knowledge* (New York: Doubleday, 1966).

10. Charles Taylor, *The Malaise of Modernity* (Concord, ON: House of Anansi, 1994), 35–37. The notion of "horizons of significance" has its roots in phenomenology and historicist hermeneutics.

11. This is a paraphrased allusion to a song by Jerry Garcia and Robert Hunter, "Eyes of the World," *Wake of the Flood* (album), (Sausalito, CA: Grateful Dead Records, 1973). Readers might wish sing along to the song for the full effect.

12. This is the story of Malunkyaputta, which can be found in Culamalunkya Sutta of the *Middle Length Discourses* [*Majjhima Nikaya*]. See Bhikkhu Bodhi and Bhikkhu Nanāmoli, *The Middle Length Discourses of the Buddha: A New Translation of the Majjhima Nikāya*, 4th ed., trans, ed. and rev. Bhikkhu Bodhi (Kandi, Sri Lanka: Buddhist Publication Society, 1995), no. 63, 533ff.

13. William James, "Does 'Consciousness' Exist?" (1904), in *The Writings of William James: A Comprehensive Edition* (1904), ed. John J. McDermott (Chicago: University of Chicago Press, 1977), 169.

14. James, "Does 'Consciousness' Exist?" (1904), in *Writings*, ed. McDermott, 183. By his "larger Psychology" James refers to his two-volume work, *Principles of Psychology*, 301.

15. *Cogito* is Latin for "I think" and a reference to *cogito ergo sum*, (I think, therefore I am), René Descartes' celebrated one-premise argument for the existence of a substantial mind (=ego=spirit), symbolically regarded as the starting point of modern philosophy. See Descartes, *Meditations on First Philosophy* (1641); and *Discourse on Method* (1637), pt. 5; where his *cogito* argument actually occurs. Both are in *The Philosophical Writings of Descartes*, trans. John Cottingham, Robert Stoothoff, and Dugald Murdoch (Cambridge: Cambridge University Press, 1984–1985).

16. For David Hume's skeptical reply to Descartes' *cogito*, see Hume, *A Treatise of Human Nature* (1739–1740), ed. L. A. Selby-Bigge, 2nd ed., ed. P. H. Nidditch (Oxford: Clarendon Press, 1978), pt. 4, sect. 6, 251–63. Immanuel Kant's response in turn to Hume can be found in part in his *Critique of Pure Reason* (1781/1787), ed. and trans. Paul Guyer and Allen W. Wood (Cambridge: Cambridge University Press. 1998); see (1781) A107–10; and esp. (1787) B131–35.

17. For Aristotle's theory of the *psyche*, see his *On the Soul*; but since what is "ensouled" is just what is alive, Aristotle's biological works are also broadly related to his account of the soul, esp. *Parts of Animals*. Related ideas also come up in the *Nicomachean Ethics*, 1.13; 4.1–2; and the *Metaphysics*, for example, 1035b–36a. All are in the *Complete Works of Aristotle: The Revised Oxford Translation*, ed. Jonathan Barnes (Princeton, NJ: Princeton University Press, 1984), in 2 vols.

18. Genesis 1:2. The Authorized (King James) Version (AV) is quoted. The Tiamat myth is based on the *Enûma Elish*, the Babylonian epic of creation. See *Myths from Mesopotamia: Creation, the Flood, Gilgamesh, and Others,* trans. Stephanie Dalley, rev. ed. (Oxford: Oxford University Press, 2000).

19. Allusions here are to karma yoga as in the *Bhagavad Gitā*, of which Gandhi made so much. Find an exhaustive translation in *The Bhagavad Gitā*, trans. Winthrop Sargeant, ed. Christopher Key Chapple (Albany: State University of New York, 2009). The dualist Sankhya philosophy, embraced in the great synthesis that is the *Gitā,* is also invoked in this paragraph, though still partly in mythic garb.

20. Shout out to the Canadian ethics-in-sport organization, *True Sport*, who promote sports as a (non-patriarchal) character-building opportunity, and advocate an ethical code for all levels and kinds of sports. In their honor, I have called Philosophy Sports like Tug of Logic *truth sports* (*alḗtheia athletica*).

21. Noam Chomsky in particular has made similar claims. He reports recognizing while still young the inanity of our identifications with sports teams, and later claims that exactly this sort of mindless identification can be and is exploited by those manufacturing consent. See Chomsky, *Understanding Power: The Indispensable Chomsky*, ed. Peter R. Mitchell and John Schoeffel (New York: New Press, 2002), 98–101.

22. On the tragic death of Socrates (469–399 BCE), our main source is Plato. See especially his *Apologia*, *Crito*, and *Phaedo*, in Plato, *Complete Works*, ed. John M. Cooper (Indianapolis: Hackett, 1997).

23. On language games, see Ludwig Wittgenstein, *Philosophical Investigations*, trans. G. E. M. Anscombe (Oxford: Basil Blackwell, 1958).

Chapter 3

Play It With Feeling

At Café Philosophy, people like their topics emotional. Sometimes people want—more often, they *need*—to think about their feelings, to sort and to figure them out. Although thinking is sometimes cast as unfeeling, and the head, in opposition to the heart, is routinely made to appear out of touch, deluded, even stupid, feeling and thought are interwoven in everyday consciousness, and parts of the same system. Feeling too may be deluded, and not only *by* thought. The whole of philosophical praxis, and not just Café Philosophy, has been characterized as thinking in touch with everyday concerns, as thinking alive to feeling, as "Thinking with the Heart."[1] One might better say: thinking *through* the heart, since emotion is become both the object and means of thought. Certainly, it often was both at Café Philosophy, as the essays in this chapter attest.

DESIRE

Desire. Who can live without it? It is both torment and delight, the needy tongue and the self-satisfied taste, the fire and the ash. Who can understand it?

What is the cost of desire? Does wisdom conquer desire or require it?

The word *desire* seems almost to drip with steamy positive connotation. But it is also a seductive lie. Desire cannot hold the mind. The mind immediately flits from the thought of desire to the thought of the object of desire, to the thought of desire satisfied. A desire satisfied is delight. But a desire unsatisfied is torment, and an unsatisfiable desire is torment unrelenting. Beware of the all-too easy positive connotations. Truth loves to hide.[2]

A desire may be a generalized or passing wish, or a dark ineradicable sin. We say: be careful what you wish for. I say: pay attention to the clinging you have already become. Desire cannot hold the mind, but the mind can hold desire.

Between the light and the heavy, desire is everything from a want to a need. As a want, desire marks a lack in us. We want to be filled up. Here desire is like a hole in us we want plugged, lest our tears get out. When the edges of that want get sharp, desire becomes a cutting need. Needs lacerate like sharp desires inside us. Like wants, needs can be filled, but later they will need filling again. Needs cycle in us, desire ebbs and rises. Hunger and lust quelled will only sleep a time, then rouse themselves again against us.

Desire is also a power. It is a power over us we can overcome and direct. Or rather, we can direct it and overcome ourselves; the power we cannot halt or stay. Desire as energy can be turned about on itself, bad lashing out against bad, darkness against darkness, until suddenly our own darkness furnishes us a torch to light our way. "Be ye lamps unto yourselves"—they say the Buddha said.[3]

But beyond power, beyond lack and need, forgoing transient imagination and the devoutly wished-for consummation, desire is wise compassion, wise as a serpent, compassionate as a lake. Desire thus clarified of the sensuous and the selfish is ennobling; sublimated in purity, it is the ultimate we can become. It is not what we want, nor what we really want; but what we really, really want, the mother and trump of all desires. Catch hold of it. It is our only ticket on the last train to the final goal, to truth, to the shining bounteous spirit that has always spurred us on to attain it, this very moment, this very lifetime.

I know you want it.

INTEREST

May I not rely on my readers to find interest interesting? Perhaps only the self-interested will be unable to pull themselves away from themselves long enough to take an interest in interest. But if they manage to, it will pay them in interest.

Interest is a most interesting word, a curious word. As a transitive verb it can mean "to stimulate curiosity or to cause concern." Etymologically, it derives from Latin *inter-esse*, "to be among." Figuratively we might call it between-being, even shared essence.[4]

In a popular expression, the adjective "interesting" can be diminutive, even insulting. "Interesting!" we say in polite irony, meaning we are bored. "That is . . . *interesting*," we say, hesitantly, not wanting to say outright that it is outrageous or ridiculous. If all we can say of something is that it is interesting, we may mean that it is merely amusing, irrelevant, or a triviality.

When we go on a date with someone new, we may wonder if that person is "interested" in us, meaning sexually or personally attracted to us. Thus we speak of having a love-interest in our life. For the seducer, every body is interesting. What interests us may only be what stimulates, not curiosity or concern, but our most basic desires.

Obliquely we arrive at the question of self-interest, which is really quite another (no less interesting) subject altogether. The question here is not what merely interests us, but what is in our interest. We are no longer dealing with psychology or sensualism, but with ethics. What is in our interest is what is good or best for us; it is *our* good. But there is a metaphysical question here too, for we can ask: what does it take to have a self-interest? What kind of being has a self-interest? Can a stone or an inanimate thing have one? Can an algorithm or a law have it? Any living being, it seems, has an interest, since it may or may not thrive or flourish; it is a possible beneficiary in that something can be done for its sake. Having a self-interest, then, is like being alive, like having a self at all.[5] It is having a sake.

We are all self-regarding, in that we take our own interest into account as we think and act in the world. This is typical, but the opposite has been known to happen as well: we sometimes fail to take our own interest into account. Still, to be exclusively or predominantly self-interested is a stock moral criticism. Morality has even been associated or identified with altruism, that is, other-interest, service in the interests of others. There is even a degree of moral heroism in someone standing up for those who are not present, when, for example, others are speaking badly of them behind their back. A high moral call, a profound duty, and a grave responsibility is to be the voice for the voiceless. This silent majority includes future generations, who time alone has prevented from having a voice now. Indeed, the subject of ethics subsumes the whole concept of *sustainable development*, which may be defined generally as the imperative to live today so as not to prevent future generations from living with equal right and comfort. If the root of morality is other-interest, the fruit of it is a sustainable human ecology.

Of course, to offer oneself as the voice of the voiceless may be only to don the *mantle* of virtue, not the real thing. To wrap oneself in a flag of righteousness may or may not be righteous, and all too often has nothing to do with the real interests of the voiceless. Friedrich Wilhelm Nietzsche speaks of morality as an old debater's trick, a rhetorical device, a mere trope.[6] Sincerity in self-offering presupposes at the very least some insight into what the best interests of the voiceless are. This is not easy for us to determine, even with the best of intentions. Being other, being voiceless, the voiceless other cannot guide us, so our own heart and conscience must. Experience shows, unfortunately, that these are not altogether reliable instruments. In fact, forget other people, even in our own case we have difficulty determining what our own best interests are. The question of what is in our true interests is really a philosophical viper pit, a quagmire without limit. Heraclitus was profoundly right in reporting that, no matter which way the mind went, it could discern no limit to the self, or "You would not discover the limits of the soul although you travelled every road: so deep a *logos* does it have." Also, "The soul (*psyche*) has a self-increasing *logos*."[7]

Where, then, are the limits of self-interest?

We are, in one sense, our own best judges. For who better can say what our private wants and preferences are? But satisfying wants and preference is not necessarily in our interest, let alone our best interest. We are our own best judges in regard only to the most superficial and evident contents of our consciousness. We are also the worst judges of our own case, for we are slanted in our own favor. It would be absurd, for instance, to allow anyone to act as judge in legal cases they were themselves involved in. Our interest is vested; that is, we have an interest in the outcome; whereas a judge must preside disinterestedly over a case, if justice rather than private advantage is to be the result. Self-interest is bias. It skews our perspective and disqualifies us as impartial. How then can we even begin to be competent judges of our own *best* interest?

Not being good, we might still be best. What, after all, are the alternatives? Paternalism is the view that big daddy—some meddling parent, the church, the state or some other power—knows what is best for you. Parents of course sometimes do know best, or at least better, as when the child is an infant and knows nothing of the world. The favor may be returned at the end of life if the grown child must care for an aged and infirm parent. If we are unable to look out for our own interests, we may set up a legal trust to look after them for us. The trustee's right is an interest in a legal sense, distinguishable from the beneficiary's interest in which the trustee is compelled to act. A legal trust ideally is a kind of sensible paternalism, a licensing of others to decide and to act on your behalf and for your sake. Democracy too at its ideal core rests on such trust, in that some few run the state in the interest of the many who empowered them to do so. But such idealism, even as a definition, seems benighted and naïve. The face of paternalism today is a national security clampdown, the quiet disappearance of freedoms and ease that is said to be in the national interest. It is psychographics, the individualized algorithms that defines your information bubble at the cost of your privacy. But the citizen is not a helpless infant or a dotty invalid, and does not consent to be treated as either.

So far we have traversed from the merely curious, through the metaphysical and the ethical, to the epistemic, and now to the political. But our problem is gravely compounded by another strain of meaning, reaching back into the complex origins of the word, namely the legal-economic. One has an interest, not merely legally or psychologically; one may hold it in a portfolio. One may have, as they say, an objective concern in something, a title or right, a stake. Early forms of the word "interest" meant simply a compensation for loss, then gradually a compensation or "consideration" for the use of money or other capital. As such it could be the reward of the virtue forbearance, in allowing a debtor more time to pay. To forgive may be divine, but forbearance is profitable. Interest in this sense is profit, it is advantage. One's "interest" in a "concern" may be a minor share or it may be a substantial or even a controlling interest. It is a right to hold, a claim to a benefit, and also the discretion to sell. This is the original vested interest, that is, an investment; and one may "divest" one's self of such interests by disposing of them, alienating them. Interest as *stake* is opposed to the above sense of interest as *sake*: the one is your money, the other is your life.

To have an objective economic interest in a business venture is, in related jargon, to have a position in it. Here position and interest mean the same thing. But in the general sense, positions we take may or may not be in our own interests ultimately, so the two also come apart. Even intellectually, philosophically, we take a position, as in a debate, often only to serve some interest. Philosophy proceeds well by examining not only the positions and arguments for them, but also in seeking out the interests that lead people to adopt those positions. Truth also lies in the interests behind our positions, not merely in the content of the pro/positions we maintain.

There is another, deeper lesson for philosophy here. Conflict in philosophy often seems to the uninitiated as merely a difference of opinion or positions. In fact, it is a battle of interests. The market, politics, love, and reason all occur in and through contest and competition. Our world just is this jockeying of competing interests, and we misunderstand it if we think of it merely as differences of opinion, as when you think strawberry is best and I chocolate. Imagine a fork in a river. The fork itself is not claimed, but my people live on one of the divergent streams, yours on another. If I should go upstream and dam above the fork to divert water from your side to mine, I do not merely have a different opinion from you, but an opposed interest. The conflict I have precipitated is not a matter of ideas, but a struggle of competing livelihoods. If the whole river begins to dry up, and the resource to grow scarce, so that there is an insufficient supply for both of us, our interests may outright clash even without my precipitating action. Dialogue may be the only way out short of war, but this dialogue is not in the first instance about changing opinions or points of view. It is about realities, real interests. This actual bump and tussle of political contention is called *Realpolitke*, how things really work rather than the toned-down language of diplomats. What is at stake in the contest of philosophy is not merely ideas and opinions, but real advantage, positive being, and ultimate interests. In such circumstances, words become instrumental, and position-statements strategic and symbolic. We need a circumspect and sober *Realphilosophie*, not an idle and inner diversion. We need an *interested* philosophy, not just an interesting one.

No discussion of interest can be complete if it earns no financial interest, which though it is legal and economic, is different again from interest in those sense. Financial interest is an accrual of debt through itself, the stipulated tendency of financial holes to grow bigger if left to themselves. Someone who lends you money takes some risk. The extra you payback beyond the principal is interest, and it compensates them for that risk. You develop your credit by increasing someone else's income on schedule. In this way, you become credit-worth, credible, and your projects will be sure to increase your banker's interest, in several senses. Compound interest is geometrically delicious.

Steven R. Covey likes to picture healthy relationships as a kind of trust fund, as mutually reinforcing emotional bank accounts.[8] When we err or sin or simply rely upon the generosity and understanding of others, we make a withdrawal. Kindness, consideration, and simply being there are like deposits we spend in receiving but must pay back in kind. Love is being-together, a coalesced or joined *inter-esse* of shared being. It transforms who we are. It disqualifies us as impartial judge in our own case and, if we are found to have an interest in another's case, we lose credibility as a witness to it. Thus we borrow and lend of each other in love's commerce, building trust and sometimes destroying it. We can bankrupt a relationship by our onesidedness, to the point where no words or promises can repair it. Emotional capital is raised by our proven reliability over time. These are mutual funds of the highest order. In love itself, two become one, that is, the interests of one come together with the interests of another, they merge, become the same. What thus becomes one, becomes nothing, though we speak of Love's infinite bounty. What we owe another we owe ourselves, and vice versa. The boundaries of interest dissolve with the disappearance of the boundaries that separate us, vindicating Heraclitus interpersonally. Love abolishes interest. Thus it fascinates.

STRESS

Stress is *strain, tension, worry*. The word itself is ready to burst from semantic pressures due to internal contradictions. This is already indicated by this initial triple definitional list, which glides almost imperceptibly from the overtly physical to the inward and mental. Strain and tension are primarily physical, as is vividly brought to mind by images such as a bent but mighty bow, a tightly-pressed spring, or a taut or twisted rope. Worry is fretting, a form of distressed or anxious cognition, thus internal. When people say "I am stressing about something," they are referencing mental processes going on inside of them. The word *stress* spans the chasm, like a tightrope across two opposing cliffs, linking mental to physical as surely as it separates them, depending on their separateness to make connection possible, yet dangerous. My definition of *stress* is a tightrope. Walk with me.

Any word as profoundly ambiguous as *stress* brings with it the risk of semantic oblivion, that is, of thinking and believing total nonsense (although some would call that a condition of human existence). The semantic risks one runs when using the word *stress* are thrown into relief by Hans Selye (1907–1982), the "father of stress." This controversial Hungarian-Canadian endocrinologist's experimentation in the physiology of adaptation transformed medical thinking and put stress not only on the medical map, but on top of the public mind.[9] Selye conceived stress as a perfectly-general three-phase response within us that seeks to restore physiological homeostasis after encountering threats or other situations of concern. His triphasic "general adaptation syndrome" (alarm, resistance, exhaustion) went against the wisdom of Walter B. Cannon (1871–1945), the Harvard scientist who in 1915 had coined the phrase "fight or flight" in his own simpler account of threat-response.[10] Both theories were mechanist, construing emotions as purely physiological, and thus were opposed to William James' "theory of emotion," which crucially involved *interpretation* of bodily states.[11] The two theories were also elaborations of the "theory of homeostasis" (*millieu intérieur*), introduced into physiology by leading French physiologist, Claude Bernard (1813–1878).[12] It is worth noting that both Cannon and Selye parlayed their findings well beyond science, and laid claim to philosophical insight.

However, Selye himself did not consistently distinguish stress as cause (for example, of disease) from stress as effect (that is, from the disease process itself), an ambiguity that lingers still in common usage. An early critic, who lauded Selye, denied launching any "dialectical fireworks" when he complained that, in Selye, "stress, in addition to being itself and the result of itself, is also the cause of itself."[13] It is as if *stress* were had to mean all things to all people. It is an overworked word showing signs of strain, which over time is known to lead to cognitive break-down. Use with caution. Even the father of stress came to question its use.[14]

Strain and tension, as words, are primarily physical in their signification. That is not to say that the images of a wound-up coil or a twisted rope are not lovely metaphors for states of mind. Indeed they are. Physical strain may be the cause of mental stress, but we also conceive that mental response metaphorically in physical terms. Although "strain" (I say) is primarily physical, we can also strain to understand. Mental straining may be due to exhaustion from past over-thinking and constant worry but sometimes it stretches the mind to learn to grow. One must work the mind to grow it, like any muscle. Ignorance must be felt as a hindrance before it can be opposed.

Tension (*Spannung*, in German) keeps the tightrope tight, without which there is no traversing. Thus it holds up the middle of my triple definition too, for it prevents all sagging in the center. Tension is in the middle, since it is physical, but also felt, experiential. My image of tension is the furrowed brow, representing a stretch-sustained thought or prolonged worry. That brow is the image of philosophy as well, so I find the Chinese proverb to be very anti-philosophical: "Tension is who you think you should be. Relaxation is who you are." How much of philosophy (for example, anxiety-ridden existentialism) is stress-driven?

Tension is the taut muscle, it is how we hold ourselves a little off our feet when we are anxious. The tense muscle is an outward sign of inward stress; its outward form is chronic contraction of the muscles. One can say that we all know what tense muscle feels like, and this is passably true. But an observation of Martha Graham puts the lie to it: "tight muscles don't feel."[15] There is tonus, a healthy balanced tension, that enables use and feeling; but excess muscle tension deadens sensation, even as anxiety tucks us in thought, away from bodily feeling.

It seems pertinent to mention here that regular physical exercise, a mild routine of gently stressing one's muscles, is inversely related to psychological stress, which no doubt you hoped I would get back to. Psychologically, stress is a reaction, with physiological, cognitive, and emotional aspects. Prolonged stress is dangerous because the body's resources in response are limited and can be entirely spent, leading to system collapse (Selye's exhaustion phase). Working out physically is one way to build up the body's resources so that one comes through times of stress with greater endurance. And of course philosophy is your daily mental workout.

I have been taking these key words with the baggage they carry. But psychologists and physicians have tried to introduce some semantic order by way of technical terms. To clarify communication and thinking, they have distinguished stressors from the stress reaction (which reaction, as mentioned, has both physiological and mental components). Stress is the reaction, our response to the stressors. This distinction, if consistently used, addresses the above critique of Selye, since it allows us to say that stressors cause stress (and not that stress, like Baruch Spinoza's God, causes itself.).

Stressors are threatening or demanding situations; they may be external or internal. External stressors vary from daily hassles (which are routine but cumulative) to catastrophes, traumas, or life-changing events. Among these are: loss of job, spouse or relationship; death or illness in the family; accident; work pressures; crowding; exams. Notable among stressors are eustressors, positive events that nevertheless bring change and new demands. These can be significant causes of stress; though we welcome them and want them to happen, they can tax body and mind, much in the same way that distressing events do. Examples of eustressors might include a first date, your wedding, opening night, a new job, new responsibilities, and so on. Stressors are not necessarily bad things in our life.

Stressors may also be internal. Any internal event or inner situation that threatens us or places great demands on us is also a stressor, that is, a cause of the stress reaction (from which it is quite distinct). Self-doubt, a harsh inner critic, or anticipatory fear of any of the above external stressors is an example. Negative self-talk is talk that may spontaneously arise inside and deliver vicious and stinging self-attacks. This is also an internal stressor. Panic attacks, and even the fear of them, keep some people housebound. One can come to fear one's own thoughts, for there may be no escape from inner persecution. A guilty conscience is an internal stressor. One's pessimistic outlook that foredooms all is also a stressor, and a significant cause of stress, however virtuous, blunt, or true it may seem.

It is an oversimplification to say that stressors *cause* the organism's response, that is, that stressors cause stress. Regularity, rather than necessity or determination, is all such causation amounts to. The stress response is complex and there is much we can do to influence aspects of it. Stress, as we know it, is autonomic, involving: a dilation of pupils; perspiration; chemical conversions in the liver leading to a rise of useable blood sugars; increased heart rate and raised blood pressure; a cessation of digestion, and a diversion of the blood to the muscles for ready reaction; a release of adrenalin, lymphocytes and clotting factors. Psychologically, we grow alarmed, increasingly aroused, highly vigilant.[16] But *autonomic* does not mean automatic; it does not denote Cartesian mechanical necessity. The thinking that went into it and comes out of it can also be rethought.

The cited physiological changes and others prepare the body for fight or flight, but also (as we are social creatures) to tend and befriend.[17] They are resource-consuming, and cannot be prolonged indefinitely. Burnout and exhaustion, even delusions, hallucinations, and cognitive collapse are possible over the long term. The body is rising to the demand, resisting the threat, hunkering down, so that even thought itself may become rigid, and ego-defenses may kick into high gear. As long as the wear and tear on the body is reparable, the organism can resume its unstressed state; if not, it is just more age and death creeping up.

Yet there are many variables and intervening factors, and we are not mere hapless victims of our stressor-rich environment. There are *individual differences* in stress response, degrees of hardiness, related to style and attitude. Past experience dealing successfully with similar stressful situations can calm a person in the process, who can then assure others. Facing an unexpected pop quiz, school children were found to produce less stress hormones the higher their IQ's. Presumably, those with higher IQ had less to fear from the quiz.[18]

Social support also makes a large difference to the damage stress inflicts, which is why catastrophes, which destroy the infrastructure of support, are such devastating stressors. Preparing for unlikely emergency is something we can do that could influence greatly how well we cope with stressful events.

We also tend to make catastrophes of our own suffering, to magnify our own laments, as if there were not worse cases all around us, near and far. Seeing the suffering of others can put one's own problems in a better light. Helping is such good karma because it builds our own resources and provides support for others. Spreading an optimistic outlook is also good, and we know laughter is the best medicine.[19] While idealists with exaggerated expectations may be more subject to burnout, there is nothing like pessimistic depression to cast one into the depths, falling off the tense tightrope of life and its stressful conditions.

Something as subjective and personal as an explanatory style may influence the level of stress one reports, and even one's capacity to overcome it. An explanatory style is the sort of causal attributions one makes, the sorts of causes one cites in the story one makes up about what is happening. A depressive mentality can skew our explanatory style, so that bad things that happen to us are treated as our own fault, and we blame ourselves (we are too old or inadequate or stupid). This negative thought pattern is merely confirmed when the next bad thing happens, and thus we entrench it, along with a vicious cycle of stress enhancement, brought on by disordered thought.

I am convinced that when the Buddha said the world is mind-created, he was not espousing metaphysical idealism.[20] Rather, he meant that the fret and meaning and duty and worry of the world are all read into it by an overworked mind that is cognitively stressed by trying to make sense out of a morally senseless reality. Success is a goad, failure is a whip, but we take these weapons freely and self-apply them to get ahead. Love is a spur on our tender hide, so we go off galloping. We stoke the fire that overheats us instead of relaxing, putting our feet up and enjoying the warmth or the ride. Stress might be taken as the root meaning of *dukkha* (suffering). Its universality is indisputable.

Tie your horse up outside. Pull up a chair. Reduce stress, but keep up the tension. Maintain a moderate happy knot in your brow. It is the only way over the tightrope.

PASSION

Passion: source of vice and of crime? Or a sanctifying interest that makes life bearable? Is passion the enemy of reason or the quick of life? With passion, we lose the straight path of reason; without it we have no love of life. Is passion the involuntary thrust of impulse or the architect of meaning that transforms our dull routine? Can it really be one thing that accomplishes these opposite effects? Should we find our passion or overcome it? Can we do both?

An antidote to the unreflecting suspicion of passion (which accuses it of such vices as envy, adultery, cruelty, even murder) is to point to the tautologous solecism: "no compassion without passion." For we suppose compassion arises from calmness, never suspecting the storm at the eye of the calm. The lion is also a spiritual metaphor, not merely a political one.

In calmness, sensitivity of feeling arises. And in sensitivity of feeling, the ameliorating effects of the actual experience of passion (as opposed to the mixed effects of its socially mandated denial). For feeling and passion run away with us, but sensitivity returns us again and again to the still point, asking: what is it that I am feeling right now? Where am I running? What is the name of my passion? To watch the impassioned breath is to calm it. In the center of the agitation, your desire is still the witness: open its eyes! Passion does not sleep.

Physiologically, there are surprising similarities amongst passions.[21] That is, various whole-body indicators of arousal (change of respiration, heartbeat, blood pressure, blood-flow patterns, etc.) are remarkably alike during very different passions. In fact, it is possible in the laboratory, by manipulating social context, to influence people's cognitive/emotional interpretation of the arousal effects of injected epinephrine, a natural neurotransmitter that stimulates the autonomic nervous system, resulting in the whole-body fight-or-flight response (Selye's alarm phase). But it turns out that our cognitive *appraisal* of our body's reaction drives our subjective experience of emotion. Shall we say: the name of our feeling varies with the context in which we name it? Or is the inner world too constructed?

Reason itself has been found to require feeling. Such at least is the conclusion of neurologist Antonio Damasio, whose books hit on distinctly philosophical themes. *Descartes' Error* and *Looking for Spinoza* are the unlikely titles of this physician's popular books.[22] By linking reason and feeling, and in seeking to correct René Descartes, Damasio might seem to be reverting to the position of Aristotle, who understood virtue to involve a kind appropriate *passion*, and advised us to seek a habitual *mean* amongst extreme passions. This makes settling the question of virtue into something of a reasoning process, in that right and wrong, though matters of feeling, are not *mere* matters of feeling. Aristotle, like Damasio, was moderating the heart-mind rift, which Plato had only cut deeper, yet which, in modern times under Descartes' influence, had widened yet further. (Everything in moderation, the wisdom of Delphi dictated—"even Plato," Aristotle might have quipped.) To be sure, the "mean" that Aristotle's virtue-ethics elevates is no blind habit or moderate average; it is nothing less than the never-ending striving toward an increasingly refined excellence (=virtue). Great virtue wrestles with great passion. The moderation of mountain-climbers (or professional spelunkers) is not that of those content to reside on middle lands. Reason walks amongst the passions, as among the lilies, as a saint amid beasts (that is, *carefully!*).

Similarities notwithstanding, Aristotle and Damasio are worlds apart, each working within incommensurable horizons and having starkly different aims. Certainly Aristotle did not and would not have pitched his virtue theory as a model of neural organization. Nor, for his part, does Damasio aspire to virtue theory, and he cannot be said to be making a contribution to philosophical ethics. *Descartes' Error* begins with case studies of patients with brain damage, but sets out to outline the neural underpinnings of normal everyday cognition. Such cognition is importantly social, so already in that early book Damasio understands the human brain as a social brain (in line with Aristotle's famous definition of humans as the *zoon politikon*[23] [social animal]). Today such neurophysiological projects have become exercises in evolutionary and social theory, as Damasio's recent books show. A more relevant difference here is that Damasio almost entirely avoids the pre-scientific term "passion" (*pathos*, central in Aristotle to both psychology and ethics), preferring the terms "feeling" and "emotion," noting several senses of each. The root of "passion" connotes passivity, as if one were the perpetual victim of one's own passions, so perhaps innocent of them too; in abandoning the term, Damasio is only playing safe and being scientifically serious. That is all fine and well, but it closes off Aristotelean horizons of meaning to us. Aristotle will revisit us in later chapters.

The Cartesian "error" Damasio seeks most to correct is the dualism of reason and feeling, not that other Cartesian dualism, *substance dualism*, Descartes' notorious metaphysical theory that mind and body are distinct realities, differing in essence, though interacting during life. The so-called mind-body problem that ensued, though mentioned late in Damasio's book,[24] is not directly addressed at all, and not so much refuted as side-stepped (which again is only standard scientific practice for the last century or so). In any event, Damasio's main claim that the neural circuitry for thinking and for feeling interact in generating everyday consciousness is a reversion to Aristotle only incidentally, as already suggested. For in sidelining the concept of passion, Damasio is correcting Aristotle just as much as he is correcting Descartes; in Descartes too the "Passions of the Soul" are by definition passive. Indeed, for Descartes, passions are importantly bodily phenomenon, thus mechanical, and in general *nonvoluntary*. They cannot be virtues without reason and the soul playing a role.[25]

So put Aristotle and Descartes aside. If a philosophical precursor for Damasio's theory of the "feeling brain" is desired (and one is by no means *required*), one would do better to look to ancient India and the Buddha's analysis of experience. I contend that the broad outlines of Damasio's theory as to how feelings relate body to brain bear striking parallels to features of the Buddhist analysis of experience, known as the Theory of Aggregates. To show this, I will need first to draw out Damasio's theory in more detail.

Damasio draws a crucial though unstable distinction between "emotion" and "feeling," noting several senses of each term. Emotion "is a *mental evaluative process . . .* with *dispositional responses to that process*" in both body and brain.[26] Notice at once that, so defined, both evaluation and disposition (a tendency to act) are inherent to emotions. Among emotions (following widespread practice), Damasio recognizes both primary ("early," "innate," "basic," "universal") and secondary ("acquired," "social," mediated by "thought," "prefrontal").[27] In Damasio's terms, emotions clearly include but go beyond the traditional passions, such as anger, fear, lust and jealousy (a secondary emotion). *Feelings*, by contrast, are not emotions, on Damasio's way of speaking, but more like the subjective experience of emotions, where the latter are taken as physiological states of brain and body. He writes: "feelings [are] the subjective experiences of the momentary state of homeostasis within a living body."[28] Crudely, primary emotions refer to mostly bodily states, secondary emotions to brain and body states. The ongoing feeling feedback (in the form of "somatic markers"[29]) from these states to the decision-making circuitry is indispensable to the everyday thinking process, so the theory goes, and its disruption explains certain notable pathologies of social reasoning.

Somatic markers do not correspond to, contribute to, and partly constitute *emotional* states only, but also the emotionless middle-lands; some of them are not associated with any particular emotion. For this reason, Damasio introduces, beyond the experience of primary or secondary emotions, an obscure third sort of feeling, which he calls "background feelings."[30] These "correspond to the body states prevailing *between* emotions," he tells us, since during an emotion itself "background feeling has been superseded."[31] They are feelings as if in search of a passion or emotion. We learn that background feelings may be pleasant or unpleasant, though "neither too positive nor too negative,"[32] and they are sometimes so fine as not to be felt at all. Typically, "we are only subtly aware of a background feeling, but aware enough to be able to report instantly on its quality."[33] Though highly subtle, readily superseded, and easy to overlook, these background feelings are nevertheless what we "experience most frequently in a lifetime."[34] Damasio says that, "originating in the 'background' body states," these background feelings are "minimalist in tone and beat, the feeling of life itself, the sense of being,"[35]—statements which, I need hardly point out, are almost wholly non-clarifying. He goes so far as to "submit that without [background feelings] the very core of your representation of self would be broken."[36] We are to understand that to be a terrible outcome, but from a Buddhist perspective, which denies the very existence of self and seeks extinction (*nirvana*), the matter can appear otherwise.

The Buddhist Theory of Aggregates would appear to cover much of the same ground as Damasio's theory (taken as an account of everyday mentality), though in partly similar, partly dissimilar ways. The Theory of Aggregates is about what goes on in human experience. It relates five elements or factors of experience conditionally (that is, in law-like ways), while yet leaving the door of freedom ajar. Two key elements of the theory are *saññā* (re/cognition) and *sankhāra* (often rendered as volitional reaction, habit-pattern). *Saññā* is not pure intellect, but the element of experience that learns, thinks, mis/understands, and evaluates the situation, mostly from a first-person perspective (is this good for me or bad for me?). Our re-action (*sankhāra*) to the situation, whether at the mental, vocal, or bodily level, accords with this evaluation. These first two elements seem to fit more or less happily with Damasio's double-barreled definition of emotion as a "*mental evaluative process* . . . with *dispositional responses*" thereto.[37] The fit seems especially clear in the case of secondary or social emotions, where opportunities to make ourselves miserable abound. But the most characteristic claim of Damasio's somatic marker hypothesis (that bodily feeling provides indispensable input to the cognitive, evaluative process resulting in behavior) is also prefigured in the unique and surprising function assigned by the Buddha to a third element, the bodily sensations (or *vedanās*, anything we feel physically in or on the body). The special place in the Buddhist theory for *vedanās*, which are called the deepest part of the mind,[38] makes the parallels to Damasio, even though differences also exist, worth noticing.

To understand the *vedanās* as the linch-pin of everyday mentality, it is necessary to explain how the Theory of Aggregates works. To illustrate (and oversimplify), the theory kicks in when "object comes into contact with object,"[39] as for example when using our sense organs we perceive someone or some words or some external thing or event. First a kind of awareness (*viññāna*) arises, but this is bare awareness specific to the sense-modality,[40] and prior even to recognition and evaluation (*saññā*), which come next. Like a vigilant sentry, this prior organ-awareness sends or is a signal that something has occurred, raising a question, though not yet alarm, about its nature. Only *after* recognition and evaluation do *vedanās* (or bodily sensations) come into the picture, and these (which always exist, even in deep sleep) are only altered *according to the evaluation*. We feel the *vedanās* in and on the body; they are there throughout the body, and may be pleasant or unpleasant, subtle or intense, as they reflect our passing thoughts. Importantly, our volitional response (*sankhāra*; the karmic element and the only one involving choice), which we might think springs immediately from our evaluative understanding of the object, actually takes the bodily sensations (*vedanās*) as its proximal cause (though of these causative feelings we are only inconsistently aware). In the words of S. N. Goenka: "Sensation is the forgotten missing link between the external object and the reaction."[41]

This late arrival in the cognitive thought-process of "feelings" or bodily "sensations" marks them off as totally distinct in function from the sensory inputs that in the West have been called "sensations" since Descartes and David Hume.[42] Of course they may become input, and they are, insofar as we are aware of and think about bodily sensations; but it is their role *after* evaluation and causally inducing action (with or without our awareness) that is unique in the Buddhist theory, until, as I say, Damasio's somatic marker hypothesis. Put simply, I propose that the "background feelings" in Damasio's account are what Buddha called *vedanās.*

The *vedanās* play a role in cognition that, if not quite the same as in Damasio, is nevertheless empirically (rather than conceptually) distinct. *Vedanās* may be highly subtle, are hard to notice, and our attention is drawn away from them when we are dealing with the world around us; they are easily superseded, that is, *unattended.* They are pleasant or unpleasant "background" experiences, sometimes literally gut feelings, that contribute to mood, and are not just frequently experienced, but they are there day and night, even in deep sleep. *Vedanās* never sleep. But the habit pattern (*sankhāra*) of the mind is to react to them, much as we unconsciously swat away a mosquito that troubles us in the night, or roll over in deep sleep (that is, to end discomfort). In context, *vedanās* are whatever you feel when in meditation you scan your body. By practicing non-reaction to bodily feelings, one slowly replaces the reactive habit-patterns that we all recognize as the throes of passion.

Damasio writes: "In standard circumstances, feelings tell the mind, without any word being spoken, about the good or bad direction of the life-process at any moment."[43] They tell us, from a gut perspective, how well our current action, project, or dream is going, so we can adjust course if needed. Goenka writes: "Sensations arise on the body and are felt by the mind; this is the function [aggregate] called *vedanā.*"[44] By mastering our reaction to the on-going bodily sensations, we can break the habits of passion that bind us in knots. *Vedanās* therefore are the ground on which the illusion ("representation") of self is broken.

There remain, to be sure, notable differences between the two theories. On Damasio's account, background feelings are not connected with any "dispositional responses," at least not in the way that emotional feelings are. Although on the Theory of Aggregates too, *vedanās* are not inherently dispositional, they do importantly *condition* our volitional responses (notably, desire, *tanhā*, identified by the Buddha as the principal cause of our self-made misery). This conditioning, however, is what body-scan mediation seeks to undo. The yoga involved is a sort of autonomic retraining, the replacement of unwholesome response patterns with a perfect autonomy. If you are master of your reactions to *vedanās*, nothing anyone does to you can ever provoke you to (passionately) overreact, since it only ever does get to you through unpleasant bodily sensations. There is nothing in Damasio like this sort of aim to liberation from passions. Neuroscience has no yoga (nor did Descartes).

The difference is not entirely academic, but utterly practical, even soteriological. By practicing a steady awareness of bodily sensations, meaning a non-reactive non-response to them, pleasant or not, we defeat the default connection that results in impulsive actions often later regretted. Sin and vice arise due to ignorance of the bodily sensations, ignorance and the non-conscious habit of reacting to them. To come out of that, on the Buddhist view, we must come to feel the subtlest and also the most intense of sensations without responding, not to become vegetables inactive in the world; not so that, like bitter Schopenhauerian[45] pessimists, we withdraw our will from the world and run away. On the contrary, with long practice, we become responsive in a refined way, reflecting best-interests, and enlightened response. No longer running, we know what we are feeling in the most direct manner possible.

If, as Damasio says, emotion supersedes background feeling, it leaves us ignorant of ourselves. By contrast, in dispassion, the background feelings become salient to a vigilant consciousness. Dispassion with steadfast consciousness intensifies feeling, in that stillness increases sensitivity, and this leads even to compassion. When you can feel everything inside you, you cannot help but feel the pain of others. Prolonged dispassion is by no means easy, nor is it easy to be impervious to pain and—harder still—to pleasure. That path is long and not, perhaps, for everyone. You cannot make progress by accident. To make headway, it really needs to become . . . your passion. You need the determination of a lion.

A better antidote to the unreflecting rejection of passion is a heated chinfest of philosophy. Cure yourself. Let the lion roar. Explore the extremes of reason and passion in your community think pit.

GUILT

Guilt, in its plainest psychological sense, is simply the painful consciousness of having done wrong. Problems with guilt arise when the sphere of wrong-doing expands to swallow up life choices, narrowing the individual to an obsequious cog, a duty slave, a moral robot. Or, when the wrong done is not specific, a vague hovering self-suspicion that cannot be discharged, like an inner crime investigation force which harasses with spying and general accusation but never lays any concrete charges. Or in the case of so-called psychopaths, antisocial personalities that lack a *painful consciousness of having done wrong*, and yet are perfectly aware of having done something illegal, socially unacceptable, and considered immoral. But note carefully—there are two absences here, relative to the presumed moral normal: the absence of pain or sympathy is most notable, but less important than the subtler lack, namely *consciousness of having done wrong*, which is itself decidedly different from *consciousness of having done something illegal, socially unacceptable and considered immoral*. For one can know that something is against the law, not acceptable to others, and considered by them to be immoral, without thinking that thing is wrong (for instance, if the concept *morally wrong* is lacking in me, I may still be perfectly able to understand concepts like *illegal, unacceptable to others*, and even *considered by others to be morally wrong*, in much the same way as the blind can know that something is considered by others to be chartreuse without knowing what chartreuse looks like). I am driving a wedge between a moral concept and a social one. By my account, *guilt involves moral knowledge*. The wrong must be known, not merely vicariously inferred. Psychopaths may be ignorant of wrong, but they know that others are not.

Thus, I assume that seeing our own wrong-doing hurts. *Guilt is pain.* It is the inner penal system, not the inner prosecutor, who simply derives high fees by exploiting that system. There are exceptions, good inner lawyers, as it were. And it helps to have a constitution, even more to have a revisable one. But the individual psyche is about as lucky on this score as the average global citizen when it comes to actual recognition of inalienable human rights. Due process is often denied. The wheels of inner justice also grind slow. One is often guilty unless proved innocent. And proof is sadly lacking.

Original sin is often represented as a blanket accusation, an extravagant case of collective punishment. As a doctrine, it is often unfairly reduced to the advice to always feel bad about yourself. Can one inherit guilt? Come to think of it, how else is it acquired? Is guilt not a legacy of past circumstance?

Guilt ought to be distinguished from shame. They exhibit different cultural complexions. Shame is the introjection of public humiliation. Out of fear of our thoughts or actions being exposed, we refrain. Shame is all about the public gaze. There is a Confucian line somewhere that reads more or less: *Ten fingers pointing. What could be worse*.[46] That is shame.

Guilt is a more personal form of persecution. Guilt is more a sense of personal culpability than of public humiliation. Guilt is the introjection, not of public embarrassment, but of cosmic judgment. When Jesus says that you violate the law when you lust after your neighbor's spouse or harbor anger toward your brother, that is about love. It is about taking stock of one's insides on a higher standard than inherited law. In short, it is about guilt. Forget shame and public perception. Now you can judge yourself. But is this not in effect shuffling off original sin, a rejection of public and shared perceptions? There is a new law, a new standard, a higher law invisible to the public gaze.

Those who would perceive themselves without guilt had best try. Before long they will try their own tolerance. They will long for their sense of guilt to return, for we find it hard to face ourselves without our moral filters.

Nietzsche asks: "what is the seal of achieved freedom?" He answers: "to stand before oneself without shame."[47]

Spare no pains. You will not regret it.

A guilty conscience suddenly leads me to confess that I do not believe in original sin. I stress this with uncharacteristic openness because it would appear to follow from what I said above (*guilt=knowledge* and *guilt=pain*) that *knowledge=pain*, which sounds like eating an apple and getting turned on. However, my faults are my present construction, and fall into the domain of rhetorical over-enthusiasm, rather than eating forbidden fruit and getting all worked up.

DENIAL

Refusal, denial, saying no: such a negative topic we have before us!

There are, it may be said, two main kinds of denials: those that arrive at the truth, and those that maintain a falsehood. The first is largely logical, the second is mostly psychological. The denial of an untruth is, after all, a truth. Let's have more of that. But denial is also a psychological defense mechanism, a self-deception, a declaration of fantasy, and a will against reality. We deny the truth we do not want to be true, cannot admit it to be true, or cannot even imagine to be true. Death we cover with the polite pall cloth of denial.

Psychological denial is a form of illusion, an intolerance for the truth, often temporary, but sometimes successful. It is a separation from reality, engaged in for avoidance purposes, and with the price of self-deceit. It is presumed that our "passional nature"[48] is so powerful that it manufactures an alternate reality which it interposes between us and the truth, while mollifying scruple and doubt. It is also presumed that we are so dainty and timid and fearful of pain that we require a power greater than ourselves to hoodwink and protect ourselves. Psychological denial is a picture of weakness and strength. Once, playing the smart-aleck, I said "denial is the first truth in psychology." It is a slur that works at many levels. My current employ in a psychology department forbids me such wicked thoughts.

Some denial is mere inertia. Often after a life-changing event, like a death in the family, we find ourselves in old habits, thinking in old ways, as if nothing had changed. It takes time to get used to the new reality; thinking is slow to adjust. We catch ourselves once or twice, weep all over again, and gradually learn. But to call slowness to change denial suggests that there is something willful, self-delusional, unconsciously effortful about it. There is a difference between not adjusting to the truth and not being able to handle it. Denial is an aspersion; inertia is a law.

The aspersion of denial is sometimes itself denial. We come together, we argue, you are not persuaded of my point of view. "Denial!" I cry. "Your refusal to accept my position is your denial of reality. Your disagreement with me is just your failure to face facts." Denial is not only a defense mechanism. It is also an offensive tactic. The accusation of denial is sometimes even a preemptive attack.

All the celebrated psychological defense mechanisms are mere elaborations of denial, which is really only the bluntest of such weapons.[49] *Repression* itself would be ineffective if denial of it were not involved. One must forget that one is forgetting something to successfully repress it. It does not work to go around consciously repressing it—that is called daily struggling. *Projection*, another defense mechanism, is like a source attribution error in perception, rather than in memory (that is, it is comparable to when we remember hearing something said, but mistake who said it). I have impossibly conflicted infantile ideals, and then find them manifest in you as your fine attributes. I forget that I saw that image first in myself before I fell in love with what I am calling you. Projection is a denial of origin of mental contents.

The aficionado of denial will go in for *reaction formation*, a defense mechanism with real flair. Here an unacceptable impulse (of which the ego firmly denies the existence) is mastered by hypertrophy or exaggeration of the opposite tendency. Here solicitude is evidence of repressed cruelty, cleanliness of a secret interest in feces, and of course the notorious homophobe who loves who he beats. Here we find the art of denial at its most flamboyant and invisible, excepting only *sublimation*. In sublimation, our negative and unacceptable impulses are transformed by the artistry of denial into socially productive causes. Wracked by *eros*, the artist sublimates upon the canvas, instead of sinking to perversion. The violent man who finds cover in becoming a policeman has (we may only hope) sublimated his vicious urge. Sublimation is denial with a noble mien.

There can be no denying my negative slant on denial. My critics will charge that I am in denial about denial, and trying to sweep the whole concept of defense mechanism under the conceptual rug. But they just cannot handle the truth. Myself, I find the double negative not hardly enough. I must go on to positive assertion. Yes. I must say yes to denial.

Logical denial is denial of falsehood. It is saying no to bullshit. No is a very powerful little word. No means no. Your power to say no is sacred. Use it, or you will lose it. Just say yes to your power of no.

The pressures to conform being real and insidious, the bad influence of low karma being pervasive, and the perquisites of corruption being so very appealing, the power of "no" can mean your salvation. Action often being habit, the act of saying no can be your liberation. There are some who contend that there is no free will, only a *free won't*.[50] Veto power may be our fundamental liberty, symbolized by stopping and thinking. Denial is refusal to go along, to be a sheep, to fit in. Freedom just may start with logical denial.

Our actions have many explanations, although we prefer to assert our ownership when things are going well, when we are comfortable in our actions. (When things go wrong, we would rather blame circumstance, and implement our perpetual stand-by procedure, called plausible deniability). Though we claim responsibility for our (fruitful) actions, the histories of reinforcements, dangling inducements, and plain old routine account for many of them. Causes of our behavior range from near to far, from genetic to cultural, from custom to duty, from biochemical to behavioral reinforcement. If we do not step up to deny the over-determination of action, we will be swept up by the world, and be left with no choice for ourselves.

Saying no to oneself is the highest form of self-affirmation. It overrides the inner automaton. We have a weakness of ease, and aversion to struggle. Saying no to these, we take on difficult battles we would not otherwise win. No stand on principle ever began with a yes. It began with a no in the face of its violation. Standing up for oneself is saying no to those who would walk all over you. Denial pokes a finger in the chest of all oppressors. No means revolution.

It has not gone unmentioned before that two negatives make a positive. Two positives rarely make a negative, except in the sarcastic doubter's reply, "yeah, right!". One has to shake one's head at jokes that bad.

Say no to your sofa. Stop and think this very night. Float your philosophical barge along denial.

ANGER

Anger ranks as one of the great delusions of all time. It is also a creator and a perfector. Anger rises from pain, but pays in secret joy. Anger is a kick, not only in the ass, but also for the gleeful, vindictive heart. Anger is the bribe and reward of ignorance, but also the fount of just revolution and a righter of wrongs.

Dignity spurned works for justice, but only if it is self-aware, only if it knows its own dignity. Dignity ignorant of itself, when spurned, may instead strike out, or grow cold and silent, fearful, a victim, waiting in revenge. There is, put dubiously simply, a righteous anger, which is both the very worst and the very best sort of anger. It is the worst anger, since it is anger hyped up within itself, anger certain of its right and of the virtue of the destruction it is about to unleash. We live in righteous times.

Yet anger that is truly righteous does not claim righteousness out of hurt or ignorance, but out of a calm awareness that knows what is right. Let us not argue about what is right. I suppose only that you recognize *something* as right. Let me speak of that. I appeal to some deep central truth of your worldview, something vital and important to your sense of justice, fairness, and self-respect. For there are such "rights," and they do get wronged. In these cases, anger is indignation, and justly so. There are senseless wrongs in the world, no shortage in fact of great injustices; for the world is unfair, and humanity is not universally led by the pure or the humane. If any such world tragedy should land close to your door, like a plane falling out of the sky, or an accidental pandemic, then you too may know a rightful anger, a sore outrage grounded in high principle.

Still, a right to feelings (even right feeling) is not a right to act impulsively out of those feelings. The best and noblest motives lie behind many a terrible atrocity. That of course does not make them right, at best only well-intentioned. But let us not argue about what is right. I assure you there are many examples on which we would agree. For all our talk of moral differences, moral commonalities are profound and abound. We are right to rage at indignity; but only right, and not rage, should lead us.

Rage is no guide. Anger is not wisdom. But anger comes. We do well to feel it and to find it. We do better to name it. We each have our triggers that stick us and irritate the craw. A trigger may be as sudden or as simple as a pistol shot, or it may be cumulative, building slowly over time like a slight but steady nagging. Bit by bit the sensitive self is engorged; anger escalates; little digs accumulate until suddenly, like a geyser, a stream of bitterness and invective erupts. In the heat and crisis of this moment, reason and cognition are suppressed. It is no time to think. Reason here has nothing to say, but proves itself in patience. When the worst is over, the adrenaline takes some time to drain; only slowly are energy and balance restored. The next step may be depression, regret, and tears. These too pass, and thus the cycle continues. Thus we roll and roil in anger. But by knowing this, and naming the cycle while it is unraveling, we can, with sufficient inner skill, come to stop it.

Anger begins in pain, but pain does not cause anger. Anger is only one option in response to pain. But anger often bursts, and people say they had no choice. Later it subsides, and the explanations of helplessness get constructed.

Denial and justification are the typical aftermath. "The god Ares possessed him," "a natural instinct to survive kicked in," "the testosterone did it," "she was asking for it." Here free will is given a terrific pretext, a bad excuse, and a sham moral cover. Anger overtakes us, overcomes us, and we play passive hostage to our passions. (Here reason disproves itself with impatience, and spins lies whenever self-disapproval grows intolerable.)

Anger feels like a triumph and a liberation, but it is a capture. The will feels like it is free, but there is the press of the moment, and reason standing by ready to concoct a self-serving account *post-facto*. Anger is ignorance and unfreedom. But anger is also choice, not in the way that one may choose to raise one hand, then the other; but in the way that education is a choice. The choice, once taken, is *followed by* all the hard work. It must be made once and for all, but thereafter again and again to advance. Anger is a choice in that there are alternatives to acting out of anger. These opportunities may already be lost when the great swell of anger has arisen. But like the choice for an education, the choice against anger is (dependent on conditions and) *prospective*, that is, made with reference to the improvements next time. The hard work begins *after* the choice, to which one must recommit over and over for success to be assured.

If pain makes us vulnerable, anger provides a shield. While it defends from without, it provides cover for what is within, hiding it from scrutiny and awareness. Under the protection of darkness, the energy circles, waiting, hoping for a moment of release. If it cannot find one, or if it is fearful of finding one (for anger expressed may invite a worse reply, and only the wrathful Lord knows where that will lead . . .), it can do only one thing, namely find an inner object to abuse, something below the shield, like the self-image. Thus pain leads to anger and anger is thwarted to self-abuse and depression.

Bottling up anger is natural and understandable, but it is folly as well. Breaking the bottle, striking out in anger, is also natural and understandable, but it is equally folly.

I end with the reward of righteousness, false and true. Anger pays. Anger rewards. Know the deep abandon and joy in the center of your anger. It is your fix, the habit you may only renounce once you admit it. The Germans have a lovely name for it: *Schadenfreude*, the joy we find in the suffering of others. The honest soul must confess it. Anger exploits this feeling, boosting it with the sadistic pleasure of creating the very suffering that it is gloating over. The moment of righteous rage is its own reward (the costs show up later). Nietzsche, the inflamed philosopher, has charted this ground very well. He quipped that Dante got it wrong in saying Hell was created by the love of God; rather, Heaven, the reward of the righteous, was created by the stifled fury and hatred of . . . the lovers of God.[51] Inverting the moral dictum that we love those who hate us, he challenged us to conceive a contempt for what we love. Nietzsche reclaimed a conscious righteous anger.

One hears it said: *Don't get mad, get even.* I say: "don't get even, get even better. Reward yourselves. Kick loose. Storm the gates of truth."

ENVY

Envy makes the world go round. Therefore those who hate envy are often found to hate the world.

Envy is one of the great vices that became a virtue. This ugly duckling story may also be seen, from a different perspective, as the killing of the goose that lays the golden egg (if I may, in one sentence, mix metaphors, fables and waterfowl). Let me explain.

Envy begins its life as a vice. For you late moderns, who think of vice as a police department, let us recall that vice is the opposite of virtue or excellence, the linchpin concept of ethics before the notion of universal human rights ushered in the modern age. The word *vice* has an old-fashioned ring. Today we simply call it a lifestyle choice, at least whenever it is not a police matter.

So to say that envy is a vice, we must transport our mindsets back to another time. The very roots of the word betray its vulgar history.[52] *Envy* derives from the Latin *invidere*, which means to look askance at. Our word *invidious*, derived from the same root, refers to a tendency to cause discontent, animosity or envy. The oldest meanings of *envy* in English are now obsolete, but they include: malignant or hostile feeling, ill-will, a malicious look, an active evil, harm, mischief, odium, and holding a grudge.[53] So it is not too much to say that envy began as a vice, but was only later rehabilitated as a middle class virtue.

Apart from these ancient attenuated negative connotations, there is the chief and core meaning of *envy*, from which we shall not, unfortunately, be able to remove all negativity. Whatever one's final assessment of envy as virtue or vice, one must agree that envy, as an emotional experience, is unquestionably a negative feeling. Envy is mortification, a discontent, a miserableness, a sadness occasioned by the good fortune of another. *There is no joyful envy*. Hunger is a negative experience; but we eat to satisfy it, and we are benefited. Envy too, may carry such indirect benefits (at least, that is what all the controversy is about). But, like hunger, the immediate experience of it is—without controversy—an unpleasant state.

Fortune may bestow a wide variety of gifts, and accordingly one can distinguish kinds of envy by attention to the envied object. Broadly, there are three main categories of goods that others may enjoy, and each type may evoke a corresponding and characteristic envy. Envy may have a material complexion, as one feels chagrin at the wealth, prowess, or physical comforts of another. Or envy has a social complexion, and we are discomfited by the reputation, status, or social circle of someone else. Thirdly, we may envy the inner attributes of another, whether intellectual, ethical, aesthetic, psychological, or spiritual. Thus we may distinguish (inexhaustively) among material, social, and psychological objects of envy.

In addition to distinguishing envy by its objects, one may look to the intentions that accompany the core feeling. Here we find a snake pit. At its most innocent, envy merely wishes to enjoy boons equal and equivalent to those of our rival. Envy here is mere emulation. But it is one thing to wish to be as rich as Joe Tycoon; it is quite another to deprive him of his wealth, or to steal from him, or to desire to eliminate him and take over his empire. And when one begins to lay plans for the seizure, it is no longer a matter of mere wish. Envy has gone beyond emulation.

Similarly, one may wish to match the wedded bliss of another. This can take the form of imitation (as a wish to find one's own mate) or the form of replacement (as a wish to seduce that happy person's spouse in a vain attempt to take part in the existing bliss). Again there are a variety of intentions possible, even relative to the same object.

One may be miserable until one has as much and as good; or one may insist on having the exact items the other owns, in effect supplanting the other and taking his or her place. Beyond these strategic intentions, there is the scorched earth policy: If I cannot have it, no one will. Envy can be purely destructive of the happiness of others, and is more likely to be such whenever it despairs of its own consummation. The insides of envy are uglier than its outsides.

Categorizing envy by its objects is a little like classifying stars by who looks at them. Such means are not likely to advance astronomy, much less to shed light on envy. Mostly, distinctions by object are made by apologists, who wish to defend the indirect benefits of one or another sort of envy. Thus I have heard spiritual envy extolled, while material envy is scorned. The idea is that if we envy the wealth of others, we are entering into vain competition with them. But if we envy the spiritual perfections of a saint, *bodhisattva*, or deity, we have no wish to win out over them, but at best to join them as equals in spiritual attainment. Far from competitive, our envy of them is praise to their ears, and they may magnificently grant us boons that elevate us to their peerage. They help us up; we do not wish to out-glorify them, but to honor them. What is so bad about such envy? Earnest emulation of virtue is virtue.

A related perspective holds that envy is ethically neutral. If one envies good things, and if this envy is without spite, or leads to personal improvement through emulation, then it is a good thing. If one envies evil things, or if one's envy is spiteful and malicious, then it is evil, even absent of all emulation (which would make it still worse). Envy is only a means. It is the end for which it is used, and the manner of its employment, that is good or evil. Envy is instrumental. This is consistent with the previous view (distinction by object), since it assumes that we should not envy sinners or the arrogant; but envying the spiritually great might be okay, if it is done in the right way for the right reasons.

A predominant view since Bernard Mandeville's *Fable of the Bees* has been that private envy leads to public wealth.[54] The very competition that spiritualists demean is the great engine of growth and hope. It is envy that sparks competition, and the desire to better one's own position, to stand out amongst one's peers, to live on the top of the hill. The general struggle for relative wealth leads to absolute wealth creation. While individuals may or may not survive, the market grows and gets more goods to more people, eventually better goods to richer people. We have a right to our envy, on this view, which claims that envy is the goose that lays golden eggs. The spiritualist disdain of envy would kill this squawking goose. Let us rather emulate the Joneses to keep up with them. If such envy is evil, at least it pays the bills.

The beneficence of the invisible hand is just the asymmetrical mirror-image and license of the principle of envy.

So envy has been extolled as the ecstatic admiration of the spiritually great, defended as a neutral tool that can be used either for good or for evil, and lionized as the innate will to self-improvement, thanks to which we have all progress. It has come a long way from being a mere vice, a malicious twinkling of the eye. To those who hate envy, these benefits will hardly seem impressive. What have we established? That envy fuels the rat race? Can what is so joyless and inwardly ugly fail to transgress against the spirit? Even spiritual envy seems to violate a spirit of generosity. It is an expression of spiritual poverty, a desperate admission of a spiritual lack. It is already seeing the divine as other. This is the first mistake of believers (the second being seeing the divine as self). And as for the moneyed apologists who are feigning sympathy for fowl, all they actually have to show for their case are the golden eggs; the spirit of the goose has long since died in the sweatshops of progress, its carcass carved and served with a sauce of gloating at their annual opulent thanksgiving dinner.

NOTES

1. Günter Albrecht Zehm [Pankraz],"Pankraz, Dr. Achenbach and das denkende Herz" [Pankraz, Dr. Achenbach and the thinking heart], *Die Welt* 38 (February 15, 1982). Achenbach, a pioneer of philosophical praxis, was an inspiration to Marc

Sautet, who created Café Philosophy; see Sautet, *Un café pour Socrate: Comment la philosophie peut nous aider à comprendre le monde d'aujourdh'hui* (Paris: Robert Laffont, 1995), 61. See also Andrew MacLeod, "Thinking with the Heart," *Monday Magazine* (1998), an early media report on Café Philosophy in Victoria.

2. Heraclitus, Fragment B123: "Nature (physis) loves to hide," in *A PreSocratics Reader: Selected Fragments and Testimonia*, 2nd ed., ed. Patricia Curd, trans. Richard D. McKirahan and Patricia Curd (Indianapolis: Hackett, 2011).

3. Here, I use the Rhys David translation, taking *dipa* as lamp rather than as *dvipa* (island). See *The Long Discourses of the Buddha: A Translation of the Dīgha Nikāya*, trans. Maurice Walshe (Boston: Wisdom Publications, 1987), 245. Scholarly consensus now prefers the latter reading, which does make rather more sense in the context. But Walshe advises "it is perhaps best not to be too dogmatic about the meaning" (569n395). See also "With Yourselves as an Island," in Samyutta Nikaya 22.43, translated in *The Connected Discourse of the Buddha: A New Translation of the Samyutta Nikāya*, trans. Bhikkhu Bodhi (Boston: Wisdom Publications, 2000), vol. 1, 882; as well as 1055n53.

4. This essay makes evident use of the *Oxford English Dictionary* (*OED*), 22nd printing, compact ed. (Oxford: Oxford University Press, 1982), s.v. "interest."

5. The word "like" is important. Presumably corporate entities and the state can have an interest. Though not alive, they are expressions of (social) life, and their interest, in so far as it is legitimate, originates in those underling lives.

6. Friedrich Wilhelm Nietzsche, *Daybreak: Thoughts on the Prejudices of Morality* (1881), trans. R. J. Hollingdale (Cambridge: Cambridge University Press, 1982), 2: "Morality has from of old been master of every diabolical nuance of the art of persuasion: there is no orator, even today, who does not have recourse to its assistance."

7. Diels Fragment, B45, and B115. For easy identification, the Heraclitus fragments that remain have been given numbers (B numbers or Diels numbers). Translations of Heraclitus in English are adapted from *A PreSocratics Reader*, ed. Curd, trans. McKirahan and Curd, 41–53.

8. Steven R. Covey, *The Seven Habits of Highly Effective People: Restoring the Character Ethic* (New York: Free Press, 1989), 55–59.

9. See Hans Selye, *The Stress of Life* (New York: McGraw-Hill; 1956); and Selye, *Stress Without Distress* (Philadelphia: Lippincott, 1974).

10. Walter B. Cannon, *The Wisdom of the Body*, rev. and enlarged ed. (New York: W. W. Norton, 1939). Dedicated to Ralph Barton Perry, "Guide, Philosopher Friend." Cannon hoped applied scientific theories like his would lead to "a wise life"; see his final chapter on "social homeostasis." It was not the first time life-philosophy resorted to physiology, nor the last time physiology would make itself out to be a life-philosophy; see Antonio Damasio, *The Strange Order of Things: Life, Feeling, and the Making of Cultures* (New York: Pantheon, 2018).

11. See William James, *The Principles of Psychology* (1890), authorized ed. (New York: Dover, 1950).

12. See Cannon, *Wisdom of the Body*, 37–40.

13. Ff. Roberts, "Stress and the General Adaptation Syndrome," *British Medical Journal* 2, no. 4670 (July 1950): 105. It will be recalled that being self-caused is a

divine attribute, a defining feature of what Baruch Spinoza (1632–1677) called "God or Nature." Amusingly, the withering Roberts quotation is not infrequently attributed to Selye himself. It is in fact no flippant remark but is more or less deduced from quotations showing inconsistency in Selye's early usage of the term.

14. Lila MacLellan, "The Scientist Who Coined 'Stress' Wished He Had Chosen a Different Word for It," *Quartz at Work*, June 29, 2018; last updated July 2, 2018, https://qz.com/work/1316277/ (accessed July 2, 2021). In retrospect, the word strain apparently seemed a better choice.

15. See Don McDonagh, *Martha Graham: A Biography* (New York: Popular Library, 1975). Carrie Stern attributes a similar line to Erick Hawkins, the first man Graham asked to join her company: "'Tight muscles cannot feel,' Hawkins often admonished." See Carrie Stern, "Erick Hawkins," *Dance Teacher*, September 29, 2007, https://dance-teacher.com/erick-hawkins/ (accessed June 6, 2012).

16. See D. Stephen Lindsay, Delroy L. Paulhus, and James S. Nairne, *Psychology: The Adaptive Mind*, 3rd Canadian ed. (Toronto: Thomson Nelson, 2008), 108–9, 638.

17. Shelley E. Taylor, Laura Cousino Klein, Brian P. Lewis, Tara L. Grunewald, Regan A. R. Gurung, and John A. Updegraff, "Biobehavioral Responses to Stress in Females: Tend-and-Befriend, Not Fight-or-Flight," *Psychological Review* 107, no. 3 (2000): 411–29, https://doi.org/10.1037/0033-295x.107.3.411.

18. See Lindsay et al., *Psychology*, 640–42, which also covers facts mentioned in this and the next paragraph.

19. Selye's came to advocate gratitude and "altruistic egotism" as an antidote to harmful stress. See his *Stress Without Distress*.

20. I have developed this theme in greater detail in Michael Picard, "Bewusstsein und Realität: Die Frage des Idealismus in der frühen indischen Philosophie" [Consciousness and Reality: The Question of Idealism in early Indian Philsophy], unpublished invited lecture, Gesellschaft für Philosophische Praxis, Bergisch-Gladbach, Germany, August 16, 2019. Audio recording also available online at Douglas College Open Repository.

21. By its nature, this "fact"—though it masquerades as physiological insight—is really only a comment on the state of the technology of measurement (in other words, about relative ignorance). That there should be some physiological difference in different states of passion was predicted by James' *Principles of Psychology* (1890) theory of emotion, but the initial physiological measures of arousal offered little to go on (Cannon, *Wisdom of the Body*; Selye, *Stress of Life*). It was in this context that the 1962 Stanley Schacter and Jerome E. Singer epinephrine experiments next referred to were undertaken, with such surprising results, partly confirming the cognitive appraisal theory of emotions. When this piece was originally written, I was teaching psychology, and reflected the state of the art as reported in a textbook I was using, cowritten by a colleague, namely, Stephen D. Lindsay, Delroy L. Paulhus, and James S. Nairne, *Psychology: The Adaptive Mind*, 3rd Canadian ed. (Toronto: Thomson Nelson, 2008), which has references to the underlying literature mentioned here.

22. Antonio Damasio, *Descartes' Error: Emotion, Reason, and the Human Brain* (New York: Avon, 1994; repr. New York: Penguin, 2005); Damasio, *Looking for Spinoza: Joy, Sorrow, and the Feeling Brain* (Orlando, FL: Harcourt, 2003); and Damasio, *Strange Order of Things*, among others.

23. Aristotle, *Politics*, I, 2, 1253a2. See also N*icomachean Ethics*, bk. I, 2 1094a–b, and I, 7, 1097b11.

24. Damasio, *Descartes' Error*, 247–52.

25. René Descartes, "Passions of the Soul," in *The Philosophical Writings of Descartes*, trans. John Cottingham, Robert Stoothoff, and Dugald Murdoch. (Cambridge: Cambridge University Press, 1984–1985), vol .1, 337–39.

26. Damasio, *Descartes' Error*, 139; emphasis in the original.

27. Damasio, *Descartes' Error*, 131–34 (primary emotions); and 134–39 (secondary emotions).

28. Damasio, *Strange Order*, 27.

29. Damasio, *Descartes' Error*, 165–201.

30. Damasio, *Descartes' Error*, 150–55.

31. Damasio, *Descartes' Error*, 150.

32. Damasio, *Descartes' Error*, 150.

33. Damasio, *Descartes' Error*, 150.

34. Damasio, *Descartes' Error*, 150.

35. Damasio, *Descartes' Error*, 150.

36. Damasio, *Descartes' Error*, 151.

37. Damasio, *Descartes' Error*, 139; emphasis in the original. There is nothing particularly surprising in this alignment, even if through it we indirectly associate certain brain structures with these Buddhist psychological terms. I would note that the question of the role for *vedanās* in everyday cognition, which is raised next, also becomes, through this alignment, a testable neural hypothesis.

38. I take this point from S. N. Goenka, *The Discourse Summaries* (Bombay: Vipashyana Vishodhan Vinyas, 1987), 41. "Unless one deals with sensations, one will be working only at the superficial level of the mind." I reply in this essay on his exposition of the Theory of Aggregates.

39. The word for object is *rūpa*, which may be an external material object or an object of thought. Thought too is understood to have a material basis or organ (*āyatana*), and in that regard to be just like the senses. Clearly, contact (*phassa*) is no mere mechanical meeting of surfaces, but more like contact in the sense of communication theory, or perhaps complex chemical binding, both of which are wholly appropriate in a neural context. *Rūpa* is one of the five Aggregates, the other four being mental (awareness; recognition/evaluation; feeling/sensation; volition). All five, aggregated and unanalyzed as we find them in experience, make up the "framework of the mind-body," in the Buddhist perspective, what I above called a theory of what goes on in experience.

40. This too is an empirically testable hypothesis of the Theory of Aggregates. Is the Buddha not referring to activation of cortico-thalamic loops? See Susan Blackmore, *Consciousness: An Introduction*, 2nd ed. (Oxford: Oxford University Press, 2012), 154, 158, 181, 237, 374. Note that Buddhist theory recognizes numerous classes of consciousness (*viññāna*) beyond these pre-cognitive, sense-modality-specific sorts of awareness.

41. Goenka, *Discourse Summaries*, 40.

42. For David Hume "all the perceptions of the human mind resolve themselves into two distinct kinds . . . : impressions and ideas" (*A Treatise of Human Nature*

[1739–1740], ed. L. A. Selby-Bigge. 2nd ed., ed. P. H. Nidditch [Oxford: Clarendon Press, 1978], 1). All (legitimate) ideas arise as "faint copies" of impression (so that impressions provide the only content of our ideas, which gives Hume a criterion to distinguish sense from non-sense, a weapon he uses to raze the history of ideas). Impressions include not only the "original impressions of sense," but also "reflective" impressions that arise when an idea is interposed (275). Passions are reflective impressions, and arise, either directly or indirectly, from pleasure and pain, which for Hume are among the "original impressions of sense" (276). By contrast, neither "background feelings" nor *vedanās* (which include "physical" pleasure and pain) are sensory inputs to a concept-forming process. *Vedanās* do not make up the content of our concepts (unless our thinking happens to relate to them).

43. Damasio, *Strange Order*, 12.

44. Goenka, *Discourse Summaries*, 27.

45. I refer here to Arthur Schopenhauer (1788–1860), a Kantian who embraced Indian philosophy and bringing it into relation, perhaps for the first time, with Western philosophy. Philosophically a pessimist, and personally embittered, Schopenhauer praised but also misinterpreted Indian philosophy, especially Buddhism, as pessimist. His classic work, *The World as Will and Representation* (New York: Dover, 1969) is among the most accessible of all great works in philosophy.

46. Despite efforts, I have not been able to trace the source of this remembered attribution.?

47. Friedrich Nietzsche, *Die fröhliche Wissenschaft* ("la gaya scienza") [Gay Science] (München: Wilhelm Goldmann, 1887), no. 275. Here is my more faithful translation of the complete aphorism: "What is the seal of attained freedom?—To no longer stand ashamed before oneself."

48. The phrase derives from William James, "The Will to Believe," in *The Writings of William James: A Comprehensive Edition* (1904), ed. John J. McDermott (Chicago: University of Chicago Press, 1977), pt. 4, 723.

49. Defense mechanism are widely discussed, originally in Sigmund Freud. For a recent review, see Phebe Cramer, ed., "Defensiveness and Defense Mechanisms," special issue, *Journal of Personality* 66 no. 6 (December 1998): 879–1157, https://onlinelibrary.wiley.com/toc/14676494/1998/66/6 (accessed September 14, 2021).

50. "Free won't"—a widely attributed expression used to suggest that we have no free will except as a veto, an ability to turn back the "necessity" of instinct or action unconsciously initiated—is credited by Susan Blackmore to Richard L. Gregory in 1990. See Blackmore, *Consciousness*, 141, 479.

51. Friedrich Nietzsche, *On the Genealogy of Morals* (1887), ed. Keith Ansell-Pearson, trans. Carol Diethe (Cambridge: Cambridge University Press, 2007), first essay, sect. 15, 29.

52. I rely in this essay on the inestimable *OED* s.vv "envy," "invidious," 231–32, 459.

53. *OED* s.v. "envy," 231–32.

54. Bernard Mandeville, *The Fable of the Bees and Other Writings*, abridged ed., ed. E. J. Hundert (Indianapolis: Hackett, 1997). The view is often mistakenly attributed to Adam Smith, who in *The Wealth of Nations* (1776), rev. ed. (London:

Penguin, 1986), famously wrote: "It is not from the benevolence of the butcher, the brewer, or the baker that we expect our dinner, but from their regard to their own interest." (bk. 1, chap. 2, 119). And then there is the notorious "invisible hand" (from bk. 4, chap. 5, but see Adam Smith, *The Theory of Moral Sentiments* [1759], ed. D. D. Raphael and A. L. Macfie [Indianapolis: Liberty Classics, 1982], 184–85) by which individuals, not intending the public good, nevertheless add to it in pursuing their own interests. *But neither of these have anything to do with envy.* Moreover Smith regarded sympathy as a fundamental human motivation, and envy as a vice, even if its "principle," when well-directed and in moderation, need not be. But we can also have too little of that of which envy is too much. In *Moral Sentiments*, Smith wrote: "Even that principle, in the excess and improper direction of which consists the odious and detestable passion of envy, may be defective [that is, in deficient supply]. Envy is that passion which views with malignant dislike the superiority of those who are really entitled to all the superiority they possess" (*Theory of Moral Sentiments*, bk. 6, iii, para. 16, 243–44). Thus, although "improper direction" is inherent to envy, we can also fall short of virtue by a deficiency in that "principle" which makes envy. Smith "justly condemns" the person who "tamely suffers other people, who are entitled to no such superiority, to rise above him or get before him" as "mean-spirited"; which in all by name is envy deficit. Thus, we ought not to envy our superiors, but we ought to accord them their "dignity and rank." If we trim our desire and guide it properly, and *bolster it when it flags*, we may enjoy all the virtues of envy short of its name.

Chapter 4

Games We Play

In the intricacies of intimate interrelations there is much room for foul play, from forms of self-deceit to running mind-games in other minds. The stakes are high and the subterfuge deep. We want true love, and we are prepared to pretend in order to get it. Antics arise already in front of our mirror, where we practice our moves alone. They extend into relationships, where we also seek to find our self, all the while doing our best to reveal only our good side. How can I be your mirror when I cannot bear my own? It is uplifting to highlight the flaws in *your* self-image, but one word against *my* dazzling self and things get darkly serious. In these sometimes-sordid sports, where lies and love look so alike, some words are weapons, and others mend wounds. Why do we scrap and scar when we could make beautiful music together? Are we not overly-entertained by our own soap-operas? The games we play in relationship were regular themes of our Café Philosophy confabs.

SURRENDER

Surrender—the all but final act in love and war. The humiliation of the white flag and the exhilaration of a whispered *yes*—how can these two worlds exist under one roof, come under the cover of this single word, *surrender*?

But then again the language and strategy of war have long since invaded the territory of love. Cupid was armed from birth. Conquests are tallied as notches on the player's thigh. Even marriage can be a military operation. . . . But my topic is surrender. How did I drift off onto marriage?

From a first-person perspective, and again in a military context, surrender is of course defeat, and therefore hardly the optimal outcome. But when surrender comes, it is because it is preferred over the imminent alternative, usually a more eviscerating defeat. Surrender saves us from certain death, or rather makes that death a little less certain. For we throw ourselves on the mercy of the martial court.

Is it so different in the case of love? Does love, when it comes, finally defeat us? Is there not a kind of ego-humiliation that occurs due to genuine care for another? And if our defenses still hold, how can we say we are yet in love? Now, if the comparison were just, then in the crisis provoked by love, the option of surrender should arise as our next to worse alternative. That is, love's surrender should lead to hope, however uncertain, that utter annihilation will be forestalled. And is just this not so? Call that utter annihilation the loneliness of existence. Does love's surrender not save us from this? The heart's surrender—is it not just our visceral last chance bid to not die alone by dying for another? Is the bet of love not the uncertain hope to put off our isolation, perhaps thereby even to eternize our existence? *I shall be with you always.*

In love, two become one, and the other's interest becomes one's own. Where else have we heard that? Aristotle: "master and slave have the same interest."[1]

If surrender is the penultimate act in war, what is its last act? One may sue for peace, but peace comes only if the suit is accepted. For the plaintive, that final act is experienced from the other end. To be accepted as bond-servant, captive of war, to be slave and prisoner. To be lorded over by the victors. To all this surrender opens oneself. And perhaps also to mercy. Can you see where I am going?

O you captives of love! Willing prisoners and slaves to your beloved! Are you not bond-servants of your vows? Lorded-over while you whisper, "yes! yes!," is this not after all your optimal outcome? Have you not been fighting all these long years for your present . . . defeat?

Come willingly to Philosophy, hands in the air. Get your mercy at the court of social reason.

LONELINESS

Loneliness is the pain of the illusion of separate existence. As we are each constitutionally subject to this illusion, we are each given the ill-wrapped gift of loneliness. We have no choice but to be offered this bitter gift, though we have wide latitude in the manner and style of our reception. Most of us find some way to refuse it.

Loneliness has many faces, mostly sad and long. Perhaps the most poignant is the imagined face of a far away loved one. Here loneliness takes on the face of the one missed. This one is lonely because that one is not present. It would be easier to bear being alone if we did not long for our distant beloved; it is not so much being alone we feel as being without them. Love bestows a world upon the one loved, which is reflected in the way our family becomes our world, our private realm within the home. One misses hearth, and is only homesick. When one misses family, one is lonely.

Another face of loneliness is the wayfarer, who is not homesick but sick of home, and so has gone off a-wandering. The homeless traveler has a loneliness that is not simply a longing to be with one's own. It is the loneliness that is felt when one lifts one's pack and knows, all one's belongings are on one's back. It is the trackless wanderer looking for their own way, the pilgrim, who only now and then is troubled or delighted by memory of those left behind. This is the loneliness of going it alone.

A third face of loneliness is the blank stare of social isolation. These are the nameless faces going by on subway cars, focused on the infinite distance to avoid any dangerous interaction. This is the loneliness of the long-distance plodder, the tendency toward mindless repetition and empty formalities. Drudgery is friend to this loneliness, for at least it whiles away the hours and minimizes change. It also takes root in families that do not communicate, in the silences where things that should be said never get said. Isolation within intimacy, a kind of homesickness at home, is suffered by anyone whose relationships have become routine, and whose passions conventional.

We can even miss the people we are with if they (or we) have built a wall of silent toleration or contempt between us. We can isolate ourselves within the very relationships we enter in order to stave off our loneliness. As this shows, the logic of loneliness can be an intricate dialectic, but it is no less strong for being delicate. Suffice it to say that we are often in some measure the architects of our own social isolation, that we can fear togetherness just as much or even more than we fear our aloneness. A silence that destroys togetherness (communication) can also preserve togetherness (maintain a stable status quo).

A fourth face of loneliness is an aging face, for age has its own loneliness. Each of us faces death alone, and age brings us swifter and swifter toward that lonely existential question which will have its answer. Older eyes look more steadily upon death. I do not mean that the young face death less than the old, only that any older self has reflected more on it than that same self younger. This face of loneliness may be found by looking in the mirror, and seeing the lines around the eyes, increasing yearly, reminding us of our future. Such loneliness is a condition of existence, even as death is our unconditional nonexistence. Loneliness is here the mirror image of death, and the lines of age are just existential worry lines, deepening with age. How much fear of loneliness is really only a masked fear of our death? Nor is this fourth face capable only of a worried look; it tolerates different expressions, as many as there are different attitudes to death.

But now I discern in this crowd another lonely face, not this aged mortal one that deepens furrowed brows and gives crow's feet to eyes, but a youthful face, a youthful fear. Is there not a kind of loneliness shown in the timid stare of innocence, fearful that it may be wrong, or inadequate, or unlovable, or simply missed? This is a bright face pained by the prospect of never being picked, of being overlooked, of being left undiscovered, unable to attract anyone toward oneself. The aged fear ultimate or the last aloneness; youth fear never being found. Behold the loneliness of the green wallflower, standing off, at the edge of the crowd. This is the pitied periphery, not the invisibility amid the elderly or other lost minorities. The loneliness of the ripe apple, left on the tree at harvest, of being passed over in one's prime, unrecognized and thus never given the opportunity to grow through relationship. This loneliness we each feel a little when we are shown in public to have been in error. It is like the loneliness of being singled out as wrong.

This fifth face of loneliness expresses the awkward uncertainty of young adults and of all novice lovers. It can be shown by shy gawking, a nervous glare, or a quick looking away. This loneliness stares at its feet and hides its hands. It is no more the reserve of the young, than the isolation of death is exclusively felt by the old. Whatever frightens us silly, and makes our speech mumbled and hesitant, dresses us in this fifth mask of aloneness.

Yet there is something sacred in this changeable innocence, as it is a fear of being found wanting, and of being accountable for one's failures, of being responsible for what happens. It powers great reforms in us, which may be superficial attempts to shape up appearances, or deeper reflections that transform us from the inside out. If we reflect on our aloneness long enough, we realize no one else is there to deal with it. We must either paper it over, or learn to live with it. By long looking at it, gradually the eyes open, and one sees that this loneliness-blight afflicts one and all, a universal malady. This may seem to make matters worse, but actually the paradox of the shared experience of aloneness is enough to destroy the illusion of separateness, if only the eyes are allowed time to adjust to the new light.

In this light another face of loneliness arises, the face of truth, an honest expression, a radiant hue. This face shines almost to holiness, knowing it is alone before its god. And it is okay with that, except for this infinite flame of longing that leaps from it toward the divine bosom. But this is a joyful longing, and though the pain of truth sings its lament of separation, the song its god hears is a happy paean. For truly the very boundaries of my body depend on the pressure and temperatures at which I find myself. What is inside me was once outside me, and then it was no other stuff than it is now. The food on my plate is the labor and life of others, and only it maintains me. I do not retain it or anything, for it all passes through me, like these words, which are just another bridge to the other, to you all. The face of truth smiles its slight smile and gets along, but how lonely, how alone, how wayward! The only self it expresses is its relation to other, and how lonely this path, when the world is run by self-interest and competitive self-serving. Where indeed is this face to be found in this world? For I have heard of the face of truth, but I have never seen it, and I am a long-time mirror-gazer.

"Truth is a pathless land," said J. Krishnamurti.[2] It is a wilderness in which one must make one's own way. There is no road carved out of the mountain, and we all know where the well-intentioned paved road leads. This is the loneliness of truth I mean, not unlike that wayfarer face already mentioned. Since the topic is personal, I will mention a personal story, as it relates to Café Philosophy and its origin, and it allows me a graceful exit from this crowd of lonely faces I have drawn.

Years ago, finding myself credentialed but without employment, yet with an undimmed love of philosophy, I vowed to take it to the cafés. But this vow was peculiarly inactive, even lethargic. Only when a new café in my neighborhood graciously put itself at my disposal did I do anything. As it happened, my initial reaction to the offer, to my own surprise, was anger. I stomped out of the café in a huff. In a few moments, I found myself at my place in front of a mirror. Only then the oddity of my emotion became clear to me. Why was I angry? The answer came after some staring: there was no one to show me how. I had to do it alone. Nobody had prepared me for this. The beginning of Café Philosophy in Victoria, Canada, was this pathless loneliness. I never dreamed it would grow into a community that abates the pandemic of loneliness in our world, at least locally. It began in a daunting loneness; but it was not an attempt to erase or address that loneness. If it has provided me with a sense of belonging, a welter of friends and philosophical companions, then I take that all as bonus. Though I did not foresee this, I am no less grateful for it. So I end with thanks everyone who attends and who reads this. I am glad to have so many interesting people each week to talk to![3]

INTIMACY

The word "intimate" has two curiously opposite meanings. On the one hand, as an adjective, "intimate" applies to what is innermost and closest to one's private nature; but as a verb, "to intimate" means to tell, to announce, to disclose or make known. Of course, the two meanings come together in the intimate confab, where two people share their secret struggles toward intimacy, revealing and healing in ever-closer rounds of pillow talk.

Intimacy is a most vulnerable being. Around this tender crouching plant crowd all manner of threats. Too much aggression, and intimacy will never reveal what it is hiding. Self-doubt, like your own hands around your throat, can choke off intimacy, and stop all growth. Betrayal is an existential threat to intimacy, but more of that later. Perhaps the most prevalent killer of intimacy is comfort, and the stasis it enjoys. Intimacy requires safety, but atrophies without risk. Thus, television is also the enemy of intimacy, as is the ubiquitous personal phone. Cellphones have invaded the intimate space of bedroom.

With these and so many other threats, intimacy clearly needs strengths, craves strengths, and indeed can build its own strength through endurance. An attitude of success can create success. Boldness pays, if it does not cross the invisible and shifting lines between it and aggression, or between it and perceived prurient interest. Intimacy needs its challenges and hurdles to grow, but it also needs its walls and protective enclosures. It needs its greenhouse, with sun, a gentle spray, and no winds. Many a bug has crept into an intimate relationship and chewed holes in it.

The space around each person has been divided into various concentric zones. We all know we can crowd someone's personal space if we stand inappropriately close to him or her. The immediate vicinity of a person's skin is sometimes called the zone of intimacy.[4] This context lends meaning to the expression "intimate aggression," which is quite literally in-your-face anger (ranging from up-close-and-personal shouting or finger-wagging to domestic abuse and sadomasochistic practices that shall remain nameless). "Intimate aggression" may sound like an oxymoron, but it is a very vivid reality. It serves the purpose as well of stripping the term from its apparently essential positivity, and reminding us that connotations deceive.

Intimidation saps intimacy, but intimacy itself can be intimidating. Intimacy is like our bedroom door: we prefer to keep it shut lest others see inside. If we have it, we may feel no need to share it. If we do not have it, we may feel uncomfortable about sharing that. If we have had it, but do not now, we may be reluctant to disclose why. But these threats to our discussion pertain directly to our topic. Be bold. Risk the truth.

An intimate is one with whom one can share one's embarrassing moments, fears, weaknesses, and frank truths. By all accounts, being loved has better health outcomes than the alternative.[5] The lonely are sicker. The lonely will not be happy to find this out. They may just get lonelier. One theory holds that human language evolved as a substitute for social grooming, in which primates for instance spend their leisure hours engaged.[6] At root, perhaps our intimate words with each other are supplements to social touching. Conversation as contact comfort—that is my prescription for those without intimacy. In short, attend philosophy and treat yourself to an intellectual massage.

Let us share sweet nothings in each others' ears. Philosophy you can coo too. Come as you are.

LOYALTY

I have all this on the authority of my dog. I obey him implicitly on all such matters. Shake hands, boy!

Loyalty is old school. Think of the workplace. Used to be, one could be a company man one's whole life. Loyalty was part of a payback scheme. Loyalty was a two-way street. All that has changed. As security has dwindled, loyalty has become flexible, adaptable, a switch. It goes and comes with the job. Globalization has shaken up and shaken down the little guy. What does he owe anyone? Loyalty now is to the next paycheck.

Marriage today is not a lifetime, but multiple over a lifetime. Monogamy has gone serial. Why shouldn't loyalty?

Voters have no loyalty, nor should they. A fickle electorate is a free electorate. For politicians, even those who deliver on promises, this can come as a bitter truth. It came home to Premier of Saskatchewan, Tommy Douglas, the father of universal health care in Canada, when he was on the hustings for re-election in 1948. The farmers to whom he had brought rural electricity, roads, schools, free hospital care, and so on, sat on their votes until they could see what he was offering this round. So he took in his stump speech to retelling a story attributed to Winston Churchill:

> A candidate calls on an old friend to ask how he intends to vote, and is told that the old friend is undecided. "What?" says the candidate, "How can you say that? When we were boys together we went skating and you fell through the ice and I pulled you out. When you wanted to get married I loaned you two hundred dollars. When your house burned down I signed a note for you at the bank. When your child needed an operation I lent you the money you needed. Isn't that so?" To which the voter replied, "That's all true, but what have you done for me lately?"[7]

Even Plato gives loyalty a second-rate status.[8] The heart, seat of courage, wellspring of anger, owes loyalty to the head, the reasoning mind. This characterizes the well-regulated *psyche*, the just soul. The heart knows nothing, but its loyalty to reason gives it true opinion. It understands not the wherefore, the reasoning, the justification of knowledge, but like the loyal sentry post, it prowls the perimeter, keeping out intruders. Between the philosopher-rulers and the peasant-producers, the loyal guard dogs form the middle tier in Plato's speculative ideal society. They sniff out difference between friend and foe, protect the city, and pay blind allegiance to the philosopher-rulers (who need that blindness to maintain their big lie). Loyalty is for soldiers. It is left for philosopher-generals to reason why.

Your dog is the true philosopher, Plato says, pandering to his middle class.[9]

Loyalty is groupthink, pressure not to break ranks, the safety of numbers, the blessed power of "we." All for one and one for all: the pledged union of *compadres* or compatriots. Loyalty is to die for, to kill for (a good line is worth re-using). Loyalty is a nod, a rubber-stamp, a knowing wink. Loyalty is clubby, a social front, the mutual covering of backs and asses. The patriarchy is a men's club, machismo is the sign of its loyalty. Loyalty is the liberty not to think.

Love induces commitment. That commitment is sometimes called loyalty. But loyalty is the outer husk of commitment, the dry shell that lasts even after the love has gone. Or it is semblance provides cover for the lost love, for disloyalty. Disloyalty looks at first just like loyalty. It is the bark before the bite.

However bad loyalty is, it is better than disloyalty. Betrayal and uprooted expectation are nobody's cup of tea. It does not help at all to know what is disloyalty to one person is to another greener pastures. The cheated are not relieved by the good time had by all others. The fink, the narc, the mole, the spy: they feign loyalty for access. Disloyalty disguised as loyalty is pernicious, a sin of malice. Loyalty that merely wanes is at worst a sin of weakness. Conscious violation, hidden and under cover, is the worst. Let no praise of loyalty detract from that, or offer umbrage.

If you cannot trust anyone, who can you trust? If loyalty is a ruse, in whom shall one place one's trust?

"O Polonius! So sanctimonious. But were you right? To thine own self be true?"[10]

Atta boy! Go fetch philosophy. Do not do it out of loyalty. Do it in order to be disloyal to illusions, yours and mine.

BETRAYAL

To betray is to break a trust. Trust may be implicit or expressed. The betrayal may be open or hidden. The drama and the ambiguity of betrayal depend on these dimensions of transparency, as does its immorality.

Betrayal does not require that the trust be explicit. An infant can be betrayed, but has no explicit understanding of the love and commitment it needs to survive. The trust is implicit, what is to be expected in the circumstance, an unearned desert. In other cases, implicit trust accrues gradually, for instance by cohabitation, or even a long sequence of dating. Commitment goes unexpressed, but silent nods preserve the (sometimes false) presumption of agreed upon terms. A so-called common-law marriage is yet another example where rights are earned by endurance, not by title. Though never spoken, nor ever expressly consented to, even unrecognized, the legitimacy of our claims upon one another sometimes builds just by sticking it out together. The trust is that legitimacy, those warranted claims, the right one holds against another to be true. Without such right, the trust is baseless, a mere hope. There is no betrayal without prior legitimate trust, though disappointment is still possible, and a lesson against silence.

Innocence can be betrayed, so the trust violated need not be explicit. The needs of the infant generate obligations in the caregiver; routine brings expectation. According to developmental psychologist, Erik H. Erikson, the first stage of life presents a crisis of trust, and sets up thereafter our personality orientation toward betrayal.[11] Are you a trusting personality? Are you comfortable in your own skin? Or have you manufactured defenses and arrayed them to protect yourself against betrayal? If you are the latter pretending to be the former, you may feel betrayed even by my questions.

Is theft betrayal? Is our trust in others not violated by it? I was robbed in Cuba once. It was a snatch and run crime, and luckily little of value was lost. Did I not implicitly trust the night with my security? Was common decency too much to expect? Or was I so naïve and over-trusting that I had it coming? Yet even the naïve can be betrayed, and not merely rolled over. Trust can be general, and perhaps spread too thin, but if it is violated in burglary, there is betrayal even in this petty crime. Theft by force of arms is betrayal in the ancient sense: knife to your neck, you hear "hand it over" (*tradere*, the Latin root of *betray*, means "hand over").

Betrayal can lead to withdrawal and risk aversion, or to independence and self-reliance. "I'll Never Love Again" might be the soundtrack for the former response.[12] The latter is represented most campily in "I Will Survive."[13] By trial and error, by trust and betrayal, we too learn to replace those senseless locks.

Yet undeniably the most flagrant betrayal is betrayal against an express agreement, an explicit trust. This is betrayal with self-consciousness, scheming betrayal, betrayal self-aware of its own violation. It is one thing to do a wrong thing, another to do it with a worked-out plan in full consciousness that it is wrong. This is betrayal with malicious intent. The pathetic plea and rhetorical excuse, "Who is to say it is wrong?" rings hollow in this case, for here one does wrong knowingly: the agent is aware of the wrong as it is committed. For wrong self-consciously done the harsh word *evil* is sometimes neatly reserved. However, if we listen to Socrates, this sense of betrayal is confused; for he held that no evil is done willfully.[14] Assuming, then, as we have been, that betrayal is evil, then willful betrayal, if not a contradiction in terms, must be an error in judgment.

Betrayal, defined as violation of trust, is one among many causes of relationship collapse. No doubt some will defensively inquire what the difference is between betrayal and change. People change. Relationships grow and wilt. When it is over anyway, what difference does this last post-fatal step make?

One can grow out of a bond as much as one can grow into it. When all trust has been sapped from a relationship, no trust remains to be betrayed. When the explicit has faded, permission becomes implicit.

There is something illicit, even rank, about such reasoning. It goes against my taste to promulgate a generic excuse, to issue a universal license for overlooking promises made, to rubber stamp in advance, or in guilty hindsight, a rationalization of sticky moral decisions. To me, this kind of moral pleading is just a call for the social validation of one's self-deception. We just want to get the story right, our story, our cover story, so we can make proper response when people ask embarrassing questions about how it all went so wrong. When we tell the story of our life, we want to have the best lies ready to hand. Revisionist autobiography thrives thanks to our tendency to excuse our behavior by extenuating circumstances. We call it making sense of what went wrong.

If trust is a precondition of betrayal, it may be implicit or explicit. Transparency favors the explicit, but our moral relations are overwhelmingly implicit. Ambiguity of the law is no excuse. But light also enters (or does not) at the other end of betrayal, in its overt or secretive nature. Betrayal hidden (and who betrays in the open?) is betrayal doubly bad. The trust is explicit, the violation is conscious, and the evidence is covered up. *Mens rea* [criminal intent] is evident in the skulking, the furtive laundry, the lies about late nights at work. Hidden betrayal is not only evil: it is a conspiracy.

One can betray without a word, but betrayal covered with a lie is the norm (statistical, not ethical). The point is not simply to betray, but to betray and not get caught. Conventional reasoning bends moral truth to adapt to the demands of everyday reality. Carrie Bradshaw of *Sex and the City* asks: "Is cheating like the proverbial tree in the forest? That it does not exist if there's no one around to catch you?"[15] A philosophical question, I guess, but one that is easier to ask the prettier you are. If it is not still cheating, it is called *defensive rationalizing*.

I have mostly considered the act of betrayal, rather than the feeling of being betrayed. I am afraid I may have betrayed that silent, sinking feeling. So I end with a remark from the done-to perspective on betrayal, that of the betrayed. The feeling of betrayal, I have observed, may or may not be accurate. It too we can evoke to justify our actions during an unhappy break up. I recall once feeling strongly betrayed when a certain relationship ended, before grudgingly realizing that the only violation had been my ex's audacity to stop loving me. The nerve of anyone, after all, to suggest that I was no longer lovable! The earth was likewise betrayed by Copernicus when he had the effrontery to suggest that the universe did not revolve around it.

Transparency in relationships allows in the sunshine of truth. Explicit agreements may encourage mutual understanding, but the world is implicit, and we bear relations of trust with all beings. In either case, our betrayal may be open or hidden. When loyalty fails, open betrayal is the honest policy, and the best bet. For instance, some of our finest politicians have been turncoats. And if you have to hide it, the inconvenience of living a lie has to be considered. Of course, not all that must be hidden is a lie, and discretion covers even wholesome relationships. Sunshine is a good thing in relationships, but sometimes one wants to draw the blinds.

Do not let me down. We are all counting on you. Bring your cheatin' heart.

FAITHFULNESS

If only the faithful may speak of faithfulness, then I should have to remain silent.

Faithfulness is a deceitful concept, inviting misunderstanding and weaselly excuses. Its literal and conventional meanings come apart, so that its own name tears at its own meaning. To believers, I would bet, faith is central to faithfulness. To unbelievers (or "Brites" as some are calling themselves) this is of course likely to be less true, at least insofar as we take *faith* to mean religion. So our first question: can there be irreligious faithfulness? For one side, the answer is tautologically no; according to the other side, that answer commits a gross fallacy of equivocation.

One needs to take special precautions discussing a misleadingly named topic. While we must acknowledge the meaning a word bears on its face, we need not slavishly respect the literal meaning of its roots. The salient meaning of the root word "faith," taken by itself, is religious or spiritual. By contrast, the most prevalent and readily accessible sense of "faithfulness" is interpersonal. Rather than falling along a human-god axis, it signifies human-to-human relationships, applying especially (though not exclusively) to married or love-committed couples. The literal significance of the verb stem, however, cannot wholly be shaken, so we get as it were two topics for one, with all the semantic risk and opportunity that such ambiguity brings. Therefore, we need to be careful *not* to switch the subject to any dispassionate religio-metaphysical musings and away from the more uncomfortable inquiry into the causes of relationship fuckup and breakdown. An over-blown and over-literal role for faith in the meaning of faithfulness must not (like a guilt trip) distract us from the more painful subject of the causes within ourselves of lost or broken love. Truth loves to hide,[16] but never so much as we love to hide it when it embarrasses us. Spirituality no less than philosophy can provide seemingly secure camouflage for such feelings.

Nevertheless, quite apart from all religious or spiritual questions, the "faith" in "faithfulness" rings a note of truth. It means to be true to, to keep true to, to keep one's faith to another alive. Faith as belief in the steadfastness of another—even if it has no basis in a divine or higher principle—is yet sacrosanct, in that a promise given generates an inviolable right in the recipient of that promise. Even without God's backing, and without reference to any eternal moral law, a promise is a promise, by which I mean there is no straight-faced denying it once it is made. It takes only two people to make a vow to each other, although a third force, a social or spiritual authority, is required to pronounce them married. Marriage requires the intervention and sanction of a state or of a god. And yet, with just the two of you, if you say "I do," and then you do not, you lie, and it is a wrong, regardless of whether there is a God watching.

It is instructive to compare faithfulness to another person (the paradigm, as I say) to faithfulness to oneself. To thine own self be true, the Shakespearian platitude runs. Of course this is easier said than done; harder still is to pin down what it might mean. Being true to oneself, one may have to depart from a relationship. But that only means that being true to oneself is a trump card one keeps in case a promise one has made becomes stale or uninteresting any longer to keep. Any self-interested act is liable to pass muster under the great warrant and rubber-stamp of a maxim, *be true to yourself.* I promise you today, then promptly tomorrow my new self requires for its truth a whole new life, and I leave you with a clear (or, rather, empty) conscience. If one identifies with one's ego, self-interest becomes momentary expediency, and all yesterday's bets are off.

For if I make a promise to myself today, I may release myself from it tomorrow. Once I am released by the recipient of my promise, it is no longer binding on me. If my betrothed calls it off, it is vain for me to keep my faith. Who can be true to a flown bird? But the self is in flight, and truth to self is therefore fickle. Now, in the case of love of another, one is not at liberty to remove the bond, though one has placed it upon oneself willfully. The other must release us, or our fickleness is a lie to them. From which I think we can conclude that truthfulness to another is the only basis of love, that human beings are not their own best keepers, and that there is no end to which they will not go to sanctify their defections with the name of virtue.

Faithfulness is a topic of much wriggling. It is instructive to listen the pious statements we hear about faithfulness with certain probing questions in mind: is this person excusing the breaking of faith, perhaps even erecting an intellectual defense against their own apostate history? Or ask: how much wiggling do they have to do to believe what they are saying? Or ask: is this a cover and excuse, a plain truth, or a broken heart? Or ask: is it vindictiveness pointing a finger to cover its own faithlessness?

Do not go out to those other Cafés tonight. Think about the children at Café Philosophy. Be there. You said you would.

SOUL MATES

The danger with this topic is a too-easy attack. Lacking a soul mate, we may impugn the very concept, like the fox that scorned unattainable grapes as being in all probability sour. The soul mate idea is foul, we say, but it is our bitter heart which speaks, under the beguiling cloak of reason. Without a soul mate we are transformed unawares into a sourpuss, and philosophize accordingly.

Can we do it? Can we maintain a sensible discussion of the concept of soul mate without insulting those who have theirs? To me, at Café Philosophy, we need to approach the question a little differently, much as we do the question of the existence of God. It is not enough for an atheist not to believe: they often feel they must attack the sanity and right of others to believe. They insist that the Most High Grapes are sour. I want to engage in dialogue about the philosophical problem of the divine with believers and non-believers alike. So at Café we ask, "what does God mean to you?" (rather than "does God exist?"). I want to dialogue with all of you about soul mates, both with the haves and the have-nots. Can we do it? Can we ask, not whether soul mates exist, but what soul mates mean to you? Or will the temptation to cry *Naïve!* sour our debate?

It is hardly to be denied that the premium conception of soul mates concerns the lifetime mating and bonding of two human beings, while hinting at an eternal aspect to this relationship. Lesser imitations exist, but this is the main idea. That there are only two involved is presumed to be key: we speak of "our other half" in ways that would never permit us to speak of "our other third" or "our other fifth." That just is not decent. Marital harmony comes in two parts only. The existence of soul mates outside of this holy union ruins the song utterly, not to mention constituting legal grounds for divorce. The only exceptions tolerable are total redefinitions, so that the new soul mate is no longer a soul mate in the same sense as the spouse (or spousal-equivalent). These secondary soul mates may be teachers who transform us; witnesses who explode our self deceptions; bosom or beer buddies; best or childhood friends—but under no circumstances can they be lovers. All of these acceptable relationships may, but none of them must, destroy the privileged oneness of "that special someone." The pristine sanctity of marriage cannot survive the other woman (or man), even if the marriage sometimes can.

Of course, second-besters everywhere will reconsider the necessary conditions for attaining that rarefied union of soulmatedness, without yet disqualifying it as a match made in heaven. After all, can't heaven make a match, then mix and match? Can't heaven want my first marriage, and then also want my second? (It begs the question as to who is to blame in the divorce; piety and decorum assumes at least 50% for each party, thus exculpating Heaven.) God may not tolerate divorce, but *we* must, at least in light of demographic trends. Serial monogamy is the order of the day. Tomorrow, who knows?

What is sacrificed by this diminished form of the ideal is the eternal glint of our love pairings. Soul mates are only for now or for a time, not for all time. Later, during the next phase of my life, I will have someone else. If you are here now meaningfully for me, and I for you, so that you want no more, and I want no more, are we not for the nonce soul mates? If later we squabble and separate, are we bound to admit our soul mating was mutual illusion, or can we still say that it was right and true for us both then, though no longer? Perhaps, as sequential soul mates, we are still amid the stars, but the stars themselves now die.

If the ideal of soul mate can theoretically dispense with eternity, it can arguably dispense with God as well, that great match-maker and marriage-arranger, who winks at the blushing of adolescents. The stars themselves may guide us. The astrology of love is no doubt more profitable than chance at predicting love's inception and its success. But even without God or the stars, numinous demi-agents such as archetypes shrouded in the transpersonal unconscious can provide the requisite solemnity and prearrangements. Synchronicity can fix the meetings, appoint the dates, and otherwise blindly lead lover by meaningful coincidence to the beloved. We shall have our soul mates regardless of the prevailing theology.

Though it is a climb-down, the *Occasional Soul Mate* suggests itself as a more affordable model. That holiday romance that left you transfigured; that intense all-night conversation on a train with a stranger you never saw again; that illicit fling that was sweet through and through before it dissipated suddenly, to your secret mutual relief; that teacher whom the night brings when the soul is ready to be taught; that improbable dating ad success; many are the ways for our innumerable pointillist soul mates to manifest! If now the term has been diluted to mean random meaningful encounters, perhaps none but the most acute will notice. The lonely will not lament it.

This weakest definition of soul mates is probably the most democratic. Any old liaison that works for a while is a tawdry definition of soul mate, but it has the merit of ensuring that the majority of people have had at least one. The dilution of ideals is often popular, but mine is not the lament of a nostalgic conservative, pining for the restoration of divorce-free matrimony (legally-enforced eternity). Soulmate-lite is good enough for sitcoms and for putting up appearances; and it is good enough to arouse the reminiscence of reactionaries. More inwardly, the picture is bleaker, of a kind of soulless mating, the presumed salve for the unmentionable horror of solitary existence. This is clinging to fight the void.

But the soul mate myth might yet be rehabilitated by endowing it with metaphysical or cosmic (if not theological) significance. Sigmund Freud attempted to do so in the name of science, no less. A straight debunking would never do, for all myths, like dreams, express latent truths. So Freud looks back to Plato's *Symposium*[17] in which the great playwright, Aristophanes, is made to articulate the theory that, originally, some human beings were spherical and had a third, combined gender, male *and* female. The two-sexed beings, who had four arms and legs, were later split apart by the Gods, who grew jealous of how much pleasure these globular "two-spirit" humans were enjoying. Since then, the resulting unisexual half-humans have had to search, often through multiple lifetimes, to find their "other half." The myth of soul mates has this origin in Plato, yet it also points farther back, some say to India, where four-armed four-legged androgynous gods have long been familiar. India: home of the great "other half" of Western philosophy.

Freud, who thought everyone was inherently bisexual, could not resist the myth. He had referred indirectly to the Aristophanes story already in [1899], where he takes it to summarize the "popular view of sexuality."[18] By [1920], Freud had come to see rather more in the tale. He introduces it in one of his most remarkable later flights of theoretical fancy. To reveal the primordial origins of the sexual instinct, Freud traces it back "to *a need to restore an earlier state of things*."[19] (It will be recalled that Freud, around this time, had introduced the radical *thanatos* or death instinct, which was also conceived to have a restorative effect, restoring an original dissolution.) The [1920] discussion of Aristophanes comes on the heels of a discussion of protozoa conjugation, which apparently has an invigorating effect comparable to sexual union. Freud, still laboring under the misconceptions of Lamarck and Haeckel, saw the coming together of germs cells in sexual reproduction as the very recapitulation of the origin of organic life. So when Freud comes back to the Aristophanes' myth in Plato, he introduces it gingerly, only after precautions and excuses, and his primary application is *at the cellular level.* The original life substance, it seems, was torn apart and now perpetually seeks to restore its unity; sexual dimorphism is merely a late expression of this vital will to reunite, one which is preceded by cells coming together to form multicellular organisms, and then developing a "protective cortical layer"[20] to defend against a dangerous environment. Here Freud suddenly breaks off his theoretical reverie, pausing only to lament the great uncertainties involved, which nevertheless do not prevent him from accepting his musings as reasonable if tentative hypotheses going forward. From philosophical myth we move to mythical science

In 1921, Freud added a footnote, which cites Prof. Heinrich Gomperz of Vienna on the Indian origin of the Aristophanes myth. He directly cites the

Bṛhadāraṇyaka Upaniṣad,[21] where a cosmic origin story is related involving an androgynous being (*ātman*). Freud writes:

> the Brihad-aranyaka-upanishad is the most ancient of all the Upanishads, and no competent authority dates it later than about the year 800 BC. In contradiction to the prevailing opinion, I should hesitate to give an unqualified denial to the possibility of Plato's myth being derived, even if it were only indirectly, from the Indian source, since a similar possibility cannot be excluded in the case of [Plato's] doctrine of transmigration.[22]

So Freud suspects that Plato has his Indian sources, and his evidence is the soul mate theory Aristophanes presents in the *Symposium*, which offers so striking a parallel to a many-armed Indian deity overseeing the transmigration of souls. But for its cosmic significance he looks to his romantic life-philosophy of protozoa.

Let me end by mentioning an error opposite to the easy one with which I began. The soul mate can be like candy we never get to taste, all the sweeter for the constant longing, imagined to be sweeter than it is because it is unknown. We magnify it by comparing it to all we have ever known, this desperately lonely existential anguish sequestered in radical, opaque subjectivity, without even a self to knit one's private experiences together. Tell me you feel the same way! If I cannot have my soul mate, can't I at least have some existential twin, to co-ponder with me the same abyss, if only from the other side of the chasm?

Gather round the chasm. Come be clever foxes! Bark up the soul mate tree. Sweet are the grapes of philosophy.

NOTES

1. Aristotle, *Politics*, trans. Benjamin Jowett, in *Complete Works*, ed. by Jonathan Barnes. (Princeton, NJ: Princeton University Press, 1984), bk. 1, 1252a33–34, 2129.

2. [Jiddu] J. Krishnamurti, "Truth Is a Pathless Land," Speech dissolving the Order of the Star of the East, Ommen, Holland, August 3, 1929, https://jkrishnamurti.org/about-dissolution-speech (accessed August 8, 2021). In *Freedom from the Known*, ed. Mary Lutyens (Chennai: Krishnamurti Foundation, 1969), Krishnamurti writes "Truth has no path" (10).

3. My loneness in this case was my ignorance. The occasion of the offer from the café owner was a *Sunday Telegraph* article (Patricia Cleveland-Peck, "I Drink, Therefore I Am," *Sunday Telegraph*, November 10, 1996) that had been posted to a café bulletin board, to which one of the owners drew my attention. It was about Marc Sautet and his Café Philo in Paris. So I knew a little about Sautet, but nothing at all about his method. I have since translated Sautet's account (Sautet, *Un café*

pour Socrate: Comment la philosophie peut nous aider à comprendre le monde d'aujourdh'hui [A Café for Socrates: How Philosophy can help us understand Today's World] [Paris: Robert Laffont, 1995]) of the birth of Café Philosophy; it appears in a collection of essays I edited on public participatory philosophy. See *Cafe Conversations: Democracy and Dialogue in Public Spaces*, ed. Michael Picard (Vancouver, BC: Anvil Press, 2022). There the origin story of my own Café Philosophy is told in more detail.

4. The idea of interpersonal zones (intimate, personal, social, etc.) has its roots in the important work of social psychologist, Kurt Lewin, a Gestalt theorist who pioneered attempts to map the immediate social environment of the individual organism. He also invented sensitivity training and action research. See Kurt Lewin, *A Dynamic Theory of Personality: Selected papers*, trans. Donald K. Adams and Karl E. Zener (New York: McGraw-Hill, 1935); and Lewin, *Principles of Topological Psychology*, ed. Fritz Heider and Grace M. Heider (New York: McGraw-Hill, 1936).

5. Helen Riess, *The Empathy Effect: Seven Neuroscience-Based Keys for Transforming the Way We Live, Love, Work, and Connect Across Differences* (Boulder, CO: Sounds True, 2018).

6. See [Robin] R. I. M. Dunbar, "Group Size, Vocal Grooming and the Origins of Language," *Psychonomic Bulletin & Review* 24, no. 1 (February 2017): 209–12, https://doi.org/10.3758/s13423-016-1122-6. See also Dunbar's *Grooming, Gossip, and the Evolution of Languag*e (Boston, MA: Harvard University Press, 1998).

7. Doris French Shackleton, *Tommy Douglas* (Halifax, NS: McClelland and Stewart, 1975), 172.

8. I allude here to the ideal city sketched in Plato's *Republic*, bks. 2–4. See the *Republic*, trans. by G.M.W Grube (Indianapolis: Hackett, 1974), 29–109. Plato lays out an ideal society with three classes, which are the social manifestation of three psychic organs (functional parts) as follows: peasant-producers (corresponding to our soul's appetites); police-army guardians (reflecting the sense of anger and honor seated in our "hearts"); and wise-rulers—male and female—(the reason in our heads that ought to rule our passions). Plato jokingly compares the mid-tier guardians to loyal guard dogs, who can tell friend from stranger, but needs to be leashed and kept away from the reigns of power. Thus my tail-wagging jokes. See the Plato, *Republic*, 375a–376b.

9. A loose translation of 376a. The joke is explained by Grube's translation of *Plato's Republic* (46n11). Plato extends the metaphor at 404a; 416a–b (clarifying that sheep-dogs are intended, not wolves, who are not good to the sheep); 422d ("hardened and spare" dogs fight best), and at 440d (where the guard dogs are called to heel). At 459a, a dog-breeding argument underlies the great *eugenic* political lie at the heart of Plato's utopia.

10. William Shakespeare, *The Tragedy of Hamlet, Prince of Denmark: Text of 1603 and 1623*, 3rd. series, ed. Ann Thompson and Neil Taylor (London: Arden, Thomson Learning, 2006), act 1, scene 3, http://shakespeare.mit.edu/hamlet/ (accessed September 14 , 2021).

11. Erik H. Erikson, *Childhood and Society*, 2nd ed. (New York: W. W. Norton, 1950), esp. 247–74.

12. Lady Gaga, Natalie Hemby, Hillary Lindsey, and Aaron Raitiere. "I'll Never Love Again," *A Star Is Born* (album) (Los Angeles: Sony Records, 2018).

13. Dino Fekaris and Frederick J. Perren, "I Will Survive," *Love Tracks* (album), by Gloria Gaynor (London: Polydor, 1978). The song was made famous by Gloria Gaynor. Please sing along.

14. This is one of the so-called Socratic Paradoxes: virtue is knowledge (or a science); sin or vice is ignorance; so no evil is done intentionally, but only by mistaking what is right. For a good discussion, see W. K. C. Guthrie, *Socrates* (Cambridge: Cambridge University Press, 1971), 130–42.

15. Darren Star, "The Cheating Curve," dir. John David Coles, *Sex and the City*, July 11, 1999, no. 206, season 2, episode 6 (New York: HBO, 1999). Samantha had just corrupted logic and ethics thus: "the act of cheating is defined by the act of getting caught. One doesn't exist without the other."

16. Heraclitus, Fragment B123: "Nature (*physis*) loves to hide". In Patricia Curd's *A PreSocratics Reader: Selected Fragments and Testimonia*, 2nd ed., trans. Richard D. McKirahan and Patricia Curd (Indianapolis: Hackett, 2011).

17. Plato, *Symposium*, 189d ff, trans. A. Nehamas and P. Woodruff, in Plato, *Complete Works*, 457–505.

18. Sigmund Freud, *Three Essays on the Theory of Sexuality* (1899), trans. and ed. James Strachey (New York: Avon, 1962). 22.

19. Sigmund Freud, *Beyond the Pleasure Principle* (1920), trans. James Strachey. (New York: Bantam Books, 1959), 100; emphasis in the original.

20. Freud, *Beyond the Pleasure Principle*, 102.

21. *Bṛhadāraṇyaka Upaniṣad*, in *Upaniṣads*, trans. Patrick Olivelle (Oxford: Oxford University Press, 2007), 1.4.3. The story reads in part: "Now he was as large as a man and a woman in close embrace. So he split (*pat*) his body into two, giving rise to husband (*pati*) and wife (*patnī*). Surely this is why [the great sage] Yājnavalka used to say [to his wife]: 'The two of us are like two halves of a block.'. . . He copulated with her, and from their union human beings were born." As far as I can tell, there is no spherical being, no lunar origin, as in Plato, and no four arms (although *purusa*, the self that became big as two, is called "a thousand-limbed" in the famous Vedic *Puruṣa Sukta*, where it is also a union both male and female, the self-fecund male womb. See *Ṛg Veda*, 10.90. See *The Rigveda: The Earliest Religious Poetry of India*, trans. by Stephanie W. Jamison and Joel P. Brereton (Oxford: Oxford University Press, 2014).

22. Freud, *Beyond the Pleasure Principle*, 101–2.

Chapter 5

Playing Fair

When rules give out, what becomes of fairness? What is fair is what is beautiful and right. But who can lay down rules of beauty or exhaustively define what is right? We must play by the rules, but they have not been spelled out; they remain unsaid and subject to interpretation, yet are not reducible, for that reason, to *anything goes*. Interpretation brings bias, a kind of playing unfair in meanings; but it is not optional. So can we still play clean? There are no logic referees; we have to play that role ourselves, even while we hash out our differences. We need to play together, making up the rules as we go, which can and sometimes does go terribly wrong. But that only shows that opinion alone does not determine right and wrong, that rules have a basis beyond belief, and that belief needs the check of reason. Beauty and the Good are not our playthings. Let us be theirs.

VALUES

What are values? That question is curiously different from this one: What is valued? When asked the first, we often reply with an answer to the second. What you value shows your values, and maybe also your value. But *what* you value is not what it is *to value*.

The word *value* has many meanings, many values.[1] A value is a fair return, a denomination, an importance, worth, or usefulness. In music, the value of a note is its duration. In visual arts, the value of a color is its luminosity, or relative lightness. One of the word's meanings is what is valued. Thus value is also what is valued. Some say there is not much more to it. Even value may be useless. Some values are not worthwhile. The paradox is slight, because the values of *value* are many. Some worths are not worthwhile: a mild ungrammaticality is needed to render the contradiction salient. The easier reading is trite: some things valued are not valuable; or even easier: some things considered valuable are not valuable. It is curious how ambiguity places a contradiction alongside a banality separated only by a philosophy.

We no longer consider things to have a worth. That only people do, and it is a net worth. Forget that this consideration cheapens us. The prevailing doctrine is that things have value only because they are valued, because someone values them. Value is no longer a feature of anything, but simply an assigned quantity representing an offer of a fair exchange. The philosopher Immanuel Kant took pains to distinguish all appearances from the unknown reality "x," the thing-in-itself beyond all our intuitions and categories.[2] The self-in-itself was such an x, but it had a value surpassing any price.[3] Today every x has its price, the cost to pry it from the dead hands of those who prize it. To be a value is to be perceived as valuable.

If you ask people what their values are, they will provide a list. Usually it is a list of valued things and people. Values are what is valued. Or they may list abstract nouns like *peace*, *justice*, *truth*, and *freedom*. It will be said that to value these things is to enjoy pleasant sensations when relating to, or reflecting upon them. In other words, to value is to gush. Value, it is said, is noncognitive, merely the regular occurrence of positive affect when presented with the beloved, a fair outcome, non-deception, or a reduction of external restraint. But outside the valuer there is no value.

A value is a rating, an appraisal, an assigned quantity, capable of more or less. No ratings without raters. There are no values without subjects assigning values, or placing value upon inert and valueless things. Value is utility. And when all utility is stripped from nature its value will be reduced to zero, along with human being. The value of human value has yet to be determined, but the chart is drifting downward and into the red.

The process of value-adding is a sacred economic engine. If you are not profiting from that, you are skimming from the reusers and recyclers. But, as a pundit once told me, to render an old-growth forest into ready lumber is really only profiting by *value subtraction*.[4]

The purchase of persons is illegal, which only drives up their price. In this market, price never exceed costs, which are incalculable. Or rather, costs are externalized as the product. Our religions require that we not put prices on heads, and avoid attaching labels generally. But we have technocrats and actuaries to fix the price without need of a tag. And if the value of untrammeled nature cannot properly be assessed, we have environmental economists to calculate a perfect proxy in average willingness to pay. We cannot attach a dollar value to the forest and its biodiverse habitats; but we can estimate how much the average tourist would pay to visit there, or how much its proximity affects house prices, and thus obtain objective numbers to be assigned a putative scientific reality, in this way presuming forests are fungible after all. The value of clean air may likewise be assessed by the willingness of the taxpayer to bleed on tax day in order to breathe freely the rest of the year.

Values may be effective or aspirational. We routinely ignore the distinction when it is in our perceived interest. (Thus we approve of ourselves based on our excellent aspirational values, but we condemn others for the least unfortunate lapse.) If we want to know what someone values, we have to ask them, for values are opinions and opinions are best assessed by survey. But if we really want to know what someone values, we would not dream of asking them: we would watch them, and read their values off their choices. Actions speak louder than words. "50,000,000 Elvis Presley fans can't be wrong."[5] Market value is objective, positive; it is effective demand. We all love animals, but most of us eat them. The stomach trumps sentiment, the hand triumphs over the heart.

The above list of valued abstractions suggests that values are warm and fuzzy if deep. We forget the depths to which love of evil can go. We forget the power of revenge, the sweep of vanity, the pride of place—values are what we value. We forget that we must rate the valuer to evaluate the value. That jealousy is widely valued (enacted) makes jealousy human, understandable, but no less evil. Selfishness is universal but so is ignorance. Should we love that? What is most valued may be least valuable. Heraclitus already knew: "it is not better for humans to get all they want."[6]

We think value is born of the heart, and thus is born pure. But whose heart is pure? Not all values are created equal, because not all valuations are equally valid. We forget how much cunning goes into our values, how many concurrent and crossed purposes they serve. We think of values as born of love, as what we love. We forget how we love to hate, how we delight in contempt and spite. Our love affair with evil must needs be kept secret, and appearances kept up that our marriage to the good is made in heaven. So we equate the good and pleasure to maintain the illusion during the day, while at night we pay obeisance to the dark saint with engorged libido. Happiness is what we value. The appearance of truth will do.

The gods love what is good because it is good; it is not good because the gods love it.[7] And we are fools to think we are the gods of value. Value is also a rock, the one we live on, our immovable center. It resists the labels and price-tags we affix to it. It proves itself in enduring our onslaught of self-deception, in outlasting us. To rent it is to destroy it, to own it is to serve it. We try to ride it, but we are eroded. It rights itself against all our wrongs. Value devalues all our valuations. We think we define it at our own cost and peril. But it awaits discovery and the chance to define us.

Be careful what you wish for.

GOOD

Etymologically, *good* means favorable, advantageous, worthy, or wholesome. It is a term of general approbation, a salutary tag, applied to whatever functions or works well. *Good* connotes positive value, yet enjoys a variety of opposites and negative correlatives, ranging from poor, bad, and evil, to ugly, harmful, and unfortunate. Having many opposites, *good* is deeply and multiply ambiguous; it is consequently a dangerous and deceptive word, more so whenever its significance is taken for granted (as it usually is). I might almost say that *good* is a bad word. It would be good if I could leave it out of this essay entirely. But I can hardly make good on my title with that approach. I shall have to make the best out of a bad situation.

What follows is framed for the most part as a series of semantic pointers, observations on how the word *good* works differently in different contexts. These contexts may be differentiated by contrasting the good with a variety of contextual contraries and things it is not. Nothing particularly novel, deep or insightful is intended here. What I seek is more like a settling of terms, or perhaps, in the end, an unsettling. Along the way we dip our toes in the deep end of Ancient Greek ethical philosophy. But it suffices to say for now that my aim is to reveal the conflicting burdens carried by this overloaded workhorse of a word, and to dispel the illusion that somehow mere insight into its moral connotations will make better persons of us. Moral insight, in any case, is not into the good, but into ourselves. So there shall be no question here of defining moral goodness, only cautionary tales as to how ambiguity unaware of itself is the bane of philosophy.

All Value Spheres

Whatever else *good* applies to in philosophy, a chief concern has almost always been good actions, good persons and a good life. Although the principal semantic field of the word *good* in philosophy is thus ethics or morality, that is by no means its sole domain. In the wide swath of everyday life too, the adjective *good* has its uses in all the major value spheres. Thus, for example, in aesthetics—good as fair, beautiful, handsome, delicious, even fun (as in "s/he is good looking"; "we had a good time"); in the market—good as profitable, enriching (as in "this is a good deal"; compared to goods as wares, commodities, merchandise); in ecology—good as healthy, salutary, fertile, even uninjured (as in "this is good land," "I have one good leg"). Even in logic, *good* means true, valid or cogent (as in "good point!" or "that's a good argument"). What it takes to be a good doctor is different than what it takes to be a good father, and good painters are not necessarily good people. What the word gains in breadth, it loses in clarity.

So to begin let us beware that the meaning of a word often depends on the words next to it. This is especially true of the philosophically important word *good.* The point is by no means new. Aristotle finds the word *good* (*agathón*, in Greek) to be hopelessly ambiguous for similar reasons. He says:

> Again, the word "good" is used in as many senses as the word "is"; for we may predicate good in the Category of Substance, for instance of God, or intelligence; in that of Quality—the excellences [that is, the virtues]; in that of Quantity—moderate in amount; in that of Relation—useful; in that of Time—a favorable opportunity; in that of Place—a suitable "habitat"; and so on. So clearly good cannot be a single and universal general notion; if it were, it would not be predicable in all the Categories, but only in one.[8]

The Aristotelean categories mentioned here come up again elsewhere in this book (especially chapter 7). The ones listed here are Substance, Quality, Quantity, Relation, Time, Place, but there are four others. What are Aristotle's categories?[9] To simplify, for Aristotle, the categories are ambiguities of "is"; that is, ways to be, meanings of *to be* (of the Greek *on*, *onta*). Put critically, Aristotle offers a *grammatical* analysis of being. Categories are classes of predicates, or different sorts of things we want to say (assert). His point in this passage is metaphysical (even if he bases his conclusion on an understanding of language), and directly critical of Plato's view of the "single and universal" Good. In contrast, my point is grammatical or semantic, but I can use Aristotle's words to make it: "good cannot be a single and universal general notion."

What is more: even the ethical good, I would say, "cannot be a single and universal general notion." This is *not* to say that ethical goodness is subjective or a mere matter of taste. Objectivity does not need to be singular: it can be plural. Universality is not required of objectivity. Let me now return to the meaning of *good.*

A Good Job?

One basic source of confusion is the contrast between what is functional and what is ethical. From a practical perspective, what is good is what works, what gets the job done. This is *effectiveness.* Only results matter if effectiveness is our concern. Of course, to be practical, we must also be concerned with costs, with *efficiency*, in other words, with the rate of return on the initial outlay. An *effective* policy or program is simply one that accomplishes what it is designed to accomplish, that fulfills its stipulated end or purpose (however noble or base that final cause may be). An *efficient* policy, in contrast, is effective at least cost. Efficiency quibbles over the various means to a settled purpose, recommending least bucks for the loudest bang; but like its cousin, effectiveness, it knows its place and does not fret over which bangs are best. Thus, functional good is always relative to some presumed end or purpose: a good shoe is good for what shoes are good for. The same applies to rifles. There can be no question here of moral (let alone universal) goodness inherent in a gun or a shoe.

Different though these concepts be, the functional good and the moral good are readily confused. Aristotle asks: "just as eye, hand, foot and, in general, every [bodily] part apparently has its functions, may we likewise ascribe to a human being some function besides all of theirs?"[10] Aristotle answers that indeed we may, and the good life in the ethical sense will turn out to be just the functional good of human life, or living well *as human beings*. Thus being all we are formed to be is flourishing (*eudaimonia*) or happiness. So it turns out, with certain qualifications, that happiness is the virtuous life. We have to get the ends right, and not merely haggle over the means to our own unhappiness. But they were happier times when we could easily presume that there is some natural or god-given function or end (*telos*) for human being, for that is what Aristotle took to underlie virtue and the principles of ethics.

To be clear, efficiency and effectiveness are (positive) instrumental and prudential values (prudence is a virtue). They are the *expedient*. They make very fine morally-neutral bureaucratic virtues. We ought to care about them, but they concern themselves with means only. They do not care about ends at all (one might even say, they do not *care* at all). Ethics, by contrast, needs to be more choosy. *Ethics is care*. Whereas the instrumental sense of *good* restricts itself to a consideration of means, ethics is bound also to consider ends, to evaluate, reject or approve of some ends as worthier or less worthy than others. Of course, ethics also adjudicates means, but it does so with a richer palette of value terms than efficiency, effectiveness, and other prudential values. Ethics may safely be regarded as a species of self-restraint, a limiting of oneself to certain ends. But that is not enough, for ethics cannot simply be the most efficient means to a noble end, as in a spate of brutality to restore the peace. Indeed, ethical good must concern itself with means *and* ends in ways totally alien to what mere expediency demands, which prizes efficiency exclusively and effectiveness above all, and is interested only in results, like a falsely-sacred bottom-line. Such so-called pragmatism is a philosophy despite itself, a kind of anti-philosophy that tramples over what it pretends to prize. (It is not to be confused with its namesake, philosophic pragmatism, as found in Charles Sanders Pierce, William James, John Dewey, or George H. Mead, and which has a place elsewhere in this book—for example, chapters 2 and 6).

Unphilosophical pragmatism runs roughshod over morality, one sort of good overcoming another. But the danger—a sort of semantic imperialism—is that the crude meaning crowds out the subtle one, as bad money chases out good. Expedience drowns out the ethical good as it rallies people around worldly necessities as pretexts for action. In everyday life, the good is assumed, implicit, unstated. How can we distinguish clearly what remains buried in the daylight? Only when the everyday is interrupted does the good emerge as problematic, and philosophical analysis can begin. Yet often the instrumental meaning condemns the moral good to a grave-like silence; and that is why philosophy appears akin to the impractical and to what does not work. These are semantic slurs, but they trace lineaments of objective faults of subterranean meaning.

In (unsubverted) philosophy, as mentioned, the moral sense of *good* is paramount, though it is a struggle to keep it so, and even what that means exactly remains open to debate. The moral good is the virtuous, the just, the commendable, the benevolent, and what is right. But these are rough verbal stand-ins, demarcating a terrain, not logical equivalents, still less definitions. Or rather, as definitions they beg questions and are logically circular, since any inquiry into their meanings would eventually lead back to the moral term *good* itself. Folly and wisdom alike seek definitions, but folly alone finds them. The point for now, however, is not finally to define, only to mark off for special consideration, to contrast for perspicacity. Let us now put aside the narrow focus on means and all questions of prudence, and look instead to ethics proper.

Sin and Sinner

Within ethics, it becomes imperative to distinguish among the various objects to which *good*, as a moral adjective, is to be affirmed or denied. As mentioned above, both a person and an act may be good, but already here the word is taken in distinct yet related senses. Let us say that an act *does good* if it is beneficial at all in any way; and an act i*s good* if the good it does overall (the sum of its beneficent outcomes) outweighs any non-beneficent effects the act has. The logical circularity here may be excused, as it does not prevent a clear contrast between the notion of a good act and that of a good person. A person is not just the sum of their acts. Note first, that a g*ood person* may do something that *does no good* or *is not good overall*; that is, nobody is perfect, not even the best. To be a good person does not require that every last act one commits be good, virtuous, or right; indeed, those are far from preconditions even for being a saint. A person is good depending, at least in part, on the tendency of their acts over their lifetime, not on any single snapshot of their behavior. And yet, what good a person has the opportunity to do depends also on factors beyond their ken or control, a *fact* (empirical circumstance) sometimes referred to as moral luck. If two people do acts that are equally good, but one overcomes much adversity to accomplish what the other does as a relaxing hobby in their spare time, how could we call them equally good persons? The good a person is not reducible to the good they do. No simple bridge from action to person can be built, which perhaps shows the limitations of the definitions just introduced. Those circular definitions will not do, so we drop them now; but they have served to make the point that act and agent must be evaluated in complex, related, though importantly different, ways. Likewise, evil may be an angry outburst, a weak moment, or an entire career. Alone, the first two make at most for evil acts; whereas a pattern, or something more like the third, is needed for an evil person. We hear that we are not to judge the sinner, only the sin. Certainly, we cannot use the same criteria for each. And thou shalt employ proper criteria to evaluate, or improper criteria shall be employed to evaluate thee!

We see in other ways that one cannot safely infer that a person is good or evil from a good or evil act alone (tempted though we are to infer just that, almost irresistibly so when the single act is sensational). For instance, a good person who has done wrong reacts differently upon discovering this, than an malevolent person does who has realized own wrongdoing. The former regrets, apologizes, and, where possible, makes amends; the latter cares not, derisively laughs, and resumes or intensifies their vicious conduct. (If pressed, they may, in low style, angrily scream a facetious apology.) Generally, it is wiser to condemn actions than persons, lest one cause what one says to become true; but also too because evil persons are worse than evil acts, as good people are worth more than the good they do. Praise too is best specific, for actions can be repeated but people gone are gone forever.

Good, Right, Virtue: Arch-Concepts in the Moral Value Sphere

Let me now turn to another well-worn distinction, still within the moral sphere, which may dispel the fog somewhat, even if it does not pretend to absolute definition. It can be strangely clarifying to replace one unanswerable question with a raft of related unanswerable questions. One comes to survey the same terrain with incommensurable maps. Consulting many maps reduces the risk of not finding what is there, but not represented on any map; yet our terrain is more complex than any (finite) stack of maps, so the risk of getting lost in confusion also increases.[11]

Dauntless, let us contrast the question as to the nature of the Good with that of the Right, on the one hand, and of Virtue, or excellence, on the other. Good, Right, Virtue: objective ethics may take its grounding in any of these basic concepts, and the resulting philosophy will vary considerably.

While the term "good" in most cases affirms (as we have seen) a variable positive value upon its object, the term "right" signifies a principle, something which (other things being equal) must not be violated. If the gesture of the good is a thumbs up, and that of its denial is a thumbs down, the gesture of what is right is a line drawn, as if in the sand, as if to say: "thou shalt come this far, but no farther!" There is a holy shroud of necessity surrounding the right, whereas the good is optional, and may even be inadvisable. Too much good *can* be a bad thing. But so is not enough. Why pay a certain amount for a good, when you could get double for that amount elsewhere? The good is not even necessarily the best; so unless you intend to give up on the best, you may have to forgo many a lesser good, as when driven to trade-offs. In a race, fast is good, but fastest is best. When it comes to compassion, even a little is nice; rarely are we called upon to exert the maximum; but let us agree that there is some minimum which ought to be extended in reward. A good may be any little, or it may come in heaps. Rights are a moral minimum, and duty is the least you can do.

Clearly, then, there are wrongful goods; that is, good deeds that are morally wrong (so not right). To take another instance, a good turn done to one in need may be grossly unfair to others in as much or more need. Yet its wrongness does not erase the good done. It is a good deed that should not have happened, illustrating that ethical values and ethical norms may collide, even where the question of individual or cultural relativism is wholly irrelevant (since these conflicts arise within contexts as specific as you like).

Though the good and the right may thus diverge, in the general course of events they track together. It is another matter when it comes to virtue, those moral excellences that call upon us to go beyond mere duty and to what is right, and beyond the good too, to reach toward the best, and to take the crown. The hero is not obliged to risk all, yet they do it. Compassion is cramped that restricts itself to what is meet, owed, or to what is right. The best soars beyond even the last best, which is always only the best "so far." Virtue is not humbled even by the impossible, and will not confine itself to the lawful or the general good. Virtue demands its superstars, and always a new and more excellent crop. If doing good is insufficient, and doing right is the minimum, who but Virtue will guide us to and in the upper reaches of the good? Thus the good has friendly competitors in the conceptual terrain of ethics, and both are more high-minded than simple goodness need understand. To misuse Aristotle once more, in ethics we cannot get by with "a single and universal general notion."

Having laid out this threefold distinction, let me for the remainder hone in on the philosophical question about the meaning of the word *good* (continuing to take this in the moral sense), with an eye to clarifying the important ethical question, so far only hinted at, *what is the good life?* So first we ask about the meaning of moral goodness.

Not What Is Desired, but What Is Desirable

What we like we call *good*. What is moral we call *good*. What bears the same name we too easily confuse. Yet these two senses of *good* are as different as what we desire is from what is desirable, which are tragically distinct. Or perhaps we should say that a tragedy arises from not recognizing the vast chasm between the two. This was touched upon in the previous essay on Value, summed up most poignantly by Heraclitus: "It is not better for humans to get all they want."[12] But let's here pursue the matter further.

People differ in what they (say they) like. This is a difference in (espoused) preferences. People differ in how they define *morally good*. This is a difference in moral values, not a difference in preferences. Put aside the first fact (that there are differences in preferences), so we can focus on the second: differences in conceptions of the good. The nature of the ethical good is a topic of vast and significant controversy. But it is *not* the unremarkable fact just put aside that people have widely different preferences. Even if we virtuous types happen to prefer something we recognize as morally good, we can also recognize the difference between preferring that thing and assessing it as morally good. Put differently, *to be good* in the moral sense does not equate with *to be preferred*. Without this distinction, philosophical moral thinking can scarcely begin. (Though it can cave in.)

For, many times we see cases where what is morally good is not in fact preferred, even if it should be. Pleasure is chosen over principle. What is preferred is often, by consensus, not what is morally right or good. What we want is therefore not the same as what we call morally good, even if we want the latter, and it is good that we do. Of course, it may yet be the case that morally educated preference is a rough guide to what is morally good. This raises the normative question: what should our preferences (be educated to) be? And this question marks progress. The issue before us is not *What do we prefer?* But, *What ought we to prefer?* It is not the question of empirical fact, *What is desired?* But, the question of principle, *What is desirable?*

What Is It to Be a Duck?

Look carefully at these last two contrasting pairs of questions. The first question in each pair goes to matters of actual (though psychological) fact. The second question of each pair is about not what is actual, but what is ideal. They are normative questions, and take us beyond mere matters of fact and (even) opinion. Yet also these normative questions I wish now to put aside, in order to place in view a yet deeper philosophical question, which otherwise might get confused with those raised so far. The distinctions just drawn and just now sidelined allow us to see that our original question, *What is good?*, is simply too clumsy for present purposes. It dangerously straddles two logically distinct questions, as if attempting to climb two ladders at once. It conceals within itself both the normative (or evaluative) question *Which things are good?* and also a *definitional* question, *What is the nature of the Good?*. We want to know, not what acts or other things in the world are exemplars of moral goodness, but, much more fundamentally, what it means for those things to be good (in the moral sense). So do not quack, and do not line up all the ducks; just tell me what it is to be a duck.

This new question as to the nature or essence of the good seems to require a definition for an answer. Socrates was the first Greek philosopher to ask after the universal essence (*eidos*), to demand a definition (*horos*) to disclose the nature of a thing; and he was interested before all else in moral or ethical ideals, like Justice, Righteousness and the Good. On such moral ground angels need not fear to tread, but fools wander boldly. Socrates required definitions, but was never fool enough to be wholly satisfied with any he found. This essay will follow that wise and diffident course. Nevertheless we must here at long last raise and squarely face the question of definition, of essence: what is the nature of the Good?

Plato, picking up the Socratic leitmotiv, took contemplation of the Good (*agathón*) to be the philosophers' chief duty, which amounts in the end to participating in *agathón* itself, in that the philosophical *psyche* (soul or life) is to become as good as possible. Thus the Good, in Plato, takes on a central governing role not only for the wise *psyche*, but also in the ideal city (or *polis*), and even in the cosmos itself; or rather outside it, since *agathón* is also the point of transcendence (*hyperousia*) in the Platonic worldview. In his *Timaeus*, we learn that *care of the soul*—the Socratic ambition to make the soul as good as possible—requires cathartic harmonizing with the cosmic music through contemplation of things eternal.[13] Only the philosophical life will do that for you.

Plato and Aristotle agree in defining the good, *agathón*, as "that at which all things aim."[14] The Good is the universal end of all. This metaphysical claim one cannot find Socrates pronouncing, but one can perhaps discern it in the calm of his death-bed smile.[15] Taking the Good to be the very *raison d'être* of the cosmos is a striking instance of the moral conception of the universe (which Friedrich Wilhelm Nietzsche attributes originally to the ancient Persian sage, Zarathustra, a predecessor of Plato). No doubt the law of karma, in so far as it governs rebirth according to good deeds (*karma* means deed or act), also institutes a sort of moral order in the universe, albeit quite a different one than this Greek conceit. Still, ethics, in all these philosophies, rests on cosmic or metaphysical principles: the Good is grounded in the nature of reality itself. Or *vice versa*? Reality is a mere reflection of the Ideal. One is no longer sure if the metaphysics is driving the ethics, or the ethics the metaphysics.

The Good Life

One philosophical role of a concept of the Good is to buttress one's conception of the cosmos; a closely related role is to spell out the contours of the Good Life while we yet linger in that cosmos. If the universe is the ultimate good vibe, you've got to get on its wavelength. Soul harmony lies in that direction. Ethical philosophy wants to know what the good life is for human beings, not just what a good act is and what good persons are. The good life is an ethical ideal, it is not a lifestyle based on wealth and privilege (which, alas, today is the picture that first comes to mind in response to this lamentably blithe term). A principal preoccupation of ancient Greek ethical philosophy was to conceive the Good Life, rather than articulating rules for proper action. Indeed right action was only to be understood through a conception of the virtuous person ("what Socrates would do"), the virtuous person being understood as the one excelling in said Good Life.

Although Aristotle disagreed with his friend and mentor, Plato, that the Good (*agathón*) was a transcendent reality, he sided with him in regarding the highest human life to be a philosophical life, a life of *theoria*, which involved contemplation for its own sake, ultimately about the sake or purpose (*telos*) of the cosmos itself. In the *Philebus*, Plato debates whether pleasure (*hedone*) or wisdom (*phronesis*) has the better claim to be the good at which the highest human life should aim, settling for a higher blend of the two. In the *Republic*, he argues that a just soul, even with the worst possible false reputation, who was trash in the eyes of the world, would yet be happier than an evil and unjust person whom none suspected, and who all hailed as the great and beneficent ruler;—not only happier, but 729 ($=(3^3)^2$) times happier.[16] So for Plato it is in your interests to be good; and yet the good is objectively defined independent of you. *You should be good because it is good*, not *you should be good because it is good for you* (although it is). The Good determines your interest, not your interests determine what is good. Today it is an almost forgotten perspective.

On the question of the Good Life, and the highest good for which we may aim, Aristotle also starts out from a distinction that more or less tracks Plato's contest (happily resolved) between pleasure and wisdom. Speaking of the "highest of all goods achievable by action," Aristotle writes:

> Verbally there is very generally agreement; for both the general run of men and people of superior refinement say that it is happiness (*eudaimonia*), and

> identify living well and faring well with being happy; but with regard to what happiness is they differ, and the many do not give the same account as the wise. For the former think it is some plain and obvious thing, like pleasure, wealth, or honour.[17]

As is suggested at the end of this quotation, Aristotle goes beyond the two distinct conceptions of the good life discussed by Plato to consider a third. For, although honor is a "plain and obvious thing," it is *not* sought by the many. Most people prefer gratification and a life of pleasure, but Aristotle dismisses them out of hand: "the mass of mankind are evidently quite slavish in their tastes, preferring a life suitable to beasts."[18] By contrast, says Aristotle,

> people of superior refinement and of active disposition identify happiness with honour; for this is, roughly speaking, the end [*telos*] of the political life. But it too seems too superficial to be what we are looking for, since it is thought to depend on those who bestow honour rather than on him who receives it, but the good we divine [is thought] to be something of one's own and not easily taken from one.[19]

So "people of superior refinement," the better sorts amongst us, will prize honor, but not too highly. A more stable and lasting good of one's own that cannot be taken away is what the wise person will seek. This leads us to virtue or excellence, which is precisely the Socratic and Platonic line on happiness (*eudaimonia*). Indeed Aristotle will not fall far from this tree, yet virtue alone, he tells us, will not do.

> even [virtue] appears somewhat incomplete, for possession of excellence seems actually compatible with being asleep, or with lifelong inactivity, and further, with the greatest sufferings and misfortunes; but a man who was living so no one would call happy, unless he were maintaining a thesis at all costs.[20]

Yet something like that thesis had indeed been maintained, and at considerable cost. Specifically, one who is (*not* sleeping or inactive but) virtuous, yet afflicted "with the greatest sufferings and misfortunes" could and did claim to be happy. The radical and controversial claim from which Aristotle here steps back is that virtue is sufficient for happiness (*eudaimonia*) and the Good Life. Our reputation may be in the mud; we may have lost our health and family to the ravages of disease; we may be bankrupt, imprisoned, even tortured, and yet happy if virtuous. The fate of Socrates comes to mind, or perhaps the trials of Job (he certainly was *not* happy, though he might be called blessed). Aristotle shrinks back from endorsing such moral heroism or purifying moral supremacy. (Is he implying that Socrates did not die happy after all, as if his were only the play act of a great tragedian? "Count no man happy till he is dead," Aristotle reminded us.)[21]

We might try to understand the three competing accounts of the good life that Aristotle lays out by pointing to different personality types. Some people prefer money and pleasure over reputations and power, while others have the reverse preference ranking; yet others value knowledge over any of these two. Put like this, it seems to be a matter of differing preferences, of individual differences, and not a matter for resolution once for all. And yet, spiritual wisdom from all ages and all the great ancient religions say the first two conceptions of the Good are ill-advised, "less reasoned," and false paths.

With this Aristotle is in complete accord. The good life is a happy life, but happiness consists in the excellent fulfillment of human function, in the virtues of realizing our specifically-human capacities. Aristotle ties virtue to function, to excellence of functioning, so that seeing would be the soul of the eye, if the eye had a soul, and the virtue of the would-be soul of the eye is seeing well. So the soul is the living of the whole organism, and we must ask, as above: what is the function (or purpose) of being human? The good life in the ethical sense will turn out to be just the "best and complete" functional good of human life, or living well *as human beings.* What then are we? We are the *zoon logon echon*, the animal capable of reasoned speech. We are the deliberative animal, deliberating on ourselves and on how to live. Though we can think on our own, we "do so better [with] fellow-workers"[22]; for we are, as he puts it elsewhere, a social animal (*zoon politikon*): "it is evident that the *polis* is a creation of nature, and that man is by nature a political animal."[23] But the *polis* is the community, the city, society, as much as it is the state. Thus what makes us most human is our reasoning together, our s*ocial reasoning*.[24] And this at least puts our community conversations is a grander light we may not always appreciate.

We should take what we can from Aristotle, but leave with him all that is not good. And clearly, in a different sense than above, the Good is not for him a universal notion. And that is shown by the fact that his conclusions about the good life are *not* based on universal human being. He brushes aside as irrelevant those "with slavish tastes," as well as "barbarians," and he caters to "people of superior refinement." The *polis* or sociality that is essential to us is no egalitarian community, but one resting on slavery and in which "silence is a woman's glory."[25] Not all are citizens, or deserve to be: "For that which can foresee by the exercise of mind is by nature lord and master, and that which can with its body give effect to such foresight is a subject, and by nature a slave."[26] The leisure that Aristotle takes as evidence that his conception of the good life is the right one, rests on some people owning others, and others being silenced. The virtues of masters and not those of slaves. So clearly we cannot transpose Aristotle's model of happy flourishing onto us.

Perhaps we are, after all, the animal that reasons together. But what reason is and can be for us is not what it was for Aristotle. What our sociality is or can be is not what it was for Aristotle, nor even what history has left to us, but what we can hash out together. And what animals and our own animality are and must be for us must break free of the hierarchical mentality in Aristotle of lesser and greater, of the lesser existing for the sake of the greater, and the idea that nature is there for our use. The universal Good we must now discuss and grapple to frame must encompass the ecosphere. We can no longer be ends-in ourselves; we must find our ends in the world we are destroying by taking it as our means. The Good Life needs an ecology. "May all beings be happy."

To End: Ethical Means, and What the Ethical Means

I said above that ethics is distinguished from a thoroughly results-oriented attitude to life by a certain restraint, grounded in concerned for both means and ends, or indeed by *caring* about both means and ends. Most helpful in any such careful inquiry would be to know ultimate ends, over which, unfortunately, debate lingers. In the time-honored tradition of giving over what we do not have, many have sought to spiritualize the ethical, to ground it in some higher quest. One might point to Søren Kierkegaard or Nietzsche on this head, but let me end instead with Mahatma Gandhi, who wrote "realization of the goal is in exact proportion to the purity of our means."[27] Similarly, he tells us "Impure means result in an impure end."[28] One might well ask what purity and impurity amount to, and perhaps the rough idea is clear enough if it be embodied in his famous political campaigns of non-violent action, including boycotts and civil disobedience. But it may be more precisely conceived as *satyagraha*, (freely, "truth-holding"), which requires forswearing all dessert of any reward for virtue, in other words, the total renunciation of the fruits of one's action (karma). It is the bodhisatvic moment of refusing earned admission to Heaven.

Indeed, though he smugly predicted to those who sentenced him to death that he would soon play the gadfly in the Elysian fields, is this moment not equivalent to the heroic spiritual surrender of Socrates? If we too boldly follow the argument wherever it leads, does it not lead us to a humbling of ego?

We must choose peaceful means to achieve peaceful ends. Whatever purity is, it is not mere prudence, not merely an instrumental value, and no bureaucratic virtue. A species of wild care, it is ethics, but not mere ethics. If it be pure, it is not pure the way reason is in the Kantian context. It is characteristic of ethics, I said, to assess means with a wider palette of values than mere practicality. Let us sketch alternative rainbows.

In Gandhi's *karma yoga*, spiritual purity involves renouncing the fruits of one's actions, thus subverting the law of reward against one's own ego-interests. Thus purity goes beyond good and evil, beyond morality, if only to return in the end to sanctify it. This is a higher good. If it is the will of God that we should do good, then the aims of ethics are the purposes of God. And how are we to know those? When it comes to ultimate ends, Gandhi does not claim to know the will of God. (Thus, his move is available not only to believers; something similar is open to non-theists as well). Gandhi writes: "We must thus rest satisfied with a knowledge only of the means, and if these are pure, we can fearlessly leave the end to take care of itself."[29] For humans, in the end, it is only means that we can know. This is not just an ethicizing of politics, it is a spiritualizing of ethics. So let us end here, on the far side of ethics.

***

What is good? Alas!, as foretold, and despite our long journey, before us lies no answer to this question. If I had an answer, I would be richer than I am, but I would probably have given it all away, too.

Come. Attend to philosophy. It is wrong not to. Socrates still wants your soul to be as good as it can be. A laurel wreath for your virtue. Philosophy needs its heroes.

INTEGRITY

Integrity is the sort of subject that most properly demands philosophical silence.[30] If it is spoken about at all, it should be spoken about in others. But it should not be spoken about in others, unless it is resident in oneself (for how can a witness without integrity attest to integrity in others?). Yet speaking of your own integrity is moral braggadocio (how can a witness be judge in his own case?). It is invariably more effective to have others do your bragging for you. Of course, my concern here with the effectiveness of moral bragging no doubt taints any moral sense I may be speaking, and casts a question and a shadow over my own integrity. But I will bear these aspersions and go on.

First, one's own integrity ought to be kept silent for prudential reasons. Pure self-interest alone insists one shut up about one's own integrity. To speak in public of one's virtues is to raise the eyebrow of the crowd. The more one emphasizes it, the more one appears to be drawing attention to oneself, to be trying to establish a reputation, which integrity does not inherently seek or require. The more one openly touts one's integrity, the more one seems to be managing impressions, putting on a show or a mask, even covering something up. People feel the compensatory defense mechanism at work, so that it would in no way serve one's integrity, if one had it, to promote it so proudly.

Second, speaking up about one's integrity is simply not credible. To speak publicly of one's public virtues would seem to be redundant. But to speak publicly of one's private virtues is the moral equivalent of telling fishing stories, except in this case it is about the big one that did not get away. Conveniently, as in fishing tales, there was no one else there to witness it, or the witnesses are out of reach, so all one has to go on is the bare words of the storyteller. And that is enough, if one is content with stories. But if one is curious about the truth, one has nothing. For integrity revolves around the relationship of word and deed; words alone, even our track record, is insufficient proof. The public is intelligent enough to know that insufficient proof is insufficient.

Whenever anyone commends themselves too handsomely, we instinctively feel we are being sold to. And who believes a salesman uncritically, but the naïve and gullible? Or we interpret claims of integrity as we do a political campaign, expecting each side to put its best foot forward and to paint its opponent's boots the blackest. We expect the skewing, and adjust our ears to cancel its effect. And we expect the best foot forward to be a false foot, polished up to look nice, a foot in the door, and just another sales job. It is easiest above the fray to maintain integrity, or rather, to maintain the perception of integrity. And there is the prudential point: except under compulsion, one should say little or nothing openly of one's integrity, or it costs you the perception of integrity, which means you are spreading falsehoods even if you are speaking the truth. Rather cultivate it in private and in a clear quiescent conscience just for oneself. This plant grows best in silence.

We are suspicious of politicians when they think they are so great that they can help us, and so virtuous that they will. They tout their own integrity directly and indirectly in the struggle to come out on top, but mostly integrity comes up as an issue in an attack on opponents. It is generally more effective to attack the integrity of opponents than to broadcast one's own. But people know how to compensate for the bullshit that is derived from self-interest. Integrity—this silent unknown—is like the joker of the deck, it has shifting value, the highest and sometimes the lowest card amongst the virtues. And when you find out the truth, it is usually game over. Public figures who appear to have the most integrity are those who speak low of themselves, if not identifying with the people, enabling the people to identify with them. It also helps to put shared higher principles ahead of personal gain and private interest. To say you have it may suggest that you do not have it, insofar as it implies there is some doubt and an implicit critique to which one owes a response. Generally, if you have it, it speaks for itself; so you do not have to say it. And yet, however hard it may be to affirm outright, it is fatal outright to deny it—like death by shooting yourself in the foot.

Integrity in the moral sense means sticking to principles over convenience, to what is right over expediency. But *integrity* also has a non-moral sense, that is, a physical or a metaphysical sense. Integrity means wholeness, without necessary reference to the right or the good. This ambiguity tracks quite closely to that of *compromise*, which also has both a moral sense (a sell-out) and a physical sense (as in an unsafe bridge or other architectural structure). Just as the material integrity of a structure may be compromised, leading to physical collapse, so too the slings and arrows of fortune may impugn our moral integrity, leading to moral collapse. But all this is but metaphors abounding. Is there anything of non-verbal knowledge in it at all? Is any of it worth saying at all? Silence has its advantages over even the best of metaphors.

Integrity is a feeling. It is very personal, very quiet. The entire world may doubt one's integrity, and yet it remain true. One's integrity may be perfect, though one's reputation is in the mud. Your reputation is in the hands of others. But no one can take away your integrity, except only you yourself, since it is an inward orientation, an inward gesture, toward whatever principled truth you may recognize. Integrity can only be faithfulness to one's own principles, not to anyone else's. Herein lies another reason not to publicize one's integrity: it does not concern anybody but you and your relationship to your god or to the truth. To feel what one feels, it is not necessary to proclaim it.

And yet this inner feeling—so positive, so sanctifying, so heart-warming—is also subject to delusion. Indeed, every great scoundrel is bound to persuade himself of his own integrity. Obstinacy prolonged produces its own principles, and we may cleave to these with great pertinacity; it will be hard to resist styling this as our integrity, at least whenever we are questioned. The feeling of integrity is a moral slap on the back, and who could not use one of those every now and then? So what if we smugly congratulate ourselves on integrity attained? The slightest breach in our own perceived integrity is experienced as a fatal compromise, and covered up as quickly as if we were found suddenly nude in public. More painful still is the perception by a loved one of one's own inner dis-integral fault lines. So the whole energy and full devotion of the waking consciousness is normally directed toward maintaining the appearance of integrity, and to self-generate the feeling of integrity, so that our performance comes off well. From great evil-doers to common ego-dwellers, the appearance of integrity must be maintained at all costs, even integrity.

What is so intensely private does not bear publication; but it is also wise to hold one's tongue about what is so liable to delusion, lest it shift and change again. Again silence is cautious, silence is wise.

Integrity means to be everywhere the same, but also nowhere indifferent. It means to be wholly present everywhere you are, and to leave nothing hidden.

Integrity is a moving target. Stephen R. Covey has anchored his concept of integrity in certain "lighthouse principles," certain fixed points and guiding lights not adjustable by the trends and tastes of the age.[31] Much may be said in favor of the maintenance of old lighthouses, but this alone rather binds one to the same old harbor, to home port, to the well-trodden, and to the well-known. Integrity to the known in the end confines one to the known. Integrity to the unknown, to foreign ports, and to uncharted seas, serves even when the old beacons have gone out. It allows us to travel to new harbors and to explore without harm and without harming. What is needed for that is an integrity that moves in the world but is not moved by the world. And for that, perhaps, a whole new world will be required. Integrity to the known is a tether and a leash; integrity to the unknown is openness and sensitivity.

Notes from the road. Let me end with this one qualification to my long-winded silence on this issue: if in the end integrity must break its silence, let it speak in foreign languages.

BEAUTY

I am Beauty's butler: silent, observant, of service. I see her closely, perhaps too closely. I zip her up in back. Then I bow out.

There is a discretion I owe my mistress. How can I speak of Beauty behind her back? It is certainly not in my self-interest to reveal the secrets of my employ. Yet, if I sound coy, it is not my own doing, but my faithful reflection of her manner.

Once long ago, chance threw me into her company. I was entirely naive and I had no idea of my place. To stand beside her and see—*feel*—every head turn! The glare was insufferable, and I could not long stay so close. But her terrible image has remained with me ever since. I say *terrible*, for no other word can cloak her so well. O Beauty! Your comely aspect draws one and all—but how awful and awesome the vortex of attraction you create! A veritable maelstrom of hidden power, to die for, and to be killed over, lies just beneath your glowing skin.

Thus one bows before beauty, takes rest to best enjoy it. One who claims it, properly stoops to do so. Possession is death in Beauty's arms. Therefore, one who wants it, gives it away. The wise seek not to own Beauty, but to be owned by her. And to be an asset to art, one must serve Beauty. Then she will surround you with her self, and your riches will attest to your lowly status—as a slave.

This at least has been my long-term strategy. And look, I am already a footman! Once, holding her boots for her, my hand, almost by accident, touched her calf. Suddenly flush, I continued my duties as if nothing had happened. She grew still, but said nothing, so I knew it had been permitted. She misses nothing. I run out in front of her to make her way, the low signaling the high. So far, she permits me.

I come when I am called. I am always calling myself, to keep in practice, but only rarely do I hear her service bell. The old house is so lonely when she is away. And for long stretches, I only have my images of her all around me. But I keep attentive for a moment to serve, or to make labour for her. I know one person who was allowed once to brush her hair, long endless hours, while she softly sang. None of us admirers could survive a moment of her absence, were it not for her endless songs that everywhere fill the air, for those with ears to hear.

Beauty needs all the assistance you can afford. This goes beyond an arm to hang on, a shoulder to cry on, and a neck for her deadly stiletto heels. It is the moral support that is so urgent. I mean, the cruel things people say! Out of the blindness of ignorance or the malice of envy, who can tell? Most hurtful to her personally, I know, is the aspersion of mere subjectivity. As if vision were not so widely and variously impaired! To be merely in the eye of the beholder—what a dreadful taunt! You try that on a date: *Are you beautiful? Or is that just me?* Yet people persist in saying it, as if trying to be inclusive. Beauty, I tell you, is very exclusive. It is kindness that is everywhere; and *that* even the ugly can manage.

One might as soon rip the God from a devout believer's heart as slander Beauty by saying she exists only in her admirers' eyes. Not only is it a sleight to her bounty and her magnanimity, but also it accuses us acolytes of delusions tantamount to hallucinations, of outright making things up. As everybody knows, artists have never created anything out of thin air, but always only from the breath that carries her song. It is she who signs every great work of art.

The insult that cuts most deeply is that she herself is only skin-deep. That is a most superficial saying. At least it gives her credit for her most alluring surface, though her lovers all know that the real joy comes from penetrating to her depths. Skin itself is misunderstood as the exterior only, whereas physiologically it is her living, feeling and most wholesome flesh. Her beauty is palpable, can be felt, and gave birth to movement and dance. None who have seen Beauty dance can deny that her muscles lend her skin those gorgeous contours. Inside, outside, she is who she is all the way through. O you slanderers! Close your eyes and see that Beauty exists within your skin, as well as without your eyes.

The charges of subjectivity and of superficiality are painful enough. A subtler indignity is offered by the claim that beauty is only relative. She is so manifestly incomparable, only the rudest ignoramus could suggest she is only relatively beautiful. "How do I look?" she asks. Only poetry is the appropriate reply. Instead she hears "not bad," "better in Rome," "okay from here." That relativistic nonsense is no way to treat a lady! *Marvelous! Stunning! Breathtaking!* There are your proper responses.

Her universal charm has lately been snubbed by being called average. It turns out that if one visually averages, pixel-by-pixel, pictures of innumerable faces, one obtains an average face, which passes everywhere for an ideal. The resultant average face is highly symmetrical, and is rated by viewers across cultures as more attractive than the original mugs on which it was based. Research continues as the methodology is spread to other domains, to see if the average smell, the average song, the average modern dance, and the average sculpture might also be the most beautiful. I only know that my Beauty has her quirks, all totally endearing, but she is sheer maximum, and no mixed average.

I think too much of her, I know. I see her in everything. I am lovesick, mad, I know, but I only redouble my devotions. I see her in the innumerable stars, in the auburn sunset with its great orange streaks and strange green cloud-bellies. I see her in the incessant shifting of the water's surface, before her image is replaced by my own reflection. I see her in the valiant shoot, a new spring green, breaking through the impossible soil. I see her, eyes closed, in the dark of the meditation hall. She is in the gesture of mother love, a help to the helpless, a consoler of the shadows. She is half-shrouded, but you can feel her peeking out from behind the world-veil. She is kind to strangers. Ever-dying, she dwells with melancholy. Ever-reborn, she springs eternal in the playing child. Everywhere, but never spread too thin. This whole cosmos—but the flit of her eyelash. I live for a mere wink from her.

What is that? Is that her bell? Then I am off.

Do not ask for whom her bell tolls. It tolls for thee.

Come. You are needed. Beauty serves you philosophy.

NOTES

1. This paragraph makes use, as do many other essays in this book, of the extensive entries in the full *Oxford English Dictionary* (*OED*), 22nd printing, compact ed. (Oxford: Oxford University Press, 1982). s.v. "value."

2. These points about Immanuel Kant that I have made quickly in passing deserve clarification, as they are relevant in other chapters. Such clarification, if added to this essay, would spoil its tone, so two footnotes will have to do. As a transcendental

idealist, Kant distinguishes all phenomena as they appear to us from the things as they are apart from us, that is, from the "noumenal" thing-in-itself. Yet Kant claims that "we can . . . have no knowledge of any object as a thing in itself" (Kant, *Critique of Pure Reason* [1781/1787], trans. Norman Kemp Smith [New York: St. Martin's Press, 1929], Bxxvi). Though Kant also self-identifies as an empirical realist, he concludes that "external objects (bodies) are mere appearances, and are therefore nothing but a species of my representations. . . . Apart from them they are nothing." (*Critique*, trans. Kemp Smith, A370–71). Noting that "while much can be said a priori as regards the form of appearances,"—including, as it turns out, all of arithmetic and geometry—nevertheless "nothing whatsoever can be asserted of the thing in itself, which may underlie these appearances" (*Critique*, trans. Kemp Smith, A49, B66). Among those forms of appearance, we find space and time. "But this space and this time, and with them all appearances, are not in themselves things; they are nothing but representations, and cannot exist outside the mind" (*Critique of Pure Reason*, [1781/1787], trans. Paul Guyer and Allen W. Wood, [Cambridge: Cambridge University Press. 1998.] A491–92, B520). Finally—to anticipate my next point in the text—if we turn within in search of our very self, we encounter again the Kantian distinction that defines transcendental idealism: "we know our own subject only as appearance, not as it is in itself" (*Critique*, trans. Kemp Smith, B156). "Even the inner and sensible intuition of our mind (as an object of consciousness) . . . is not the real self as it exists in itself, or the transcendental subject, but only an appearance of this to us unknown being, which was given to sensibility" (*Critique*, trans. Guyer and Wood, A492, B521).

3. "In the kingdom of ends everything has either a price or a dignity. Whatever has a price can be replaced by something else as its equivalent; . . . whatever is above all price, and therefore admits of no equivalent, has a dignity" (Immanuel Kant, *Grounding for the Metaphysics of Morals* [1785], 2nd ed., trans. James W. Ellington [Indianapolis: Hackett, 1983], 40–41). Here Kant is trying to articulate the irreplaceability of individual persons, who as "ends-in-themselves" enjoy "not merely a relative worth, i.e., a price, but has an intrinsic worth, i.e. dignity" (40). This absolute value of persons depends on the intentions behind their actions: it "consists, not in effects which arise from them, nor in the advantage and profit which they provide, but in mental dispositions . . . the worth of such a disposition [is to] be recognized as dignity and puts it infinitely beyond all price, with which it cannot in the least be brought into competition or comparison without, as it were, violating its sanctity" (41).

4. My pundit of "value subtraction" was Michael Brent Major (1953–2021), one-time Café Philosophy attendee, well-known in Victoria for his critical and creative environmentalist ideas. Once a logger in the woods of British Columbia, he told me that he had bought a stand of cedar trees, only to discover it was in fact one enormous tree. Like so many of us, he could not tell the forest from a tree. I am sorry to report that he died in March 2021.

5. Elvis Presley, *50,000,000 Elvis Fans Can't Be Wrong: Elvis' Gold Records, Vol. 2* (album) (Hollywood, CA: RCA Victor, 1959). When I was a child my older sister had this record.

6. The Heraclitus fragment is Diels fragment B110, cited anciently in Stobaeus, (Selections 3.1.176). See Patricia Curd, *A PreSocratics Reader: Selected Fragments*

and Testimonia, 2nd ed., trans. by Richard D. McKirahan and Patricia Curd (Indianapolis: Hackett, 2011).

7. There is allusion here to the problem set by Socrates to young Euthyphro in Plato's dialogue of that name. See Plato, *Complete Works*, ed. John M. Cooper (Indianapolis: Hackett, 1997), 7a–11b.

8. Aristotle, *Nicomachean Ethics*, trans. H. Rackman (Cambridge, MA: Harvard University Press, 1934), http://data.perseus.org/citations/urn:cts:greekLit:tlg0086.tlg010.perseus-eng1:1096a.20. I chose this older translation as it lays out the categorical applications of "good" with a level of clarity and accessibility that neither Ross nor Irwin match.

9. See Aristotle, *Categories*, in *Complete Works*, vol. 1, 3–24.

10. Aristotle, *Nicomachean Ethics*, trans. Terence Irwin (Indianapolis: Hackett, 1985), bk. 1, 1097b31–32; Irwin's insertion.

11. In "A Theory of Play and Fantasy," Gregory Bateson points to meta-communicative similarities between play (which, for example, may signify, but is not fighting) and the map-territory distinction. The map is not the territory, and a toy car is not a car. See Bateson, *Steps to an Ecology of Mind* (New York: Ballantine Books, 1972), 180–81.

12. The Heraclitus fragment is Diels fragment B110; see Curd, *A PreSocratics Reader*.

13. Plato, *Timaeus*, in *Complete Works*, edited by John M. Cooper (Indianapolis: Hackett, 1997), 90d.

14. Aristotle, *Nicomachean Ethics*, trans. Terence Irwin (Indianapolis: Hackett, 1985), bk 1, 1094b2–3. The definition occurs in the opening sentence: "the good has been well described as that at which all things aim."

15. He does seem to have thought that it should be true. In prison before his death, Socrates recalls his early disappointment upon reading Anaxagoras, who could not deliver on the promise of his premise that Intelligence (*nous*) is the origin (*arche*) of the cosmos, which should have entailed, Socrates felt, that all things are ordered for the best, in other words, a comprehensive *natural teleology*, which it took an Aristotle to deliver. See Plato, *Phaedo*, in *Complete Works*, edited by John M. Cooper (Indianapolis: Hackett, 1997), 97c–99e. The death scene comes at the end of the dialogue, 118a.

16. Plato, *Plato's Republic*, trans. G. M. A. Grube (Indianapolis: Hackett, 1974), 587b–588a. The square of a cube. The calculation is based on the three functional parts (or organs) of the soul. The happiness of the wise king is the square of the happiness of the demagogue (the "man of the people" leader), while the misery of the latter's soul, raised to the power of three (or cubed) equals the miserableness of the tyrant's soul. On the musical rationale of it all, see Ernest G. McClain, T*he Pythagorean Plato: Prelude to the Song Itself* (York Beach, ME: Nicolas-Hays, 1984), 33–39.

17. Aristotle, *Nicomachean Ethics*, trans. W. D. Ross, rev. J. O. Urmson, bk. 1, 1095a16–23.

18. Aristotle, *Nicomachean Ethics*, trans. W. D. Ross, rev. J. O. Urmson, bk. 1, 1095b20–21.

19. Aristotle, *Nicomachean Ethics*, trans. W. D. Ross, rev. J. O. Urmson, bk. 1, 1095b23–25.

20. Aristotle, *Nicomachean Ethics*, trans. W. D. Ross, rev. J. O. Urmson, bk. 1, 1095b31–1096a2. Note that the implicit notion of activity here is *energeia*, which is the realization of an end, or activity that fulfills proper function. In this sense, Aristotle's "theoretical life" (1177a7–1179a–34) is certainly an active life.

21. Aristotle, *Nicomachean Ethics*, trans. W. D. Ross, rev. J. O. Urmson, bk. 1, 1101a22–35. The quotation is a Greek saying Aristotle considers approvingly.

22. Aristotle, *Nicomachean Ethics*, trans. W. D. Ross, rev. J. O. Urmson, bk. 10, 1077b.

23. Aristotle, *Politics*, bk. 1, 1253a2–3. Adapted from the Benjamin Jowett translation, which appears in Aristotle, *Complete Works of Aristotle*, ed. Jonathan Barnes (Princeton, NJ: Princeton University Press, 1984).

24. See Anthony S. Laden, *Reasoning: A Social Picture* (Oxford: Oxford University Press, 2012).

25. Aristotle, *Politics*, in *Complete Works*, ed. Jowett, bk. 1, 1260a30, quoting a poet.

26. Aristotle, *Politics*, in *Complete Works*, ed. Jowett, bk. 1, 1252a33–34.

27. Mohendas K. [Mahatma] Gandhi. *Young India*, July 17, 1924; quoted in *All Men Are Brothers*, ed. Krishna Kripalani (Paris/NewYork: UNESCO, 1958), 74.

28. Gandhi, *Harijan*, 13–7–'47, 232; quoted in *All Men Are Brothers*, ed. Kripalani, 76.

29. Gandhi, *Satyagraha in South Africa*, 2nd ed., trans. By V. G. Desai (Ahmedabad: Navajivan Publishing, 1950), 318; repr. *Voice of Truth*, ed. Shriman Narayan (Ahmedabad: Navajivan Publishing, 1968), 112.

30. A version of this essay, "Integrity: A Philosophical Exploration," was read at the Twenty-Third World Congress of Philosophy in Athens in 2013, and was subsequently published as Michael Picard, "Integrity: A Philosophical Exploration," *Proceedings of the XXIII World Congress of Philosophy: Philosophy of Values* (Athens: Greek Philosophical Society, 2018), vol. 68, 95–98. https://doi.org/10.5840/wcp232018681518.

31. Stephen R. Covey, *The Seven Habits of Highly Effective People: Restoring the Character Ethic* (New York: Free Press, 1989).

Chapter 6

Truth Sports

Epistemological topics were not generally the most popular or most in demand at Café Philosophy, but there were a few exceptions that, if not representative of academic epistemology as a whole, are nevertheless central to it. This chapter covers some of those key exceptions. My aim in writing was only partly to introduce scholarly traditions to the Café crowd; it was far more to disentangle the multitude of roles these epistemological notions play in everyday life, in order to see each role clearly and more distinctly. In this daily play, we are pushed and pulled in a variety of conflicting ways, as if many language games were being played at the same time, so that, when it comes our turn, we do not know how to move. In the Café setting, everyone in the end played their own game. Philosophy Sports are an attempt to get all participants pulling together and, if not always agreeing, at least taking objective truth seriously. Guided by the rules of logic, Philosophy Sports are truth sports, in that they are epistemologically more serious than original Café Philosophy.

KNOWLEDGE

Knowledge. Call it the cost of wisdom. That is, the net benefit of wisdom is equal to wisdom minus knowledge.

Knowledge (what it is, what it requires, and what it confers) is indisputably central to the enterprise of philosophy. It is the subject of that primary branch of philosophy known as epistemology, a field which derives its name from the Greek word for knowledge (*episteme*). The other branches (incidentally, at least on a usual division) are metaphysics (the study of being or reality) and ethics (in the most over-general sense of the theory of principle and value). Neither of these branches could be the least viable if it were not for epistemology. It makes no sense to make claims about what is real or what is valuable in the absence of claims of knowledge. Reality and values may be as they are; if we are without knowledge of them, all theorizing is vanity.

A definition of knowledge already mooted in Plato is: justified true belief.[1] This is supposed to work both ways: to know something, one must believe it, it must be true, and one must have adequate justification for believing it. Conversely, what is believed with adequate justification, and true, is known. All three are necessary, but they are sufficient for knowledge only jointly, at least according to this definition. Let us look at the three parts of it individually.

First, knowledge is belief. This stipulation wreaks havoc with a common English convention of speech which distinguishes knowledge from mere belief. "Do you believe it, or do you know?" we might ask someone, pressing them as to whether they are to be relied upon. In a court of law, belief that Leftie did it is no evidence against Leftie. In the court of conscience, we may believe in a providential deity without such arrogance as to claim to know. These verbal facts about English language usage should not obscure the fact that, on the definition discussed by Plato, knowledge is a subset of belief, not a category exclusive of belief. Every knowing involves believing.

The word "justification" will prompt concern. A justification is not an excuse, not some mumbled cover story, not any old self-serving line. What is intended here is a reasonable or rational justification, not the psychological defense mechanism ironically called "rationalization."[2] You have to have *adequate* reasons for believing something for it to be justified. The normative power of Plato's definition is buried in this word (*logos*). A rationalization of your behavior is no justification of it. Nor is: "But they did it too!" Justification is not righteous self-defense, but logical self-defense. The justification must give sufficient reasons for believing something, or else it does not count a justification in the relevant sense.

Plato himself held famously high standards of justification, perhaps impossibly high. A lover of the mathematical arts, he envied its rigor and the certainty of its conclusions. To be justified, a belief must be capable of proof, not mere conjecture or hearsay. For instance, an unbroken chain from first principles must be exhibited, as when a theorem of geometry is derived from axioms about points and lines. Such was the aspiration of Plato, except that like his teacher Socrates he was interested above all in ethical knowledge, knowledge of right and wrong. Ethics too must be based on mathematics-like rigor, or on something yet higher. The implication: just as there is one mathematics for all, there is one set of ethical values etched in eternal stone, valid for all human beings. In practice, in fact, Plato often settled for less than proof, for verisimilitude, an analogical or allegorical truth (which is not truth at all, not by the literalist standards prevailing today).[3] A little play in the search for truth is good to begin.

While Plato's aspiration is not in keeping with the soul-less science of today, it is worth pointing out that his high standards for ethical knowledge is also a way of linking knowledge and wisdom. Just as knowledge is one species of belief (for example, justified true belief), so wisdom is knowledge of the right things. It is trenchant to distinguish knowledge and wisdom as if they existed on an entirely different order. But that is not to deny that wisdom is a subset of knowing. Knowing is believing (but not just any believing); and wisdom is knowing (but not just any knowing). Wisdom is knowledge of self. One can know much without knowing anything about the self; thus knowledge and wisdom may come apart.

Socrates famously declared that virtue is knowledge. At the same time, he held that care and improvement of the soul (making it more virtuous) was the purpose and proper aim of life. Now many had claimed that virtue was knowledge because it could be trained; they sold their services in the ethics education market, and made a handsome profit. But Socrates denied that he taught anything, although he understood virtue as knowledge. The paradox dissolves at once when virtue is recognized to rely upon self-knowledge, which cannot be taught but is the indispensable condition of virtue. So the Socratic formula is really a reduction of the virtues (justice, courage, moderation, etc.) to knowledge, specifically to self-knowledge, to wisdom.

Today, of course, the ethical pretensions of knowledge are considerably reduced. Knowledge has come down in the world. Science seeks knowledge, yet eschews wisdom, the pretension of the unscientific philosophers who are content with how they like to live. The so-called knowledge economy is all about managing inconceivable volumes of information. Information: that is knowledge in modern dress. Mere data. In former days, the skill in sifting through a haystack for needles was prized. It is enough today to be able to download the haystack; the search is automated. We do not care what you are looking for, as long as you can conveniently find it. Socrates' concern for the improvement of your soul is replaced by the latest search optimization algorithms.

The veritable flood of information has left the word *knowledge* with this positive connotation: it belongs to those who can swim, who can manage the rapids, surf the digital seas. Those who drown perish at the side of the information highway.

If you doubt what I say, you will already be thinking about my next and final subject: doubt. Doubt is the acid of epistemology, dissolving everything it touches. But a constant regulated supply is actually good for digestion. When Plato raised the bar of knowledge, by ramping up the standards of justification, he threw his weight behind certainty, and leapt over doubt. Socrates stayed closer to the ground, claiming only to know that he knew nothing. Plato fancied he glimpsed an immutable world beyond the stars, and he anchored his philosophical ship there. For to know something, for him, required that that thing be changeless. Since all local things change, truth became very remote. This is the paradox of certainty: the truth is farthest from you when you think you have it.

René Descartes ruined the epistemic tastes of generations by selling them certainty, a kind of epistemological crack cocaine. Once you get a whiff of it, you cannot help going in for more. He raised the bar of justification even higher, taking certainty (the impossibility of doubt) as the criterion of knowledge. (Actually, Descartes required only that *reasoned* doubt be impossible,[4] since wanton or groundless doubt is always possible; but such niceties do not survive long in an addictive tradition.) Doubt was elevated to an epistemological method, which succeeds only through self-elimination. To know something, one must be certain; that is, one's doubts about it must all have come to an end. However laudable or well-intentioned this may have been, the result has been a certain smugness built into the very concept of knowledge, and even the withering of the art and practice of doubt. For those who most desire to know, Descartes' criterion is like poison or a slow and gradual asphyxiation. Finally, when one is intellectually incapable of doubt, one will be omniscient.

In this way, doubt has been hounded out of philosophy, or relegated to a harping sidelined critic. Or it has been transformed into a lapdog, groomed for polite company by the handmaidens of science (how, since John Locke. so many philosophers self-identify).[5] To position oneself as a master of knowledge, as one who knows, one must stifle doubt, present an air of conviction. Yes, doubt is a method; but the sooner one is done applying it, the sooner one will begin to know. The feeling of knowing is actually augmented by the inability to doubt. So there is a built-in temptation to the laziness of the imagination, a soporific to skepticism, a death-knell to criticism. If the ship of knowledge is anchored in certainty, one may board only after abandoning doubt on the pier.

If you ask me, doubt is the companion of owls. Doubt walks with knowledge into the sunset. Doubt comforts the frayed edges of knowledge. Doubt is brother to knowledge, its friend and supporter. Doubt is the fool who makes the journey of knowledge bearable. Doubt is a condition of existence, certainty the wild craving of the self-interested mind.

Just say no to certainty. Knowledge is alive when befriended; when it is possessed it dies.

CERTAINTY

Certainty is a mythical beast. Legends of it abound, its *appearance* is common, but verifiable sightings are virtually unknown. It is reported and asserted, attested to and averred. Not a few pound the table with their fists and swear they possess it.

And yet, we all see it routinely in our intellectual opponents whom we have not yet refuted to our own satisfaction; so we ascribe their ignorance and errors to their pig-headed refusal to see the obvious. The one thing we all agree on is that people with certainty are people who are wrong (excluding ourselves, of course, since we are so obviously right). Logically, therefore, certainty is a myth, a fallacy, a bias, just a trap we fall into.

Yet the ox grazes still.

Before we turn to the uses and abuses of certainty in philosophy, it may help to reflect on the polysemous nature of the root word *certain*, which derives from Old French, reflecting the Latin *certes* (an interjection meaning "in truth," "certainly," "agreed"), and which also exists in English, though it is archaic. Our word is related to the Latin verb *cernere* (meaning to sift, to discern, to decide), akin to the Greek *krinein* (to separate, decide, judge), from which we get of our words *critical* and *critique*. A primary meaning of *certain* has it referring to what is fixed, determined, settled, but also dependable reliable, unerring, and not liable to fail. It is not far from these meanings to: inevitable, destined, incapable of failing. Clearly, there are "objective" metaphysical undercurrents in the meaning of the word *certain*, but in philosophy it mostly comes up in a derivative subjective sense, which applies to persons, that means "assured in mind or action"[6] or "fully confident upon the ground of knowledge"[7] and "having no doubt."[8] *Moral certainty* is distinguished as subjective awareness of being justified in acting upon one's convictions.

Though in philosophy the main problems concerning certainty relate to the subjective meaning, clearly we cannot suppress or deny the "objective" (quasi-substantial or elliptical) meaning, referring to *that which is* certain, to the object of our subjective sense of surety. The two meanings carry over to the substantive noun, *certainty*, which points either to the thing known (be it a fact, truth or event) or to a quality or state of knowing mind, specifically a high degree of its conviction. Yet this ambiguity is no friend of truth, for it is mischievous and causes serious and systematic error.

We must distinguish with utmost clarity between the status of the thing known and the quality of our knowing. The thing known, the fact or proposition, is true (if it is) on account of some inner grounding or some external cause or reason. By some inner or outer necessity (or by worldly chance) it is what it is. On our side lies our conviction, the degree of the intensity of our feeling that, yes, we do know. How sure we feel about something is never to be confused with the glue or ground, the sufficient cause or reason, of the thing we take ourselves to know. The same applies when we think we know the cause of a fact or event; there is the truth of the matter, on the one hand, and our inward degree of assent to it, on the other.

Put it this way: what makes things true is different from what makes us sure. What makes things so, is a question of metaphysics. What makes us sure, is a question of epistemology. Necessity is metaphysical; certainty is epistemological. Nature or God or circumstance see to a great many events in this world without our consent or knowledge. Metaphysics is about the reality of causes; epistemology is about the credibility of our knowledge claims. Doubt, certainty, uncertainty, probability, aspects of risk assessment, credibility, believability, evidence, fingerprints, smoking guns, proof, wonder, inquiry, and questioning: all these are subjects of epistemology.

So, *certainty*, in philosophy-speak, refers to the quality, degree, or felt-strength of our knowledge. Although death is properly called a certainty, it is a metaphysical issue rather than an epistemological one. Of course, we *do* have a very high degree of confidence that we will die some day; and, though we may avoid contemplating it, we cannot deny it when it confronts us. The ultimate undeniability we feel at such times is certainty. However, the inevitability of death, in technical philosophical parlance, is a necessity.

Of course, if we would but reflect on that necessity, we might experience certainty. The experience of certainty is not, however, the experience of death. Amusingly, one often hears it said that nobody can know what happens after death until they die. But then, of course, we do not know, unless Death is not the knowinglessness that from here it seems to be.

Certainty is bewitching, and part of the cause of this is its inner contradictions. One can hardly use the word without falling into them. I have already mentioned one; here is another.

Technically, certainty is reserved for the highest degree of knowing (which used to be called *science*). One does not have certainty unless one is absolutely sure. It is not a matter of degree. As the absence of all doubt, certainty cannot tolerate the slightest waffle or wavering. One chink in the armor of certainty and we have uncertainty. Once certain, one cannot become more certain. Conviction, by contrast, comes in all degrees, from the minimal (open-minded, not opposed), through all expectation and likelihood and typical regularity, to the maximal (the *Eureka!* moment, the *aha!* experience, direct revelation by god, grasping a mathematical "therefore," the self-defeat of doubt, the inevitability of evidence, the plainness of the nose on one's face). In deference to precision, one should reserve the term "certainty" for the purest, all-or-none epiphany. Our degrees of conviction would then be—not degrees of certainty—but degrees of uncertainty. Degrees of uncertainty are like various distances from that singular pinnacle.

And yet (to spite precision) we do say at times that we are "pretty certain," or "pretty sure." Or we are "not so sure." The precise signification is lost amid the flurry of everyday usage. Certainty therefore has to come in degrees after all. Indeed, you can simply define it as 1 minus uncertainty (like 100%

minus say 33% as a fudge factor, leaving 67% certainty). The technical and absolute meaning becomes rarefied, an abstraction, a formality and plaything of mathematicians, while the guesswork of the everyday most times manages perfectly well in ignorance of it and of all high philosophy.

It would not even matter, if the history of ideas and of my beloved philosophy were not abounding with claims to know with absolute certainty. Certainty is such a rare bird that it is unusual and highly suspicious, to say the least, to find philosopher after philosopher advance a system of philosophy allegedly based exclusively on pure reason, sheer deduction, or *a priori* reasoning from self-evident assertions, only to go on to explain why all their predecessors, who made similar claims to infallibility, were wrong when they spoke so boldly. Only in philosophy can the bold and the futile be so intimately combined.

I furnish examples, to persuade you of my authoritative pronouncements (which you ought to doubt anyway).

Plato held that acquaintance with the forms conferred knowledge that outranked anything the senses could produce. You cannot know the plain nose on your face, but Nose as such, universal Nose, may be grasped by the mind.[9] His philosophy has succeeded when the less evident (the invisible) has taken precedence over the visible.

The ingenious Descartes invented his method of doubt, and advanced a *general demolition of opinion*, which was to leave standing only a few epistemically primordial "clear and distinct"[10] ideas. It is the epistemological equivalent of clear-cutting old-growth forest. Descartes characterizes clear and distinct ideas as those which are not susceptible to further doubt. He bases his entire philosophy upon such doubt-tested yet rich principles as the substantial existence of soul, of god, and the reality and mechanical nature of the external world—you see how one man's certainties is someone else's doubt. What one calls riches, another calls rich.[11]

Thomas Hobbes (1588–1679) set out a political system of definitions in imitation of the geometric method. His famous opinion that the natural life of human beings is "solitary, poore, nasty, brutish, and short"[12] is actually the purported consequences of a demonstration from first principles. He goes on to deduce the necessity and reasonableness of Absolute monarchy. Politics: call it the invention of convenient necessities.

It is hard not to admire Locke for the circumspection and uncertainty with which he puzzles through many philosophical ideas. At times this famous beacon of the Enlightenment seems almost to shine from the page. Yet he lacks not for boldness on moral matters: "I am bold to think that morality is capable of demonstration, as well as mathematics."[13] Locke cannot see why, if we would but clearly define our terms and agree on their meanings at the outset, we should not be able to attain in ethics and political discourse that degree of universal and unmistakable assent that so far only mathematicians have attained amongst themselves. Such deductions also underpinned the dispossession of the lands of the First Nations, and buttressed programs that in Canada have been declared cultural genocide.[14]

David Hume, that friend of skepticism, might seem exempt from this line up of certainty-mongers. He required none of the traditional fixtures for a happy death, and went smilingly into the unknowing dark. With a simple fork, he brought down such bastions a *a priori* thinking as causation, self, beauty, substance. But with what haughty tones he dismisses what he cannot skewer on his two-pronged fork. *All truths must be matters of fact or relations of ideas.* Of anything else, including talk about the concepts just listed, he says we must "commit it then to the flames: For it can contain nothing but sophistry and illusion."[15] Hume puts the pyro in Pyrrhonic skepticism, and manages to find within himself at least an arson's certainty, which unsurprisingly turns out to be just as flammable as the traditional certainties Hume did so much to undo.

Baruch Spinoza, like Locke and Hume, is unquestionably a hero of intellectual courage. More thoroughly than Hobbes, he proceeds to ape axiomatic geometry, laying down his own explicit axioms and definitions in an effort to begin from metaphysical first principles.[16] He applies his mock-geometric method to definitions of substance, attribute, mode, finitude, cause, body, idea, good, bad, virtue, power, and so on; and is able to deduce *more geometrico*: an infinitely infinite God; the world (which turns out to be God extended in space as Nature); and, within this world, all our opportunities for freedom and blessedness. Can reason reach so far with steps so short? So admirable and honorable in mien and intent, so hopeful and hopeless in execution. The vision has been justly inspiring to many, the execution rightly a model for none. The guise of reason is the death of poetry. Johann von Wolfgang Goethe (1749–1832) said: "A Spinoza in poetry becomes a Machiavelli in philosophy."[17]

The youthful Gottfried Wilhelm Leibniz sought to identify by mathematical means the proper successor to the Polish throne.[18] A life-long champion of political and religious unity in Europe, he was dispatched as a young diplomat to Paris with a plan of his own devising to bring Europe together, but the plan, a European Holy War on Egypt, came to naught.[19] Leibniz's deductions proving the actual world to be the best of all possible worlds (despite Europe being at war with itself and not approving his war on Egypt) was ultimately about forging a scientific worldview consistent with free will, so that at Judgment Day God is not totally unaccountable (that is, found wanting). Again and again we find moral certainty, along with other forms of Enlightenment optimism, making compromising demands upon knowledge, co-opting metaphysical necessity, and hoping to make reason the basis of political legitimation (since inherited and divine right of kings and the infallibility of the pope was no longer working).

Immanuel Kant *cannot* be said to confuse necessity and certainty, as the two were distinguished above, but he does insist on aligning them. What is known through the senses is uncertain; necessity can only be grasped by reason. Throughout the *Critique of Pure Reason*, Kant's thinking, to retain the dignity of the *a priori*, must eschew intuition and sense perception, because only the universality of concepts can ensure the necessity of his conclusions. Reason grasps the universal, the senses only present a manifold. In his *Logic*, Kant writes: "Certainty is connected with the consciousness of necessity . . . uncertainty is connected with the consciousness of contingency or the possibility of the opposite."[20] But he appears to back away from this claim later in distinguishing two sorts of certainty: "Certainty is either empirical or rational," the former springing from experience, the latter from reason. Rational certainty includes knowledge of mathematics, which alone admits of genuine proof,[21] but even philosophical certainty "differs from empirical by the consciousness of *necessity* connected with it; it is thus *apodeictic certainty*, whereas empirical certainty is only assertoric"[22] (that is, a matter of mere belief, not knowledge). In the end, as for Descartes, certainty in Kant is a requirement of philosophical knowledge. The slightest doubt, therefore, and his entire system fails. Purity of reason is a gossamer structure. To make certainty a necessary condition of knowledge is grant to skeptics a loaded, sure-fire weapon.

"What I know," Kant writes, "I hold to be *apodeictically certain*, i.e., to be universally and objectively certain (valid for all)."[23] As an example of an *apodeictically certain* proposition he offers this: "so far as we all know, that there is another life like this." Yet this even believers may doubt. The situation becomes even more awkward in ethics, for Kant tries to base ethics on reason itself so as to ground the necessity of moral law. It is not really a duty unless everyone would have to do it. Reducing ethics to reason is important for Kant's project of finding religion (that is, locating Christianity) "within the realm of reason." Yet curiously enough, when it comes to morality, certainty turns out for Kant to be yet more important than knowledge itself:

> One must be completely certain whether something is right or wrong, according to or contrary to duty, licit or illicit. In things moral *nothing* can be ventured on an uncertainty, nothing *at the risk of an offense against the law.*[24]

So certainty is a prerequisite even of right and good action, for morality can never be a matter of mere belief—in total opposition, I need hardly point out, to the certitudes of today. And yet, Kant tells us: that person "is morally *unbelieving* who does not accept what indeed is *impossible* to know but is morally necessary to presuppose."[25] Kant is referring here to the very basis of his philosophical ethics.[26] The moral laws I know are valid for all, but if you will not accept them you are "morally unbelieving" (not to say unbelievably immoral).

In no other respect are the great philosophers more laughable than in the way they place so high a bar for themselves, only to fall short all the more flagrantly—like Olympic high jumpers who top out well below the crossbeam. The jumps are tremendously impressive; but why did they set the bar impossibly high? Wanting too much certainty is setting your self up for error. Of that fact, one can be certain without paradox.

But let me also now praise these intellectual giants, my boyhood heroes—though they are not all equally deserving—for their enlightened toleration (within whatever limits); for their monumental labors to establish philosophy; for the space they made for free thought and emancipated thinking; for their unpaid preoccupation with what is good and right; for their sublimation of truth and their deference to what they knew they did not know; for their *wisdom*. I do not pretend to outjump them. All honor to them; their bid to end doubt revealed the scope of the problem, also that it went so far beyond them, as it goes beyond us. There is a kindness that may arise from doubt; it arises when one begins to suspect that others may have something going for their crazy foreign way of doing things. Doubt may lead to respect, to circumspection, even when it does not arrive at certainty. Perhaps it is certainty that needs to be vanquished, not doubt.

OBJECTIVITY

There is objective multiplicity; so why not multiple objectivities? In lieu of an essay, here are a few pointed and one-sided takes on objectivity:

Objectivity: the tendency to object to other people's expressed opinions.
Objectivity: a cabal of scientists.
Objectivity: the abused child of the Enlightenment.
Objectivity: inter-subjective agreement; or, two minds are better than one, or even than two that disagree.
Objectivity: fear of one's insides.
Objectivity: the timid steps of one who fears error (also known as wisdom).
Objectivity: the happiness of the mathematician.
Objectivity: the cool emotion of truth; smiling deference in the face of the unknown.
Objectivity: a category of thought, that is, of the subjective.
Objectivity: the only prayer of the scientist.
Objectivity: paid equally by both sides (a double agent).

Objectivity: not balance, but the prevailing tilt.
Objectivity: winners in the competition of ideas, or the vanquishing of all opposing ideas.

MEANING

What is meaning? Shall meaning be captured in a word or allowed to be free? Suppose I know what my meaning is, and I say it to you. Have I then transposed my meaning into words? Or into the neurons of your brain? And did not those words already have that meaning, so that I must ask: did I get my meaning from them (that is, from other people) or did I derive it from within myself? But how did meanings get into words except that I put them there? And how did other people get in here that I may name them and think of them when they're not here? Is that how meaning transcends physicality? Is meaning inherited like language from others who have gone before? Or am I myself not the inner discourse I conduct with introjected Others?

Do not let my play trip you up. You know what my meaning is. Words do not have meanings, we do. (Compare: "guns do not kill people—people do.") We have lent words meaning, they are not our meaning. Meaning is not in the words, not in the syntax or semantics. It is not the representational content of words, but the living history of usages. To give this idea a name, call it dynamic pragmatism; but naming's a mug's game, so let me now unname it.

Meaning is the act of a free mind and of a plurality of free minds coming together. The minds are free, but not all of their acts are. The minds are free, but their coming together may not be free. You do not choose your family—you come to them, and they with you. How much meaning have your chosen? You may not choose the war you or your family find yourselves in, or the other circumstances of your shared or separate existence. Families are born into worlds, they do not elect them. We do not choose our world—we come to it, and it with us. Thus social institutions like family, war, the market, government, are nets in which our meanings get caught, and thus all too often they are imprisoning, unfreeing, meaning-depriving. Instead of value-added, they are value-subtracting. We get trapped in these nets, free minds tangled in a net of words and tradition. Into a portrait of an artist's mouth, James Joyce put these words (which you see I have been stealing): "When the soul of a man is born in this country, there are nets flung at it to hold it back from flight. You talk to me of nationality, language, religion. I shall try to fly by those nets."[27] Fly by, then, friends! Fly past! Do not let the conventions of meaning catch you up or out or off guard. I say that meaning is freeing, if you want it. But you must free yourself to get it.

What am I saying? Meaning is not the fish, still less the net, but the life of the sea. It is no accident and it did not get away. Meaning is closer to us than our world, but it *is* our world, though it remains even after our world transforms or disappears. Meaning is not only private, but like our world it is shared. The sharing of meaning is the continual reconstitution of our world. Communication is this constitutive sharing, this world-making. "Language is the house of being," to appropriate a fraught phrase by Martin Heidegger (1889–1976).[28]

Where is meaning? It is so easy to say it lies in the head. But is the meaning of a word in your mind or in the public mind? Does it reside in a private space or a social space? Is it in the dictionary or is it neural in its organization? Is it the fruit of hope and the product of dream, or is it the soundness of an argument and the deduction of a logician? Is it a crux or a nub? Does it dwell close to fact or does it transcend all circumstance? Can it be misplaced like an irretrievable memory, or hidden beneath an unsuspecting surface like a symbol or a sea-beast? Does your meaning trip off your lips, or does it hide buried in your belly, waiting to be coaxed out by tongue as by some gentle lover? Is meaning not pregnant, like a pause, or is it in the punctuation (is it a gangster or a panda bear that eats shoots and leaves)?

No two bodies can be in the same place at the same time. So what? Does not it follow that the existence of ambiguity proves meaning is not bodily? But enough of these dark and ambiguous sayings. Attend philosophy—like you really mean it. Play for keeps.

NOTES

1. Plato debates the adequacy of the definition (knowledge is true belief with logos [rational account, justification]), in *Theaetetus*, starting at 201c–d, in Plato, *Complete Works*, ed. John M. Cooper (Indianapolis: Hackett, 1997), 157–234. In good Socratic style, the definition is not found wholly acceptable.

2. See the heading "Denial," in chap. 3 of this book.

3. I based myself here on Plato's "Line," the metaphysical and epistemological theories underlying the "Allegory of the Cave," both in *Plato's Republic*, trans. G. M. A. Grube (Indianapolis: Hackett, 1974), 509d–511e; and in Plato, *Complete Works*, ed. Cooper, 517a–518e. For his exposition of the theories represented on the lines cited. Also, see the heading "Metaphysics," in chap. 7 of this book.

4. See René Descartes' *Meditations*: "I should hold back my assent from opinions that are not completely certain an indubitable" and "it will be enough if I find in each of them some reason for doubt," in *The Philosophical Writings of Descartes*, trans. John Cottingham, Robert Stoothoff, and Dugald Murdoch (Cambridge: Cambridge University Press, 1984), vol. 1, 18.

5. When Sir John Locke's represented philosophy as "under-Labourer in clearing the ground a little, and removing some of the rubbish, that lies in the way to Knowledge," he befit himself humbly, as one who knows his lowly place (Locke, *An Essay Concerning Human Understanding*, ed. Peter H. Nidditch [Oxford: Clarendon Press, 1975], 11). Under Scholasticism, philosophy had been in indentured servitude to Aristotelianized theology, so Locke's move was a philosophical revolution of liberation. Greek notions of substance and cause were hollowed out, all but abandoned; and the meaning of *eidos*, of "idea," was transformed (de-Platonized, psychologized), a semantic change process that had begun earlier with Galileo (1564–1642) and Descartes or even earlier.

6. *Merriam-Webster Collegiate Dictionary*, 11th ed. (Springfield, MA: Merriam-Webster, 2003), s.v. "certain."

7. *Oxford English Dictionary* (*OED*), Compact ed. (Oxford: Oxford University Press, 1982), s.v. "certain."

8. *OED*, s.v. "certain."

9. For Plato, genuine knowledge involved acquaintance with the forms (*eide*), which are grasped by the intellect (*nous*) as the kinds or essence of a thing. Through the senses we gain impressions of particulars only, not the universal (*eidos*), so the senses offer no knowledge, or at best inferior knowledge, mere belief (*doxa*). See Plato's *Theaetetus*, in *Complete Works*, ed. Cooper, 184a–187b; and *Plato's Republic*, trans. G. M. A. Grube, 509d–511c.

10. Descartes, *Meditations*, in *Philosophical Writings*, ed. Cottingham et al., vol. 1, 17, where Descartes says he means to "demolish everything completely". In the "Second Meditation", Descartes brings up his widely-doubted criterion of certainty, namely "clear and distinct ideas" (31).

11. In the *Meditations*, Descartes doubts all he can, but is brought to a halt by the *cogito* (the argument, "I think therefore I am," *cogito ergo sum*), which he finds indubitable (others found it dubious). From this thin air, like a divine rabbit from a black hat, he produces God out of a definition due to Anselm of Canterbury (1033–1109). So wondrous a God would not leave us in doubt's thrall, but must have provided a regular world, which for Descartes means a mechanical universe, the physical world that the Church should allow philosophers to freely study. Certainty: the delusion of necessity.

12. Thomas Hobbes, *Leviathan* (1651), ed. C. B. Macpherson (London: Penguin, 1985), chap. 13, 186. The argument for it is constructed in terms defined previously. For impressive examples, see especially chap. 6, on the passions, and chap. 10, "Of Power, Worth, Dignity, Honour, and Worthiness." His certainties about dignity are directly opposed to those of Immanuel Kant (see the endnotes in heading "Values," in chap. 5 of this book).

13. Locke, *Essay Concerning Human Understanding*, bk. 3, chap. 11.

14. Truth and Reconciliation Commission of Canada, *Honouring the Truth, Reconciling for the Future: Summary of the Final Report of the Truth and Reconciliation Commission of Canada* (2015), http://www.trc.ca (accessed August 13, 2021).

15. David Hume, *Enquiries Concerning Human Understanding and Concerning the Principles of Morals*, ed. from Posthumous ed. of 1977 by L. A. Selby-Bigge, 3rd ed. ed. with rev. P. H. Nidditch (Oxford: Clarendon Press, 1978), 12.34, 165.

16. Baruch Spinoza, *The Ethics: Treatise on the Emendation of the Intellect and Selected Letters*, trans. Samuel Shirley, ed. Seymour Feldman (Indianapolis: Hackett, 1982).

17. Johann von Wolfgang Goethe, *Maxims and Reflections*, 2nd rev. ed., trans. Thomas Bailey Saunders (London: MacMillan, 1908), no. 427.

18. On Gottfried Wilhelm Leibniz's 1669 work on Poland, see G. MacDonald Ross, *Leibniz* (Oxford: Oxford University Press, 1984), 10.

19. For Leibniz's 1672 plan to invade Egypt, see Steven Nadler, "Leibniz in Paris," in *The Best of All Possible Worlds: A Story of Philosophers, God, and Evil in the Age of Reason* (Princeton, NJ: Princeton University Press, 2010), chap. 1, 3–22. (His plan would have to wait a century and a quarter until 1798–1801 when France carried out something like it.) On the need for certainty in metaphysics, Leibniz later changed his views. Eventually, according to Stuart Brown, *Leibniz* (Minneapolis: University of Minnesota Press, 1984), "Leibniz claimed no kind of self-evidence for his assumptions" (5). Brown writes: "by 1680 or so Leibniz had come to believe that the method of universal doubt was unsound" (67).

20. Immanuel Kant, *Logic* (1800), trans. Robert S. Hartman and Wolfgang Schwarz (New York: Dover, 1974), 72.

21. Immanuel Kant, *Critique of Pure Reason*, trans. by Paul Guyer and Allen (Cambridge: Cambridge University Press. 1998), B762: "Only mathematics, thus, contains demonstrations," since unlike philosophy it is based on [*a priori*] constructions in intuition (in Kant's sense of direct or immediate knowledge).

22. Kant, *Logic*, 78; emphasis in the original.

23. Kant, *Logic*, 73; emphasis in the original.

24. Kant, *Logic*, 77; emphasis in the original.

25. Kant, *Logic*, 77; emphasis in the original.

26. Kant proposes to circumscribe the limits of reason, but relies on an ancient and long-outmoded logic to spell out the limits of human understanding. To be universal, ethics must be certain; but then its principles become too thin and verbal to provide useful guidance. Kant found it literally inconceivable that space might have more than three dimensions, and was innocent of later non-Euclidean geometry. He asked, "How is pure mathematics possible?" (*Critique of Pure Reason*, B20). Then some impossible mathematics sidelined his enterprise. Caution is friend to doubt.

27. James Joyce, *A Portrait of the Artist as a Young Man* (New York: B. W. Huebsch, 1916), chap. 5, 238.

28. Martin Heidegger, *Letter on Humanism*, in *Basic Writings: From Being and Time* (1927) *to The Task of Thinking* (1964), rev. and expanded ed., ed. David Farrell Krell (London: Harper Perennial, 2008), 217–65. The phrase occurs on page 237. See also Heidegger's *On the Way to Language*, trans. Peter D. Hertz. (San Francisco: Harper & Row, 1971).

Chapter 7

Playing for Keeps

There is a traditional, narrow view of metaphysics that its exclusive concern is with eternal truths, truths that *have to be*, that are non-contingent, necessary, even absolute. No more idle play, no more provisional hypotheses, never any empirical corroboration: such metaphysics runs on a pure fuel. So let us play seriously, as Plato advised, not just with myths of becoming, but with tales of being also. And is metaphysics not play in the eternal, human dabbling in a sandbox above our grade? But the masses still hanker after the changeless, the immutable, the timeless imponderables that have been pondered since time immemorial. Those who attended Café Philosophy in order to think asked questions they knew had no answer. So they voted to know what it is best to know, but perhaps never known, what is at best surmised, and then only with an eternal glint in a winking eye.

METAPHYSICS

We gather to ask: what does *metaphysics* signify? Though we come together, we begin worlds apart. The lofty business of metaphysics as it is enshrined in the ivoriest of towers is far from that namesake science of lesser mysteries that overfills overpriced bookshelves in those incense-saturated metaphysical emporia that play soft flute or harp music to conjure an other-worldly atmosphere for spiritual consumers. Let us therefore begin with a quick survey of the ground, as best as can be made out through the thicket of ambiguity that covers it, trying not to get ourselves caught in the brambles and cross-purposes of language, nor lose sight of our moving target.

To begin in plainest terms, we can take *metaphysics* to be that core region of philosophy concerned with ultimate questions of existence, reality, and truth, and in particular with the fundamental principles thereof, where "fundamental" means *not themselves explainable in terms of other principles*. By extension, we can carry its significance beyond philosophy, in that the word *metaphysics* also refers to the underlying theoretical principles of any subject or field of inquiry. Or we can restrict it further within philosophy, as when the term refers to the view or theory of a particular philosopher or school of thinkers. Thus the word readily slips into something either less disciplinary or more specific. And it seems to slip both ways at once in what is its most popular meaning, the theme of metaphysical bookstores, with reference implicit or explicit to supernatural phenomena, supra-sensual ways of knowing, and to whatever transcends the merely physical. The gems sold in these stores are not mere stones—they are valued for something far beyond their geological attributes.

From here, it is not too far a leap to *metaphysics* in its abusive signification as unbridled speculation with regard to unknown and unknowable subjects, or simply outright nonsense. That latter slur is cast from many directions, and has different meanings, from simple silliness to a technical status of neither true nor false (which is a way philosophers cut all accounts with propositions they cannot be bothered to refute). But poets and practical people also abjure metaphysics in order thereby to appear more like themselves. For them, metaphysicians are like blind people in a dark room looking for a black hat that is not there.[1]

To prepare the way for later elucidations, let me end my precursory survey by offering one last definition of metaphysics, which also might merit a dictionary entry somewhere, but which actually represents a particular perspective within metaphysical philosophy, namely that of Aristotle. If we want to go beyond the plain and *ex*plain what metaphysics is, we can hardly go wrong in starting with Aristotle. Aristotle's *Metaphysics* is a study of first principles. It is the science of being insofar as it is being (in the parlance, being *qua* being); so in this characteristic sense, metaphysics may also properly be called ontology (*ontos*=being). In other words, in an Aristotelian context, metaphysics is the branch of philosophy that deals with questions of ultimate reality and ultimate causes, and thus contains cosmology, teleology, and even theology. When modern science, in taking cosmology over from philosophy, dropped theology and dispensed with teleology (the science of immanent purposes), metaphysics came to be seen as a bastard child, unruly, and unwilling to fit in to the new order and the progress of knowledge.

For this and other reasons, the most salient and culturally-primed usage of the ill-conceived word *metaphysics* is actually a term of abuse. This can range from gentle reprimand to censure born of bafflement, from the charge of outright inanity to consignment to the dustbin of history. Even without its charms and soothsayers, metaphysics is wanton *speculation*: idle, fanciful, vain, deluded, pernicious, and epistemically irresponsible. Scorn is heaped on metaphysics by the most diverse sorts of thinkers and non-thinkers alike (including among the latter those who pride themselves on their autonomic prowess, or their peremptory cunning, and all who valorize the deed over understanding). But it has even been a veritable compulsion for generations of philosophers (most notably those of the last few centuries in the West) to condemn as *incoherent metaphysics* all the ideas about reality ascribed to the greatest of their predecessors. The death of metaphysics is a perennial philosophical theme. The very antithesis of death by a thousand cuts, metaphysics flourishes by a thousand deaths.

The truth is, people from almost any walk of life do not mind stopping what they are doing for a moment to take a kick at metaphysics. The practical man of action may scorn as *metaphysical* any informal abstract talk that isn't actionable (to abuse a lovely word). Any chatter, reflection or theorizing considered irrelevant to cold hard deed, or to achievable fact, is readily dismissed as so much *metaphysics*. No argument is required, merely a contemptuous wave of an unthinking hand. Yet the scorn of, and for, metaphysics also runs very deep *within* metaphysics—like an underground river flowing far below a positivist desert of correlated elementary sensations. Metaphysics is rejected alike by positivists and by pragmatists; by phenomenologists and linguistic analysts; by scientists and by feminists; by politicians and by the gainfully employed; by thieves and by mystics; by clergy and by the salt of the earth. Artists may scorn it or embrace it. Only philosophers manage to do both at once.

But numerologists, alchemists, astrologers, astral-travelers, realm-climbing or plane-transcending yogis, past-life regression engineers, *I Ching* casters, energetic tao-players, rosary-counters, vision-seers, and ghost-channelers are all of them metaphysicians, implicitly if not consciously and explicitly. It is a scientistic slur to place the great philosopher-metaphysicians among this crowd, but like most effective maligning there is more than a hint of truth in it. There is, indeed, a long, long, way from the turgid deductions of Georg Wilhelm Friedrich Hegel (1770–1831) or from the grammatical-cum-metaphysical analyses of Aristotle to the little metaphysics shop with the spacey music where one buys one's necessary supply of crystals, sacred statuary, and meditation beads. Reason has no need of such paraphernalia, but philosophers (unlike magicians) have their need for the guise of reason. Magicians seem to defy logic. Philosophers wax metaphysical through the magical use of logic. Seeming logical is the point.

Let me take Plato as illustration, famous for his two-world metaphysics, his great bifurcation of Nature into a shifting shadowy realm we call our concrete existence and a timeless realm of intelligible entities, the original prototypes of the physical objects and relations surrounding us.[2] Since

Plato's epistemology tracks his metaphysics, various gradations of knowing map onto these degrees of being. Imagination and sensory-based opinion (or observation) are the lowly sorts of knowing, but only reason can encounter the intelligible eternal forms. Now reason itself bifurcates. Plato valorizes mathematical and especially geometrical thought. He famously had imprinted over the entrance to his Academy the admonition, *Only the geometer need enter*. But such deductive reasoning is strictly propaedeutic, merely preparatory, only the introductory or entry-level "mental control" portion of his yoga. The real game happens with a curious form of reason not inappropriately called intellectual intuition. It is dialectical, deals in opposites, and descends from a glorious immediate vision of truth. O Reason! How could Plato make you so mystical, *so Indian?*

Plato conceived his metaphysics before the term even existed. *Metaphysics* in its first coinage is a title, given by posthumous editors, to a particular work attributed to Aristotle.[3] Aristotle did not write a book of that title, but his lectures on *sophia*, a science of "first principles," were written down and edited during his lifetime and after. In fact, this particular treatise was named on account of its relation to his earlier work known as the *Physics*, which dealt with many of the same issues. (These include: the relation of form to matter, or universal to particular; causation and/as purpose; eternity; time; chance; continuity; infinity; cosmological order; and God as the Prime Mover and That for the Ultimate Sake of Which everything changes.) Put bluntly, there are no major differences in doctrine or methodology in the two books. For Aristotle, physics and metaphysics are hardly different at all.

Therefore, metaphysics is an original misnomer. As a discipline, it is very badly named. Originally, it signified only that this was another text by Aristotle dealing with the same sorts of issues as his book on physics (or nature). It literally meant "in addition to or besides the *Physics*," but it has come to connote "over and above the physical." Today, however, in the realm of philosophy, *metaphysics* is not synonymous with *supernatural*. The natural and the supernatural are equally metaphysical: they are just different metaphysics. (Even materialism is materialist metaphysics, despite self-identifying as a mere research program.)

It is true that Aristotle, in *Metaphysics A*, chastises the PreSocratic physicalists,[4] famed for originating Greek philosophy, for failing to recognize God as the substantial, moving and final cause of the cosmos. In this sense, the *Metaphysics* goes beyond those purely physicalist philosophies, and Aristotle seems to open up to a science of higher physics. However, Aristotle's book on Nature (*Physics*) also argues against the PreSocratic metaphysics, and features ample discussion of God in those same causal roles, plus, as mentioned, many other metaphysical topics also covered in the later book. Aficionados may continue to argue over matters of emphasis and relative weights. But the underlying continuity is undeniable.

Now within philosophy we may consider two main ways of distinguishing *metaphysics*: one in terms of its content (the subject matter of the field), the other in terms of manner (how one does metaphysics—for metaphysics is also something one *does*). The content-criterion (exemplified by most of the definitions given so far in this essay) classifies any inquiry as metaphysics if it pertains to the first principles of reality, or to being, time, space, causation, spirit (or to their respective opposites: appearance, nothingness, eternity, void, chance, and matter). This list is not meant to be exhaustive; the point is that dealing with these content areas (in *whatever* manner) is dealing in metaphysics *as so defined*. In content terms alone, it is hard to prevent metaphysics from slipping beyond philosophy and finding itself in the foundations of other fields as well.

Indeed, the trouble with this definition, some would say, is that significant portions of physics, psychology, mathematics, statistics, and biology, not to mention religion, poetry, perhaps even architecture and painting, would count as metaphysical. This is a bullet I am willing to bite; it is not the paradox it seems. The trouble arises due to the tendency to conflate this way of distinguishing metaphysics with another, namely the *methodology* or manner with which one engages in metaphysics. To see this, one must take a detour through an epoch of epistemology, namely the rise of modern science (empirical and naturalistic philosophy). Then I will quit.

Modern science was born of many mothers, so no simple or monogamous account will suffice. But in large measure one can ascribe the birth of science to an epistemological revolution, as a *new* way of ideas, new methods of attaining truths. Modern physics starting with Galileo is certainly a rejection not just of Aristotle's metaphysics of causation (his teleology), but more fundamentally of how we must come to know the truths of nature. Methods of observation and experiment (testing conjectures) replaced the old *a priori* methods of reasoning that continue to characterize philosophy. Struggles about reason continued over the centuries as the scientific method worked itself out (that is, multiplied itself into many sciences). But physics above all came to bear the stamp of science (a word that had always meant highest knowledge), and the old science, the old philosophy, formerly highest, got branded as metaphysics, due to its errors of *method*. Philosophy itself eventually comes to be seen as barren, undone by its very success. Only the sciences have the rigor sufficient to yield knowledge. This was the basic pattern of the abuse all along: all previous philosophies are metaphysics (they are wrong); true knowledge is anti-metaphysical (it is science).

But the war of metaphysics cannot be won on the battlefield of terminology. A revolution in the means of knowing will no doubt alter our metaphysical *conclusions*, but it cannot obliterate metaphysics as such (defined by its content areas). Today (just as in Aristotle) we look to physics to find our metaphysics. Atomism was a metaphysical doctrine before the molecular nature of chemical substances was experimentally demonstrated. On the whole, its metaphysics was vindicated, not vanquished. Later, when physics split the atom (*atom*=the uncut, or the indivisible) and isolated subatomic particles, this exposed additional *a priori* metaphysical preconceptions as naïve, but by the same token also opened up entirely new metaphysical vistas. By the content-criterion, relativity and quantum theory constitute an evidence-based revolution in metaphysics, not its death knell. It was not just a new oomph for *science*. The wave-particle duality; the cloud of probabilities that characterize the atomic orbitals; non-locality; holism; entropic wind-down: these are all squarely physical topics, but they represent profound metaphysical innovations as well.

Mechanism is a metaphysics. It is not the death of metaphysics (even *if* it sounds the death-knell of all supernatural metaphysics). The theory of natural selection replaces an old metaphysics, but it does not escape new metaphysical problems. Science is really only good epistemology (or rather good science is good epistemology). This is *not* to assert the converse (that all good epistemology is science, or that all knowledge comes from science). The point is simply that evidence does not cancel metaphysics: it selects among them.

I reject the idea that philosophy has its own special subjects. I recant the presumption that philosophy is its own way of knowing. *And I deny that metaphysics is a region of thought reserved for philosophers*. What philosophers call their specialization is really only their mastery/obsession with a canon. I am in favor of such mastery; and I do not mean to limit the canon to old works like those I have mentioned here. Yet to infer ownership of content from familiarity with a literature is a gross fallacy. Philosophy is too rich to own its own problems, yet it is too poor to birth its own truths. If metaphysics is a plague, it is on all of our houses.

One may reject the hypothesis of God as an answer to certain ultimate questions, but one cannot reject the ultimacy of those questions. Metaphysics is defined by first principles; it is our ultimate questions. Our encounter with the void; staring into the abyss; musing at our self-moving hand; shrinking at our finitude over against the indefinite other; balking at the thought of our own demise; negotiating our relationship with the universe (or the Beloved)—these are ways each of us enter into existential wonder, and thus into metaphysical inference and inquiry. This does not make us into philosophers (another alchemy is required for that), but it does make us, in those moments, philosophical. In an exactly similar way, we are compelled to be metaphysical, though perhaps not to be metaphysicians.

Be one among us many. Instantiate Philosophy.

CHANGE

Change is difference over time. But this plain definition hides innumerable other issues and conflicts that swarm the philosophic mind. These range from the abstruse and metaphysical to the immediate and concrete. Change is also political. Change! is even a slogan, the eternal call of political challenge. There was the voiceless Bill Clinton, not wavering from his message, at the end of his first presidential campaign, rallying a crowd with a hoarse whisper: Change! Change! As if it were no longer necessary to explain what changes were intended, as if the bare fact of change were all that people wanted. Of course, change ushered him out, too. "Voters wanted change," we (used to?) say after an election loss, as if that bland lacuna had any explanatory value at all, or even any semantic content less thin than a hoarse whisper. Were things so bad that any possible change would have been an improvement? It begs stating that a change for the worse is no less a change than change for the better.

One thing does not change: the incessant repetition of the homily that change is constant. Yet this will constantly be repeated in all philosophical conversations about change, and is the only immutable aspect of those dialogues. The philosophical problem of change has not changed much during the millennia of its discussion.

One big problem has always been how you are to change while remaining the same. If you really change, later it is not you anymore. So it is no longer correct to say that *you* changed, only that you-then is no more and in its place we have you-now. Note that the latter is true even if there is no difference at all between the two, except their location in time. Yet unless you remain the same throughout the change, you cannot yourself be said to change, or even to have changed. For you to suffer change, you must survive it.

So, can you find the immutable *sacrum* of your being, the permanent bone at the root of your existence, or do you survive only as a convention, or as we say the rope, composed of innumerable overlapping threads, is one thing? Perhaps you are only a sack of events taking place at various times, and only the fact that it is one sack makes it possible to nominally accept that you change (which then really only means that later events differ from earlier events).

The issues in play here emerge in the earliest days of Greek Ionian philosophy. Heraclitus of Ephesus asserted the constancy of change in his infamous dictum "We step into and we do not step into the same rivers." Alternatively, "it is not possible to step twice into the same river." "The sun is new each day," he said. but also "the way up and down are one and the same." "This *kosmos*," according to Heraclitus, "but it was always and is and shall be: an ever-living fire, kindled in measures and extinguished in measures."

Notice that here constancy and change get equal billing. So it misrepresents Heraclitus' view to say that change is the only constant. One final quotation, to show that in the very midst of this first philosophy of change there is a goodly measure of constancy and sameness: "what is in us is the same thing: living and dead, awake and sleeping, as well as young and old; for these things having changed round are those, and those having changed round are these."[5]

Not long later the opposite metaphysic arose, which regarded change as a flaw, origin as an illusion, and only the Immutable as true being. This was the view of Parmenides of Elea (c. late 6th cent.–mid-5th cent.), and his imp, Zeno of Elea, famous for his paradoxes.[6] They rejected the genetic explanations of the Ionians as just so many more myths of origin, no genuine advance beyond the tales of the poets. In there place they sought rational explanations of a different order. Change is metaphysically inferior to changelessness, and only the Eternal is true. This narrow (or high) redefinition of Being restricts possible candidates to one: it turns out there is only One true Reality, one Being, not becoming at all, beyond all motion, absent all change. Zeno's paradoxes were formulated to advance the Eleatic agenda, to show that all change, all motion, all difference, was illusory. The way of Becoming *is* not.

Parmenides is not the origin of origin-free explanation, at least not globally. Similar ideas were bandied about in India at an even earlier date. I have often fancied that a century before Parmenides the Buddha accepted a similar narrow and high redefinition of Being, and, seeing that we find within ourselves no such changelessness, no eternal being, argued that we ought to relinquish habitual belief in self altogether.[7] To say that there is no self is, in the first instance, to deny that there is any eternity to the self, and to claim that no eternal truth pertains to self. Confucius too, as recorded in *Analects*, is quoted as saying, while standing beside a river, "what passes away is, perhaps, like this. Day and night it never lets up."[8] The concrete is ephemeral; what co-arises with us, like us will perish.

Change of self, both voluntary and otherwise, is a topic that speaks to us today perhaps more vividly than these ancient sages, bottomless though they were. But before coming to that, I want to linger with these changeless ancients a few paragraphs longer.

Due to Leucippus, and carried forward by Democritus, the doctrine of atomism (that all matter is composed of tiny, finite, indivisible particles) emerged from the creative tension between the eternally shifting Heraclitean fire and the monistic One of Parmenides. Atoms (like the Eleatic One) were themselves eternal, without beginning or end, and incomposite (it was assumed as obvious that anything composite would eventually fall apart). The atom is the Uncut, the indivisible particle, which only ever changed its motion and location. All things were composed of atoms of different kinds arranged in various ways and, though those arrangements, mixtures and combinations could change, the atoms themselves were otherwise changeless. To anticipate Aristotle's critique, atomist philosophy reduced all categories of change to change-of-location-over-time, to motion. It would be reborn centuries later as modern mechanism.

Into this doubt-filled debate waded Aristotle, who introduced his categories of being in order to classify different kinds of change.[9] Based on a thorough logical analysis of (not reality, but) grammar, Aristotle established that there were ten ways things could (be said to) be, and correspondingly ten respects in which things could change. For instance, Quantity, Quality, and Relation are three of Aristotle's metaphysical categories. Change in Quantity is either an increase or a decrease, waxing or waning. Growth of plants and the decay of senescence are examples. Change in Quality is known as alteration, and is in some cases an alter-n-ation from opposites to opposites. To *alter* is to change in quality. To *alternate* is to switch back and forth, as from one opposite to another. Thus day turns to night, and night to day. Heat of summer becomes winter's cold, which then warms again to summer. Change of qualities often cycles, opposite to opposite, as intimated earlier in a Heraclitus fragment.

Besides Relation, the fundamental categories of Being include Place, Time, Position and Having (or State). Thus we can change our place by moving, change time by waiting until evening, change position by sitting or standing, and change our state by dressing, learning, acquiring, and so on. All these are the kinds of change, and they record changes in nine of the ten categories that Aristotle articulated. The other category is the ultimate one, the primary being of which all the others are predicated. This is the category of substance (*ousia*), ultimate being. In most instances, substances originate and cease to be; they either are or they are not. Change of substance is destruction of substance. Substances undergo other changes, but that only means that they are the ultimate subject of the change in the other categories. It is *their* qualities that change, their location, their number, their states, and their relationships, and so on. But substance itself is neither more nor less, does not come in degrees as many qualities do, and it does not exist only relatively.

So substance (*ousia*) is the unchanging substratum of all the other changes, it is the thing that remains the same throughout the change, which keeps something the same thing despite the changes that it undergoes. Your qualities, your bulk, your relations, your positions and acquisitions, your actions, and your potential like your dress all may change, but you are substantially the same as you ever were. That was you back then. You have survived all your changes, or they were not changes at all, only endings.

I fear that if I continue far on this interpretive line, I will commit a Christian sin against Aristotle.[10] I am already repentant. But I think you get the point. I am suggesting that Aristotle's notion of substance is an answer to the problem of change with which we began. It is intended to articulate the constant identity that survives and underlies natural (physical) change. The category of substance is meant to provide a substratum (like a pin cushion) that remains the same despite change in the other categories (each quality, quantity, relation, place, etc., as a pin, that may or may not inhere in the thing, the substance). (Note: All reference here to pins and pin-cushions is a cheap exegetical resort to later conventional lore, not authentic Aristotle. This metaphysical cliché is certainly not to be pinned on him. Like all metaphors, it is limited, and one can poke all manner of holes in it. But I use it not just to poke fun, but because it gets the point across so well that I am sure it will stick in your mind.)

The upshot of Aristotle's view is the strict impossibility of one substance ever literally becoming another substance, that is, a thing of one species ever metamorphosing into a specimen of another. Silk purses cannot be made from sows' ears. Impossible would be such miraculous events as that in Genesis 23:19, where Lot's wife is transformed into a pillar of salt, as penalty for looking back at burning Sodom, despite having been warned not to. Molecule by molecule, she is transformed into a pillar of salt. What begins as all human (one substance) ends as another (all salt). But a thing cannot begin as one species, and in the process of its development, switch or skip species. All such discontinuous leaping from one substance to another is abhorrent to nature, if not illogical, and is disallowed in Aristotelian metaphysics. And no reference to caterpillars-cum-butterflies, or tadpole-cum-frogs will serve as counter-example to that great and observant biologist's dictum. Of those species, it is precisely characteristic to develop in those remarkable ways, changing not in kind but in total quality, and by organic growth and change in all the other categories. Species breed true, and replicate each after its own kind. And by nature, or at least by Aristotle, one is born and dies of the same kind.[11]

Will such metaphysics never cease, my weary reader is asking? Hasten us then to the personal dimension of change, change of self, often the last resort of those who, after long assault, fail to change the world. Self-change is not merely an activity, it is an entire industry. Self-help is self-change in a helpful or positive direction, but we can take the two terms as virtually coextensive, since people are so inclined to help themselves. Self-change is the hopeful project of self-reform. More than a weekend workshop, it is a lifetime plan, a career, or a career-change. Every day in every way I get better and better. Self-change is Eldorado, it is California, new age. Self-change is the *puer eternis*, the obligation to improve, the ever-potential.

The enemy in all such projects is *not* staying the same. That is not an option. So to impose an awkward distinction (too flimsy to survive this essay) is *change of self*, for instance, the natural process of aging, which is nobody's self-change project. Strange as it may seem, then, self-change is very different from change of self. To try to link back to earlier ideas, the former belongs to Aristotle's category of activity, whereas change of self includes passive change, changes that happen to one, what one undergoes rather than undertakes. Others can change your self, but only you can initiate self-change. The optimists will tell you that, with regard to self-change, the sky is the limit. But the limit of self-change is the necessity of change of self. The change of self you do not undertake you must undergo.

The project of self-change has become mired in the mess of its own idealism. Only when we abandon all hopes for change is real change possible. When the project of change finally collapses, change will at last be able to proceed. To grasp it is to lose it. To change it is to destroy it. Happy compliance is the only freedom, the transforming touch.

Do not adjust your mental set. Network troubles are influencing your receptivity to change. Do not touch that dial. Do not change this channel. Tune in to philosophy each and every day. It will change your mind.

ENERGY

This essay explores deeply divergent sets of uses of the word "energy," one strictly physical, the other purely spiritual. The two discourses are set side by side, without any attempt to favor either. Their mutual inconsistency and joint incoherence are emphasized, but the treatment is even-handed, as if to invite camps preferring each sort of usage to sit down and talk to each other. Let spirit shake hands with spirit.

***

Energy has the aura of spirit and the sanction of science. It is a word bursting with mischief.

Energy is the ability to do work. Work is equal to mass times distance displaced. That means the more mass you move over a given distance, or the farther you move a given mass, the more work you do, and the more energy is required. This is work (hence energy) in the physical sense. Such physical work is (or has been) measured in ergs or joules. But it is not what the average joe thinks is work, or energy. To hold up a heavy stone at shoulder height is not to move it, so no work is done. But it does take effort, and it burns energy. And you should still be paid for it.

Our energy for work comes from the food we eat. In this physics and common sense coincide.

Energy is the ability to move things, but really this is just one form of energy, namely mechanical energy. There are other forms as well, including electrical, chemical, magnetic, atomic, and so on. But they are all in principle inter-convertible in such a way as to maintain quantity, which fact is enshrined in the thermodynamic law according to which energy is neither created nor destroyed. Thus every other form of energy is expressible as an equivalent of mechanical energy, of the work done, of mass moved through a distance. From this great law, it follows that the quantity of energy in the universe is unchanged, and will forever remain the same.[12]

This again appears to conflict with everyday experience, since our own sense of energy fluctuates. Sleep, rest, conviction or devotion seem to create energy. A lively speaker can energize a room. One says: there is more energy in this room than there was before the speaker. But really only more energy is being expended. Unless someone has just wheeled in a tray of snacks, the energy in the room is the same before and after. Energy can be inert, that is inactive, not doing anything. It can be energy ready to work, but currently unemployed.

And here is a window on the puzzle. Energy unused or even unusable is energy still. Though dispersed and dissipated it remains the same amount of energy. Maybe you can get no work done by it, but it is not null or destroyed or any less on that account. A ball at the top of a hill possesses an energy on account of its position relative to the center of the earth. This energy is potential, but its progressively converted into kinetic energy once the ball begins its free roll down the hill toward the earth's center of gravity. All the effort of the person with their arms up holding a stone aloft, while not work, is expended to prevent this conversion. It is easier but equivalent to hold it up by a little hill, a mound about arm's height, placed under your outstretched hand to support it. And the pay's the same too.

All the forms of matter, including all those inert solid bodies about us, the flat earth below the feet, and the dull reflecting moon, that ball and the hill itself, are all themselves energy, forms of energy convertible in principle (whether or not it is technically feasible) into radiation.

Isaac Newton had taught us to distinguish the weight of a body from its mass. Mass is constant across gravitational fields, yet a body weighing something on earth weighs something quite different on the moon, and in deep space is weightless. You would spin up a different number on your bathroom scale if you were standing on it on the moon, rather than on the earth, due to the different mass (hence gravitational force) of the two bodies. But Albert

Einstein showed that mass is not constant; rather, it increases with velocity: the faster something goes relative to an observer, the greater its mass relative to the same observer.[13] Every energy has its equivalent in mass; in the case of electromagnetic waves, it can be expressed as the quantity of energy divided by the speed of light squared.

In the radioactive decay of an atom, mass is lost to the atom, but radiation is given off. The amount of mass the atom loses is precisely related to the energy released in the form of radiation. Once again, the mass lost is equal to the quantity of energy divided by the speed of light squared.

At velocities common near the surface of the earth, where we evolved, the changes in mass are imperceptible and negligible. Thus we have evolved common preconceptions that are not in line with these technical discoveries. Our day-to-day notion of energy is also out of step with physical science, as the few examples so far given already indicate. But here I want to highlight the contradictions between *physical energy*, to which I have so far restricted my attention, and *spiritual energy*, which you cannot purchase through a public utility. For our hearts and minds, our allegiances and our vocabularies of thought are split on this issue. Energy is a contested term.

The situation is familiar enough to readers of this book: the same philosophically-important word does double duty. Histories of usage coexist side by side, but may scarcely ever intersect or overlap. This creates rich potential for confusion, error and misunderstanding. So let us now consider an alternate language, an alternate story, a new vocabulary—in short, another world.

Energy is spirit, and spirit is energy. There is no attempt here, despite appearances, to place spirit under the yolk of the thermodynamic law of the conservation of energy. Sure, some may say spirit can never be created nor destroyed, but they would no doubt fiercely resist any implication that spirit is mathematically equivalent to so many quantities of mass displaced such and such distances. Spirit is not some number of ergs or joules. Even if spirit can move matter, it does not become less spirit and more matter in the doing; for conversion implies subtraction—though only in physics. (In matters of spirit, conversion is quite another thing!) Spirit may dally in the physical realm—perhaps its self-created playground—but it never loses any of itself, however much we may lose sight of it. God does not become less god in becoming human or otherwise getting physical.

Spirit is more like a lingering infinite potential behind all things. It is an inner strengthening, independent of the waxing or waning of the body. Spiritual energy is felt energy, coursing through the body, witnessable, able to be directed by attention. The phenomenon of inner energy is an experience of opening and closing, of tensions and releases, of holding and letting go, of building up and letting pass through. While the willful mind can manipulate it, circulate it, push it and pull it, connect it or separate it, the mind is only like a river-bank, a movable barrier, or a shapeable conduit. It is not the source, and does not account for the original flow, which enters and exits the body from the transcendent beyond. The source of energy may be shown deference, but it may not be immediately known. One may adorn the temple, but the divinity may not arrive.

Spirit-energy has not been the preserve of the East. The philosophies of the West before mechanism also spoke of energy in spiritual terms, but again in its own vocabulary, terms of reference, and world of discourse. The term *energy* derives from the Greek *energeia*, which is translated as activity. The root word, *erg*, means work, and thus *energeia* too is getting work done, in the sense of doing something specific. In Aristotle, it came to mean the realization of a species-specific potential, as when an acorn grows into an oak, or a likeness is carved from a stone, or a building made according to a plan. All nature, he said, is active in this way, and so nature always works for a purpose.[14]

The mechanical picture of the world replaces these purposes (so-called final causes) with material pushes and pulls, the laws of springs and pulleys, and thereby the world was disenchanted, as the story goes; for the purpose of life was read out of the world. My point is only that in energy of the ancient sort there lurked purpose, meaning, value, and the ends of human and all life. Energy was the realization of potential, but this potential was like a star in the awesome firmament, not a stone held up with a struggle. It was human excellence, greatness, and magnanimity, superlative achievement of mind and body. It was a conception of Greek divinity, not the punishment of an overworked Sisyphus.

Even today there is a question of action, of human activity, that resists all reduction to the terms of physics. This is the question of the deed that follows upon the word, the morally accountable act. (Not to be confused with the pseudo-problem of the freedom of the will; the issue is the meaningfulness of human action, not its freedom per se.) The Greek word for deed is *ergon*, and it may be contrasted with *logos* (word or account). So you get the point: the meaningfulness of action is connected to the quality of the energy that we deploy in carrying it out. It depends on the forms and qualities of energy deployments, not merely quantitative equations. It is about the energetic/spiritual organization behind the action, in that it recognizes the constraints of human action but is not reduced to them. Explanations proceeding from a purely physical basis are not so much incorrect as misdirected.

This problem of the deed, of moral accountability of action, is not only part of the ancient notion of energy, it is equipotent to the problem of karma. For *karma* means *action, deed*, or *work*, and thus is a kind of semantic associate of *energy*.[15] The ethical issues connected to karma (responsibility, wise choice, respect, accountability) are the same as those stripped away from the ancient notion of energy by the modern juggernaut of mechanism. These issues do not have to do with the causes of our actions, but the grounds of our choices. To put it in our terms, what are we going to do with our energy? Will we belch it out into our atmospheres and destroy life as we pretend to know it? Will we devote it to goods or to good, to comfort or to learning, to war or to peace? Spirit is inevitably concerned with the morality of action in ways no physics of energy has yet attempted to comprehend.

Reenergize your mind. Attend to philosophy.

WHOLENESS

To be *whole* is to be complete. Wholeness is completion. What is whole is complete in itself, intact and entire. Wholeness is the state of entirety, of repletion, a condition in which nothing is damaged, broken, modified or missing. But this is only one part of wholeness. To be whole is also to be sound and uninjured, healthy and wholesome. And to be made whole is to be compensated for unjust loss, as when one wins suit for damages. Clearly there are many parts to wholeness, many kinds and notions of wholeness, and no coherent, integrated way to examine them in their entirety.

Nevertheless, the best way to proceed with problem of wholeness may yet be to examine it part by part. Space is lacking to cover all its innumerable parts and aspects, so completion is impossible. I will have to be selective, mentioning only the surface of a deep subject. Even then, my remarks will have to remain general, scattered, and, on the whole, of little substance. But since I am missing nothing in enthusiasm, and do my part as a champion of wholeness, I fear my remarks will come off as biased or partial. Still, I shall impart all I know, and much that I do not.

The organic whole has no artificial ingredients. The certified organic whole has come into being by a process verified for environmental sustainability. These amusing absurdities, like my opening wholesale play, bear a warning: beware of ambiguity. Irresponsible yet irrepressible puns such as these wear their nonsense openly. No less nonsensical, but more concealed, is the wondrous and magical sounding cliché, often trotted out to define a proper or organic whole: namely, it is *more than the sum of its parts*. The phrase has even been attributed to Aristotle, to whom a notion of organic whole does indeed belong. I do not know where in his works such a line occurs. However, there is a discussion of wholes and parts in his *Metaphysics* at 1045a, where it is the *assumption* that wholes (organic or not) are not mere heaps, not mere totals or sums or aggregates of parts. Today the word organic goes best with vegetables, but so-called organic wholes, or at least the famous defining formula, gets bandied about like explanatory manna from heaven. But in

Aristotle, to call anything *more than the sum of its parts* is not yet to say very much, certainly not that it is wholesome, healthy, natural or organic.

The point already in Aristotle gets to the root of why I myself find that oft-cite formula so loathsome: it promises more than it gives. It soothes the explanatory conscience, when it should irritate it to go on to ask the obvious question: *what more?* To define the whole as *more* than the sum of its parts is to define it by the indefinite, by a "more" that is itself never further specified. Logically, the definition is a failure, since it does not say what it is, but only negatively, what it is not (not the sum). It waves a mystery under our nose like bait, and few are those who cannot resist an affirmative chomp.[16]

To use examples in Aristotle, a mere artifact, a manufactured good, as we might say, though not natural, is already more than the sum of all its parts, since the sum of all its parts might be a mere heap or a scattering of parts. Yet no artifact is an organic whole. To be a *sum* or an *aggregate* or a *total* is only to be a bunch, perhaps a complete bunch, but not a whole. Completeness and wholeness are distinct: to be whole (*perhaps*!) is to be complete, but to be complete (like a set of all the parts) is not yet to be a whole (assembled). So the formula, understood aright, is trivial.

Trivial, but of interest in the limiting case of a *one-piece chair*. It too, as a whole, must be more than the sum of its (single) part. But how so, since here the part is the whole? Chair is as chair does. The function of a chair is made possible by its part(s), but it is not *reducible* to them. The function of the chair transcends all its parts. This is high-fallutin' philosophical language for saying *very little*, namely that sitting on something can make it a chair.

Now, Aristotle knew that organic wholes were not mere totalities. Let us start with a crude, verbal definition of an organic whole: an organic whole is a whole that is organic (that is, not inorganic), meaning it is alive or a product of life. The slightest hint of this plain, bluntly literal meaning is retained in our totally contemporary notion of organic as *derived directly from nature* (and *therefore* free of additives and pesticides, as the joke above had it). For life is *derived directly from nature*. Life is not man-made or artificial (*yet!*). The wholeness, the "more" beyond the parts, is naturally present, always already present, not the result of a technical process, as a table or chair results from the building. Aristotle recognized that a special part-whole relationship—a unique "more"—was required to account for biological wholes, individual organisms.

To get at this Aristotelian conception of an organic whole, one can start with a more interesting (though still seemingly trivial-sounding) definition: an organic whole is one whose parts are organs. How does an organ differ from a regular part? The word "organ" is more than the sum of its meanings. Its root *erg* is also found in *energy* and means much the same as *function* or *work*. (Think here of the word *karma*, which literally means work, deed, action, which is thus comparable to the Greek, *ergon*, meaning *work, deed, product, or function.*) An organ is a part that does something specific; it is appointed by nature to perform some special work. (All Aristotle's Nature, you will recall, works for a purpose.) Of course artifacts, like tools we make to fit our hand, have the purposes we appointed to them and, in serving our deeds, they become organ-extensions of our body.

Now suppose a hand is detached from a body so that it can no longer serve the function of a hand. It can no longer grasp or point or slap, and so on. Not part of the body, it does not serve its function; only as part of the body can it do so. That function—doable only as part of the body—is the reason a hand is not a mere part of the body but an organic part, and the body an organic whole. You will note that, not just organic wholes, but organic parts, or organs, are more than a sum of their organ-parts, for they are functionally defined. (And anyway, the function of the whole is still not reducible to the function of the parts.)

Now here you have a nice intelligible "more" to satisfy most if not all complaints of vagueness. If to enjoy this answer one must tolerate the natural teleology and the *a priori* presumption, at least it is clever and memorable. But it leaves our story here.

The so-called Gestalt whole is a whole other story.[17] But it too is saddled with the indefinite definition of being "greater than the sum of its parts." The notion, however, is squarely psychological, not organic in the foregoing literal senses. A Gestalt is a percept that goes beyond the stimulus given through sensation. Consider these now classic images:

In figure 7.1, we see four thin bars more easily than we see three wide bars, due to the preeminence given to *proximity* by the visual process.

Below that, we see a straight line intersected by a curved line, something over and above the mere bunch of dots that constitutes the stimulus. Crudely put, we sense dots, but perceive lines. The lines we see are not in the stimulus, but added to it in the perceptual imagination/apparatus. Such lines (whose existence is to be perceived) are called *subjective contours*.

On the right, we perceive rows more readily than columns, due to the similarity of the components (certainly they are not organs or functional parts!). And finally, we see one disk in front of another, and can even perceive the subjective presence of the occluded portion, giving once again a subjective contour. That contour is not in the stimulus, it is added by the perceptual process. The gestalt principle here is called closure.

There is yet another gestalt principle, too complex to articulate, that enables us to regard the closure stimulus (bottom left) for what it really is, an aerial view of a snowman from behind.

So is wholeness hallucinated? Is wholeness a subjective substance, comparable to a subjective contour? Is wholeness imagined, much as we understood

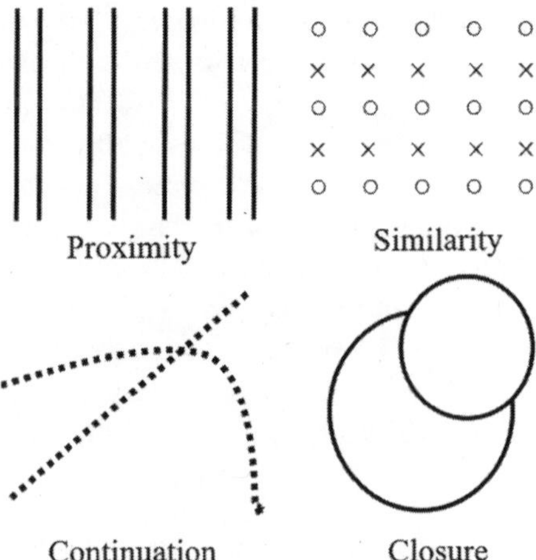

Figure 7.1 Gestalten Diagram. Illustrated Gestalt Principles.

"more" when we only sniffed mystery? Has the organic whole become mind-dependent?

Here I lamentably break off this fragment of an essay on wholeness.

HUMAN NATURE

What a crass, disordered mess, this human nature! Without maintaining the minimal politeness of logical consistency, you demand to be assessed and defined? Which mask is most you, you dissembler, you pantomime? Why so craven, so desperate, such groveling—why so much gravity and so many graves? But why then such heights, the soaring artistry, the monumental architecture, the heavenly voices, and the fantastical lies to die for in the name of Truth? Who could horizon you, define you, draw a circle to name your limit? But who could deny anything so petty and small could be other than irremediably finite?

The *essence* or *nature* of a kind of being is formulated as a *definition*. An essential definition purports to give necessary and sufficient conditions even to be something of that kind. What it is to be human, then, we might express as a definition of human nature. By articulating the essence of a kind of thing, you circumscribe or define it; what lies outside the circle is different (plant or god); what falls within the circle is one of the same (one of us). To define human beings is to fix their horizon, but our horizon moves with our being, and we will not stay still.

Smaller still than the human stature is the human thought process, a paltry if prevalent candidate for our essential nature. Prone to fallacies of feeling and reason, primed with the most recent, biased by the present, and blinded by self-interest, our thinking stumbles awkwardly through life, grasping at straws of meaning and elusive threads of significance, much as we do half-consciously in dream. The easy-to-apply principle of going with the flow also invites thoughtless entry into experience, and discourages or disguises the tragic responsibility to think for ourselves. Man: the rational animal.[18] Reason isolates us from our animality, defines us as inward beings with certain possible experiences, and makes us into what we make of the world. But the world makes us, and we make up all the rest, even this definition. Reason works much like a sieve, and we fancy that what we catch is what there is. (Metaphysics often reads like delusions of grandeur.)

The question as to our nature as human beings has provoked many divisions of opinion and numerous points of profound divergence. Perhaps none of these is more vast or fraught with tension than the opposition between the *biological* and the *social*, nature versus nurture, the genetic as against the cultural, instinct over-against education. The issue may be formulated as follows: is human nature, namely, what we are, determined by the one or by the other? Are we essentially human by Nature, or have we made ourselves into ourselves by association and social influence? Nature (so far) has bequeathed us our genes. But we are forged in experience, formed by culture, educated by society, and civilized or not in the process. Biology is not civilization. But just how uncivil are we by nature?

The issue *may* be so formulated, but then it is misformulated in the process. The oppressive dualism, the implicit either-or, is suspicious, indeed pernicious. We are not a layer cake, the lowest layer laid down by biology, with culture like an icing later laid on top. Interaction is the norm; only the nexus is concrete; the extremes are abstractions. Biology lays down tendencies, experience cultivates or neglects them. Within the ranges of likelihood established by biology, situation, and experience select an outcome. Genes can only do so much to determine your height; nutrition wreaks havoc or wonders within those limits. There is no better illustration of this reciprocal influence than the human brain. Prefigured for certain general capacities, it is wired by local experience. Neural development is a social process. Learning is physiological. The functioning adult human brain is a social product. It takes a village to raise a brain.[19]

We are biologically social, evolutionarily gregarious. We have a social nature, which rather messes up the neat layer cake model, and all circular essentialisms. We are by nature dependent on one another. Independence is a protest fetish, though often salutary. For the herd instinct runs deep, the slavish obedience and knee-jerk conformity would wholly prevail if some misfits did not lift their head above the crowd from time to time and ask: what the hell is going on? Still individuality is a social artifact, even when it is a social statement. Culture is a third parent.

It is Aristotle, as far as I know, who first speaks of custom as *second nature*. (We are social or political animals, he also says). When habits become so ingrained as to seem natural, they become *our* nature, even down to the defining quirks of particular beings. And there is the rub: what *seems* natural is *not necessarily* natural. What comes natural is often only learning that is well ingrained. *The feeling of the natural is a profound illusion, a sanctifying event, a visceral approval—and nothing more.* A theory of the Natural is only ever an ideology.

What is natural has the sanction of nature, which is a feeling of sanctity projected outwardly, and eventually of conformity with hope and expectation. The unnatural is what meets with an opposite disapproval, and is unknown, unseen, monstrous. What should be of most interest to us therefore is not *human nature* (self-sanctimonious sentiment) but *human unNature*, that is to say, our vicious unconscious cultural destruction of nature, driven by technological hubris and the illusions of acquisition and progress. We are the juggernaut we are waking up to.

Philosophical despair has led to some traditions in which the essence problem, the problem of human nature, has been long discarded. Thus existentialism is branded by Jean-Paul Sartre's slogan that existence precedes essence, that we can no longer accept any prepackaged definition of our nature, but must go out there and make it up for ourselves as we go along.[20] We are condemned to this freedom from essence, to the liberty of self-definition. The human condition—with its meaningless angst, its benign indifference, its vain and self-inflicted calamity—gives the parameters of the existential project, to forge a set of values worth living for.

Beyond this first and most divisive dualism lies another, closely related to the first. Whether we are social or natural, or a bio-social chimera, the moral question raises its ugly head: are we by nature good or evil? Are we by nature good, but corrupted by society? Or are we corrupt by nature, perfected by society? Misanthropes it seems are not content to skewer culture; they go on to condemn humanity to its very root. Those who love humanity must likewise specify whether it is some native innocence or glory that merits respect, or the cultivation of moral habits.

Political divisions—left versus right—have turned on this underlying moral question as to the worth and natural value of human beings. Are we brutes or savages without acculturation? Who are we alone and in nature, isolated without social influence? Would we be at war, all against all, with a short and nasty life? Or would we be noble beings, at peace with ourselves and our own, more contented and healthy precisely because we do not compare ourselves to others more lovely or rich? This dichotomy (Thomas Hobbes versus Jean-Jacques Rousseau) still haunts our collective imagination.[21] Do we require an absolute power over us to institute social peace? Or do we require it so we can transcend our private will and become one with the general will of a free people? Either way, to be reconciled with ourselves outside the state of nature requires grappling with the absolute power of society over individual nature. Is there not some middle path that steps over the whole question of human nature? For such fine feet I long.

Here at least is my catch, my disordered mess, my reasoned and unreasoned essay. Logic is on holiday, you shall have to sort out my contradictions for yourself. Better still, attend to yourself and give voice to your own.

ENLIGHTENMENT

It is difficult to become enlightened. Lucky for me, it is far easier simply to write about it. But what I gain in luck, you perhaps lose. Beware. Shine your own light!

These days, enlightenment is somewhat *passé*. We are post-moderns: post-industrial, post-structuralist, post-enlightenment. It is difficult to approach enlightenment when we are so far past it. Unless, like me, you approach ass-first.

One does not know whether to look East or West for Enlightenment. Like the sun, the dawn is probably in the East and the demise in the West. Certainly the elephant has a whole different feel depending on which end you happen to grab first. From conditions on this end, I would say it is facing East. I suppose you now see the wisdom of my ass-first approach.

In the East, Enlightenment is a spiritual release; in the West, it is breaking a bondage that is at once more political and epistemological—in a word, it is more scientific. Both are about knowledge and the truth, but in one Truth is God, in the other, Truth is Nature, including human nature. One is transcendent, the other opened the empire of the material, unlocking its vaults in which the secret powers of matter lay hidden. Science cracked the outer safe, exploited the codes, manufactured the technological Juggernaut we see around us. Eastern Enlightenment transcends the world; Western Enlightenment transformed it.

In Europe, as absolute monarchy began its long-lasting fall, critical minds arose that yearned to throw off the habitual dominance of ideas that Aristotelianized Catholicism had imposed. Not only authority, but the very terms in which this authority asserted itself, had to be undone, un-thought, rethought, revamped.

When faith becomes ideology, it inevitably falters in the encounter with simple facts of individual experience, so that even a dunce can pronounce against it. When Galileo appealed (in the vernacular) to the evidences to be seen in his telescope; when William Harvey (1578–1657) actually measured blood flow to prove the heart was a pump; when Newton resolved the rainbow spectrum back into white light, all were appealing to observables, which no one could deny except those who refused to look, the willfully dunce. The rest of the world, however ignorant, could not unsee just how closed the eyes of authority had become, how ideological, how false and corrupt, how blind from dogma. The filthy route to the mind, through the senses, bested the high-minded spiritualists and flattened their intellectual airs. Mechanics (as Galileo and other physicists were derisively called) trumped the scholastic hair-splitters, despite their lofty eminence. Thus was the Enlightenment ushered in on the back of an ass.

The Enlightenment is the intellectual ferment instigated by these great scientists, along with their later champions, who had begun to construct a world to replace the one inherited from Aristotle and Judaism. What was at stake was the very definition of civilization (though seldom the assumption that civilization was Europe's unique possession and birthright, and altogether absent among the dark-skinned other). Peace and prosperity, those shining angels proclaimed by Zarathustra himself, were remade in a European image, and enshrined in John Locke's eclipsed slogan, "Life, Liberty and Goods" (the latter, being more truthful but less polite, was revised by the Americans to "the pursuit of Happiness").[22] That revolutionary energy is the enlightenment energy in the West. It is the ideological revalorizing of fading deities, now called science, progress, development. Let no one today kneel before any other gods. There is no alternative.

Early on, Western Enlightenment located God conveniently outside the mechanical universe. For the traditional theist, God had been the *Summum Bonum*, the origin and end of all, the first cause and the ultimate appointer of ends (in practice, Aristotle's pointers were often followed). Now forms of Deism took over European minds, and God became a distant observer, too wise to need to intervene in the machine-world he himself had created, wound up, and set a-spinning. As God is the clockmaker, enlightenment is the making of clocks. And thus the ruthless measurement of everything existing began. The best that individual spirituality could do would be to synchronize its watch with God's. (In practice, it was good enough to assume London's Big Ben kept universal time for all the cosmos.) There was optimism that one rational system of mathematical rigor could spell out the principles of ethics and resolve all conflict by ratiocination. All we lacked was a Newton of the ethical realm.

Locke, a veritable beacon of toleration and of Enlightenment, and worthy of much admiration, nevertheless baked some ignorance and prejudice into the new mold of knowing. He dismisses the Indian fable (of the world sitting on the back of an elephant, standing on a turtle, etc.) as thoughts befitting children.[23] These children! They fondly thought of enlightenment as realizing their identity with God; they were too spiritually immature to relegate Him to the remote past or confine him to the infinite distance. Some were so naive as to consider that it was we who had to transcend the world in order to become enlightened, not god who had to depart the world in order to enlighten us.[24] Perhaps children, not understanding that knowledge is power, do not properly fear it. They cannot all receive the education Locke prescribes for a gentleman.

Adults ought to think like that stiff upright Prussian, Immanuel Kant—who was so much a part of the Enlightenment that some say he ended it—according to whose mature rationalism, space and time are mere necessities of human experience, having no reality outside the forms and categories of mind. Contrast children, who like Indians, are liable to think that the spider Goddess Maya wove the whole net of space and time, and that her world-making power resides in each individual mind, not outside it. Children just cannot understand the hair's-breadth difference between these two transcendent idealisms. They are liable to ask: is *The Critique of Pure Reason* not simply the *Upanishads* in a terrible disguise?[25] Therefore I declare that, until the myths of the primitives are interpreted as enlightened wisdom, or our enlightened wisdom is interpreted as primitive myth, we shall go on eating elephant shit.

The fire that Prometheus stole from the Gods to give a boon to human beings—how far have we seen with it? Shall we include the smelters of the Industrial Revolution and the combustion engine as products of the reason or foresight that that fire symbolized? Shall we include the mass firestorms and heat domes brought to us by global warming? The divine Self within was called a blue flame, the size of one's thumb, in the center of one's heart. To see that fire within was to realize your divine identity. How far can we see by this Eastern light? I leave you to compare. It was the Buddha who pinched out that flame of self, snuffed out the candle of identity, smothered the smut-covered lamp, instead of merely cleaning it (as the Hindus had said). There is scholarly debate as to whether it is correct to attribute the injunction, *Be lamps unto yourselves!*, directly to the Buddha. One can see why, since he understood enlightenment to be *nirvana*, which means literally extinguishing. "The world is burning"[26], he said; put it out by dowsing your own mind. How far shall we see . . . in the dark?

Do not remain in the dark. Go toward the light! Run to Philosophy.

NOTES

1. There are many versions of this well-worn insult, and almost as many alleged authors of it, so I cite none. Sometimes it is not a black hat, but a black cat, no

doubt on a black mat, possibly wearing said non-existent hat. Schrödinger's cat was not there, but it was also there. Distinguishing physics and metaphysics can be like herding cats. On Erwin Schrödinger's cat, see e.g. Gary Zukav, *The Dancing Wu Li Masters: An Overview of the New Physics* (New York: Bantam Books, 1979), 85–86.

2. I based myself here on Plato's "Allegory of the Cave" and on the "Line," the metaphysical and epistemological theories underlying the allegory, both in Plato's *Republic*, in Plato, *Complete Works*, ed. John M. Cooper (Indianapolis: Hackett, 1997). For the "Cave," see 5141–71; for the exposition of the theories represented on the "Line," see 509d–511e and 517a–518e.

3. Aristotle's *Physics* and *Metaphysics* are in vols. 1 and 2, respectively, of the *Complete Works of Aristotle*, ed. Jonathan Barnes (Princeton, NJ: Princeton University Press, 1984).

4. The PreSocractic physicalist philosophers include Thales (c. 625–545 BCE), Anaximander (c. 610–545 BCE), Heraclitus (c. 540–480 BCE), and others. Some of them are mentioned in chap. 8 of this book, along with certain non-physicalist PreSocratics.

5. Diels-Kranz numbers given are B49a, B91, B6, B60, B30, B88. Translations of Heraclitus in English are adapted from Patricia Curd's *A PreSocratics Reader*, 2nd ed., trans. by Richard D. McKirahan and Patricia Curd (Indianapolis: Hackett, 2011), 41–53.

6. Zeno of Elea (c. 490/5–430 BCE), disciple of Parmenides (c. 515–450 BCE), developed sophisticated dialectical arguments proving the impossibility of opposites, the incoherence of plurality and the self-contradictory nature of motion, from which Parmenides' monism would seem to follow. For a further treatments see *Zeno's Paradoxes*, ed. Wesley C. Salmon (Indianapolis: Hackett, 2001).

7. Buddha asks "Is what is impermanent, suffering, and subject to change fit to be regarded thus: 'This is mine, this I am, this is my self'?" –"No, venerable sir." (SN 22:59; III 66–68). Quoting Bhikkhu Bodhi's translation: from *In the Buddha's Words: An Anthology of Discourses from the Pāli Canon* (Boston: Wisdom Publications, 2005), 340.

8. Confucius, *The Analects*, trans. D. C. Lau (New York: Penguin, 1998), bk. 9, 17.

9. Aristotle's *Categories* is thought to be an early work. Key categorical terms are also discussed in *Metaphysics*, bk. 5, 1012b34–1025a30. See vols. 1 and 2 respectively, of the Aristotle, *Complete Works*, ed. Barnes.

10. That is, by continuing on the indicated line of thought, I would bring up the question of moral agency, of moral responsibility for actions, and thus of the *psyche* or soul. This in turn raises thorny questions for those who believed in an individual soul which can be singled out for judgment after death, a notion foreign to the pagan philosopher.

11. A Zen Koan runs "Though we are born of the same lineage, we do not die of the same lineage." See Isshū Miura and Ruth Fuller Sasaki, *The Zen Koan: Its History and Use in Rinzai Zen* (New York: Harvest, 1963), 100.

12. Quantum physics admits violations in the conservation law, provided they are sufficiently brief. If the violations are small enough, and quickly repaired, they may

happen at the quantum level, resulting in being popping into and out of non-being, like a white dragon hidden in clouds. For a popular treatment, see Gary Zukav, *The Dancing Wu Li Masters*, 240–42. Being, it seems, can now come from nothing, as long as it does not stay too long; and it must pay reparations for its temporary transgression by its own swift obliteration, in the manner not unlike that envisaged by Anaximander, who considered becoming definite a cosmic injustice which would be rectified in due course by a compulsory return to the primordial infinity (*apeiron*).

13. Albert Einstein, *Relativity: The Special and General Theory* (New York: Henry Holt, 1920), https://www.ibiblio.org/ebooks/Einstein/Einstein_Relativity.pdf (accessed October 8, 2021).

14. Note that *energeia* (activity) is an Aristotelean category, paired with *dunamis* (potential), so that the active-passive duality discussed earlier in regard to virtue and to passion (passivity) represents different ways to be: to change, and to be changed. This duality is intimately related to two of Aristotle's ten categories: action (*poien*, related to doing or making *poeisis*) and affection (*pashein*, related to *pathe* and passive). See *Categories*, 4, 9; see also *Metaphysics*, bk 5, 1013a29–32; 1019a15–1020a6; 1022b4–21; see also bk 11, 1065b5–1066a34.

15. *Karma* means action or work, originally ritual action, which was the cause of boons; but over time the notion was broadened to include everyday action, especially, the work required by one's station in life in the great moral order (caste system) of society, but always *spiritual* action, as in forms of yogic self-control, are included as well. But the efficacy of action in producing *fruit* is emphasized, bringing out the cosmic-moral dimension of meaning. Since attitude so influences efficacy, translating the word as "energy" (not in the sense of physics) is sometimes appropriate. In *The Tibetan Book of the Dead* (New York: Bantam Books, 1994), Robert Thurman translates "karma" as "evolution" (257).

16. My antipathy runs deep here. This was the problem I faced in my doctoral dissertation at MIT; see Joseph Romeo William Michael Picard, "Impredicativity and Turn of the Century Foundations of Mathematics: Presupposition in Poincaré and Russell" (PhD diss., Massachusetts Institute of Technology, 1993), http://hdl.handle.net/1721.1/12498. The continuum of real-numbered points is a whole that is more than a mere bunch of points, as it also involves an ordering (by <, the less than relation on the real numbers). But to define that continuous ordering requires so-called impredicative definitions, which (to put it crudely) only define the point in relation to the whole set of points, itself included. I understood the much-vaunted unity of the continuum, often regarded a secret seat of mystery, as a metaphysical (modal) relationship among the parts, as if some points could not exist unless others among them also existed. This idea of reciprocal being ("ontological interdependency") was worked out in a way that supported the legitimacy of impredicative definitions, which had been charged with vicious logical circularity. The word *impredicative* is a neologism invented around 1906, only added to the *Oxford English Dictionary* (*OED*) in a 1976 Supplement.

17. *Gestalt* is a venerable German word with many work-a-day meanings, but an illustrious philosophical history before it became gave a name to the psychological school of Max Wertheimer (1880–1943), Wolfgang Kohler (1887–1967), and Kurt

Koffka (1886–1941), some of whose principles are discussed next in relation to visual perception. Notice that the terrain shifts markedly at this point from natural wholes to psychology of mental organization. Gestalt Therapy is a different matter altogether.

18. Aristotle's famous definition. Note that above I have oversimplified his notion of essence. As mentioned later, Aristotle also characterizes human beings as a social animal. Rather than a different idea, this underlines that reason is social; see Anthony Simon Laden, *Reasoning: A Social Picture* (Oxford: Oxford University Press, 2012).

19. This was written with only a dawning awareness of epigenetics, which involves understanding how our actions and the chemical and social environment turn genes on or off, producing the proteins we are and that influence what we become. Antonio Damasio can serve as reference for the social brain hypothesis. He writes: "Nervous systems make minds not by themselves but in cooperation with the rest of their own organisms. This is a departure from the traditional view of brains as the sole source of minds" (Damasio, *The Strange Order of Things: Life, Feeling, and the Making of Cultures* [New York: Pantheon, 2018], 28). See also Damasio, *Descartes' Error: Emotion, Reason, and the Human Brain* (New York: Avon, 1994; repr. New York: Penguin, 2005).

20. Jean-Paul Sartre, *Existentialism Is a Humanism*, trans. Carol Macomber (New Haven, CT: Yale University Press, 2007); the original lecture in 1945.

21. Thomas Hobbes, *Leviathan* (1651), ed. C. B. Macpherson (London: Penguin, 1985). The "Second Discourse" (1755) of Jean-Jacques Rousseau, *Discourse on the Origin and Foundations of Inequality Among Men*, in *Basic Political Writings*, 2nd ed., trans. Donald A. Cress (Indianapolis: Hackett, 2011), 93–120.

22. For Zarathustra's *Gāthās*, see Jacques Duchesne-Guillemin, *The Hymns of Zarathustra: Being a Translation of the Gāthās Together With Introduction and Commentary*, trans. from French by Mrs. M. Henning (London: Murray, 1952). For John Locke, see his *Second Treatise of Government*, ed. C. B. Macpherson (Indianapolis: Hackett, 1980).

23. See John Locke, *An Essay Concerning Human Understanding* (1690), ed. Peter H. Nidditch (Oxford: Clarendon Press, 1975), chap. 12.19, 175; also chap. 23.2, 296. To be sure, Locke's target here is the European notion of philosophical substance (*ousia*); the "poor Indian" is a mere laughing stock one does not want to be compared to. Lest anyone mistake the bitter irony in what follows for literalism, or fail to recognize my send-up of Locke's Eurocentric paternalism, let me briefly clarify. Locke is undeniably one of the worthies of Western Enlightenment, and a beloved voice against tyranny. Yet as Plato said, "no man must be honoured more than the truth" (*Republic*, bk. 10 595c). So let it be noted that Locke is also the spiritual father both of the dispossession of Native American lands (based on misguided hearsay anthropology, his labor theory of value, and Anglican inferences of God's intentions) as well as of the residential and boarding schools in Canada and the United States that amounted to cultural genocide. Philosophy's ethical heroes are founts of racist ideology. Philosophy too has its unmarked graves.

24. On his way to arguing that "the most scrupulous or sceptical cannot from miracles raise the least doubt against the divine revelation of the gospel," Locke rejects Asian philosophy with a dismissive gesture: "For what the Persees say of

their Zoroaster [=Zarathustra], or the Indians of their Brama (not to mention all the wild stories of the religions farther east), is so obscure, or so manifestly fabulous, that no account can be made of it" (John Locke, "A Discourse of Miracles" [1702], in *The Reasonableness of Christianity*, ed. by I. T. Ramsey [Stanford, CA: Stanford University Press, 1958], 81).

25. "In essence, this view is old; . . . Heraclitus lamented the eternal flux of things; Plato spoke with contempt of its object as that which forever becomes, but never is; Spinoza called it mere accidents of the sole substance that alone is and endures; Kant opposed to the thing-in-itself that which is known as mere phenomenon; finally, the ancient wisdom of the Indians declares that 'it is Mâyâ, the veil of deception, which covers the eyes of mortals, and cause them so see a world of which one cannot say either that it is or that it is not; for it is like a dream'" (Arthur Schopenhauer, *The World as Will and Representation*, trans. E. F. J. Payne [New York: Dover, 1969], 7–8). "Now as Kant's separation of the phenomenon from the thing-in-itself . . . far surpassed in the profundity and thoughtfulness of its argument all that had ever existed, . . . For in it he propounded, quite originally and in an entirely new way, the same truth, found from a new aspect and on a new path, which Plato untiringly repeats, and generally expresses in his language as follows. . . . The same truth, though presented quite differently, is also a principal teaching of the *Vedas* and *Puranas*, namely the doctrine of Maya, by which is understood nothing but what Immanuel Kant calls the phenomenon as opposed to the thing-in-itself" (Schopenhauer, *World as Will*, appendix, 419).

26. A common paraphrase from Adittapariyaya Sutta, the Fire Sermon, the third sermon given by Buddha after enlightenment. It appears in *The Connected Discourse of the Buddha,* trans. Bhikkhu Bodhi (Boston: Wisdom Publications, 2000), 1143.

Chapter 8

Playing (With) God

We *play God* when we take life or fate into our own hands, in other words, when we are not playing at all. But when we speak *of* God, we presume to know of what we speak. So, if we would not speak *for* God, we are condemned to silence, or speak in pretense. And yet this chapter exists. Though they cannot be said to be high-profile in academic philosophy, spiritual and religious topics—I scorn to distinguish the two—were perennial favorites at Café Philosophy, and the most in demand, as measured by both votes and attendance. Yet the spirit of the age is an unbelieving spirit. At times to speak up for God at Café Philosophy was to invite mockery. Defenses were high, and some came to slay, to prove others wrong, to refute first and seek to understand later, if at all. Thus my essays on these topics, when they did not resort to literary measures, tended to adopt a tone of pleading, urging readers not so much to believe, as to think beyond their accustomed constraints of belief or unbelief.

GOD

How many gods there are, tucked mysteriously in this little word "god"! Perhaps it should not even be uttered, because it means too much, because, in respect of its surfeit of ambiguity, it means too many things to too many people. Each of us, deniers and believers, conceives a god to reject or accept after our own individual fashion, according to the limitations on our own spiritual imagination. The semantic pantheon is profuse and teeming with meaning, but here are a few limited, conflicted and competing accounts of the unaccountable, definitions of the indefinable, conceits of the inconceivable god. If you would play the God-card—so high and mighty and wild that you will never need to play another[1]—be sure to declare upfront the value of your Joker. Here, then, are some of the various values that that wild card at time may assume:

God as father, protector, guardian. Ruler and Subordinator.
God as Sky-Daddy, as Poppa.
God as object of worship, for we love to worship.
God as good listener, as Interest in human petitions, an ear for our predicaments.
God as face, as person, as the one we finally face.
God as mother, as origin of everything, and sustainer, nurturer of each after its own kind.
God as food, and as the eater of food, for the eater in the end is eaten.
God as destroyer, as the final end, as the last return; God as Death, armed with sickle.
God as justice, figuratively the Lord of Judgment Day, when final moral payback comes due.
God as a spirit troubling your samaritan bowels.
God as a voice, as instructions, as advice; God as conscience.
God as vindication, as justification, as missing premise and warrant. That Which Sanctifies.
God as mysterious explanation, or explanation of mystery. G?d the Unexplained.
God as simply everything, the surfeit of being; for nothing can be left out, and less than all is not enough.
God as the universal witness, the one eye behind every eye, the Self behind yourself.
God as love, as infinite compassion, the opener of hearts; God as friend and comforter.
God as madness, dispenser of divine frenzy; God as intoxicant, as wine.
God as ground, as Being itself, without regard for differences.
God as the divider, as individuator, i.e., as the metaphysical principle that makes each thing what it is. God is diversity.
G-d as the nameless Tao, the unutterable law of nature, the all-too-wily way Weird works.
God as silence, God beyond Being, for being points beyond itself.
God as wrath, as righteous fury, for the fear of god is the beginning of wisdom.
God as the perplexor, as mystery; God as a living question, a cry in the epistemic wilderness.
God as self, for we accept nothing higher than self, even if this is delusion.
God as the ultimate I, as Transcendent Ego, as objective subjectivity, as Objective Spirit.
God as other people, for where two are gathered in my name, I am there.
God as suffering, as the history of misery; God as the voice of the voiceless.

God as machine, as the routine confidence of lax mental habits; God as a rut.
God as dead, as crutch and coping mechanism, a false but pacifying hope.
God as unthinkable, as a feeling and the passion of faith. Kryptonite to evidence.
God as the ultimate common identity of each of us; for all is one, and that one is God.
God as energy, agency and activity, a conscious doer, awake. God is as God does. (karma)
God as the pulse of creation, the drumbeat of creation, cosmic rhythm. Vibrations.
God as explanation of the inexplicable, an assumption that soothes a wound, the assertoric Unknown.
God the drug, the opiate, a sedative, ecstasy, a high, a ketamine disintegration. Vast Soma.
God as crutch, life-support, a curative, a pain-killer. O Asklepius!
God as out for our own good, as He Who Alone Knows Best Our Best Interest.
God as sop, to pacify the aggrieved lion in us. For the lion we eat becomes us.
God as bludgeon, to rule with blind masses over blind masses. The club of epistemology.
God as time, which swallows all things, God as the final consumption. Mother Maw.
God as the thinker of all reality, for being is only an idea in the mind of God, a blink of His eye.
God as nothing, for nothing compares to God and nothing is higher than God.
God as emptiness, for all other cups are only half-full.
God as truth, for it is better to say "truth is God" than to say "God is truth."
God as laughter, because we are wont to put on divine airs. (Psalm 2.4)
God as philosopher, for God has the highest, bushiest and most furrowed brow.
God. Godot. Do not pass go. Do not collect bliss. Go forever to gaol.
Gather in the name of truth. Let the spirit of philosophy move you.

RELIGION

Religion, faith, spirituality. How do they relate? One popular usage equates faith and religion. To be sure, the word "faith" *can* literally mean religion. One speaks, for example, of the "faiths of the world," referring generally to the world's religions. But faith also is an act of assent, and as such has divergent roles within particular religions. Put differently, faith as assent to doctrine does not play the same role in all religions, even allowing for doctrinal differences. More bluntly still, not all religions require assent to their doctrines as the criteria of inclusion or of salvation. What do I mean?

As often understood, faith in Christianity may be symbolically equated with St. Peter's keys: it opens the gates to heaven. Only believers need apply. If you answer yes to all the questions, you are in; miss any, and you are out. Here faith divides us from them. What is more, if faith in dogma is the entry key, and the dogma is a mystery, then assent is valued higher than understanding, which mystery obstructs. You do not have to understand the answers to the skill-testing questions, you just have to get them right. You do not need to understand the keys, only to use them. Such faith is blind. But so is this very idea of faith.

Closely associated with this first gloss on faith is the view that faith casts out all doubt. Faith is certainty, by hook or by crook. These views are closely related because faith is quick but understanding is slow. Understanding dwells with its questions before it arrives at itself. It hovers hesitantly over its object to become acquainted with it, to let its eyes grow accustomed to the dark it strives to overcome. Understanding requires doubt even to be sure of itself. Doubt helps understanding be critical of itself, to see clearly. Faith that is blind eschews doubt that wants to see.

But faith does not always have the same role, even in Christianity. One important conception of faith in early Buddhism is effort. The image of faith is not a key, but an ox slogging through the mud of ignorance. Faith is perseverance. The reward of faith is not an easy slipping through of an unlocked gate, but it is a struggling through a swamp. Faith here is struggle. It is doubt, even ignorance, like the bull that trucks on through the muck not knowing. Such faith is a measure of the commitment of spirituality. It is not a creed, not even a belief. Take for example, reincarnation and the law of karma; these are *not* articles of faith.[2] Suddenly believing in them does not advance you one whit along the spiritual path. You get no credit for answering questions correctly, only for understanding deeply, personally, their ultimate significance. Faith here is not belief: unlike belief, it does you some good.

My point is *not* to make Buddhism appear superior to Christianity. The point is that "faith" is ambiguous. Both blind and bullish faith can exist in any religion. If you reject religion and faith based on one narrow definition, it is your logic that has become blind. Best to push through that shit.

Refuge is sometimes sought in the distinction between religion and spirituality. But it is not to be found there. What do I mean?

Religion without spirituality is dead. But spirituality without religion is crippled. Spirituality without religion will seem ideal, if religion is equated with oppressive social control. Often in contemporary speech "religion" is taken to mean *institutionalized* religion, as if that adjective were redundant. Often the institution assumed here is a church (as if churches were inherently oppressive, and) even though there are other ways, even other oppressive ways, religions institutionalize themselves besides churches, like caste, religio-political states, and the conscience or superego (which Freud, quite remarkably, characterized as a social institution in the individual mind).[3] The crutch may be a conceit. Yet beware. Spirituality without religion in practice often means "anything goes," "to each his own." It is often only idle private fantasy, with no measure of its own depth because . . . it has none. (Not that I am against spiritual innovation. . . .)

It might be more clarifying to contrast spirituality to religiosity, rather than to religion as such. Although a person could certainly be spiritual without being religious (without social institutions playing the major role), there can be no difference between the two in the case of a religious person. Their spirituality just is their religiosity. But the presence in their spirituality of societal institutions should not lazily be equated with oppression and mind-control. We must not be naive to the history of religious oppression, but equating religion with having the views of others forced upon you is no way to keep an open mind. Yet just this is common among knee-jerk atheists, who know in principle long before they understand (call them the anti-faithful).

As mentioned above, there is *an* accepted sense of the word "faith" that is synonymous with *a* sense of the word "religion."[4] Yet a person can also have faith without being a member of any religion, so the two also come apart. This semantic difference is *not* subjective, nor is it relative to situation or belief. These two senses of the term are available to believer and to atheist alike. One should not beg philosophical questions by building a selective bias into the meanings of terms, hoping others follow one's myopic example.

Though not mentioned above, there is an accepted sense of the word "belief" that is synonymous with a sense of the word "religion" (thus the religious are called believers). Yet it is not logically permissible to go on to use this one sense of the word to the exclusion of all others, thus equating non-believers with the irreligious. Just as a person can believe (that is, in God) without being a member of any religion, so too one can be religious without believing (that is, in God), since not all religions postulate God (consider Taoism, early Buddhism). These semantic differences cut across belief, they transcend faiths; they are not relative or subjective. To exploit them in stating one's positions to cop a semblance of rationality is illicit, but common in public discourse.

These thoughts may be condensed into the frustratingly ambiguous sentence: different faiths have different faiths. This is not the rank tautology that different faiths *are* different faiths. Nor is it the near-tautology that different faiths have different beliefs, a statement most naturally read as saying (what everyone knows), namely that different religions have different belief systems. But different religions or faiths or belief systems also recognize distinct roles for faith beyond credence or belief. So there is a third meaning in saying that different faiths have different faiths: faith is not mere belief, not mere adherence or acceptance, but persistence; not a key but an ox. Strictly, both may be blind, either may be knowing.

That brings me to a final point and general caveat to what I have been arguing. I have taken a Catholic metaphor for faith in the sense of belief, and have duly contrasted it with another role for faith, illustrated from Buddhist sources. But really what is being targeted here are certain narrow understandings of these rich and diverse traditions, both of which in fact contain far more sophisticated perspectives on faith than what I have appealed to here. Cultural atheism, as well as academic philosophy unduly privileging epistemic questions, conspires to feign a reduction of religion to faith, and faith to belief. But in truth faith is far more multifarious in each of these heterogeneous religions than the simplistic contrast offered here. In any case, perseverance is also a Christian virtue.

In conclusion, then, I say religion is not faith, it is not belief, it is not spirituality; yet it is nothing without these inner opposites, unless it be reduced to hollow institutions and dead formalities. And the latter describes no religion worth believing in, nor any living religion. It is wise to avoid attacking an effigy of the position you oppose. Avoid the Straw Martyr Fallacy.

FAITH

If "faith" could only be *defined* as a species of ignorance, then most of the philosophical problems pertaining to it would be resolved in a single stroke. But this easy verbal route away from the substance of the issue only succeeds in ignoring it, and ignoring here is only an active form of ignorance. Unfortunately, much popular discourse, and even some academic philosophy, starts from assumptions implying just this dismissive definition: *faith is belief despite the absence of evidence*. The deepest and most interesting philosophy lies in the idea of faith that brings knowledge, faith that keeps faith with truth, faith that *sees*. If faith is simply stipulated to be blind groping, then it is of little philosophical interest, except in the way a pest is of interest to an exterminator.

Honest atheism requires an open heart to the dead god, and decorum during mourning.

Faith on its own terms is more like seeing the invisible than seeing nothing. Can there be wisdom in such visions, or are they necessarily madness? If faith sees a ghost, how can one know whether it is holy or a hallucination? This painful question of the *verification* of faith, and of its claims to know, is often raised more or less as a knife is raised: *with violent intent*. The debate about faith as a way of knowing is as deep as it is divisive, and more than a little blood has been spilled over it. The opposing camps, it is safe to say, do not understand each other; reciprocal attacks proceed across a gulf of misunderstanding. In this essay, in order to undermine both the aggression and the ignorance, I resort to a kind of semantic violence. This is *my* struggle with faith.

In the name of a truce without lies, one might venture farther into the epistemology of faith. If one generously rejects the cynical *a priori* equation of faith and nescience, one might timidly propose that faith is belief, faith is credence. To have faith is to be a believer—what could sound more plausible? The proposal has a certain charm, in its minimal claim and its apparently neutral status. It seems like a good working compromise, an idea that promotes agreement on the meaning of terms by all parties to the debate. Believers and non-believers alike may place their trust in the equation of faith with belief, which pits believers against the faithless. But just this most tempting of conflations I shall attack, on the grounds that it promotes endless idle debate, divisive bias, and conceptual crudity. So my over-arching theme is the separation of faith from belief, strange as that may seem. I reject as confused the idea that belief is essential to faith, and deny that faith is a mere species of belief. I will be chastised for trying to divorce what God and semantics have joined together. But—*trust me!*—there is a point to my outlandish inversion.

Why go against this plainest and most flatfooted definition of *faith* as belief? The problem is that one paints oneself into a corner by this clumsy equation, a corner of futile and pernicious argument. The question gets shifted to one of the *ultimate grounds* of belief, where in practice our feet seem rarely to touch down. This sort of debate is known to all who take part in or overhear typical philosophical arguments about faith. Thus the positivists (side A) scorn the religious (side B) for having *mere* belief, for not caring about evidence. The problem with faith, from this A=Atheist view, is that it pretends to yield knowledge while only defending prejudice and blind tradition. Faith stipulates its own justification, and is therefore unjustified.

The defensive B=Believer will retort that science too has its faith, namely in the very regularities of the world. Science typically pretends not to certainty, but instead proudly boasts of its preparedness to revise its fundamental beliefs in light of new evidence (whereas faith is faith come what may). But if science is prepared to cast off one law in light of disconfirming evidence, it feels very assured that yet another law lays hidden, awaiting discovery. In short, it assumes that the world is regular whether we know that regularity or not. The faith of science denies the vanity of empirical search. Now, at the level of the logic of science, there is a logical circularity, notoriously pointed out by Hume: induction is only inductively valid.[5] We know induction is valid (that is, strong, reliable, trustworthy) because it has worked so often in the past; but this argument is itself inductive, and science seems to presume something like it continually. This ultimate logical circularity—so the retaliatory charge is leveled—papers over a scientific faith, what has been called "animal faith," an unshakable confidence in the regularity of the world, despite the epistemic regress.[6] One hears the retort: we B=Believers are entitled to our faith because you the non-believers have your inescapable faith too. You A=Atheists are really B=Bestial Believers. At worst, this argument is the fallacy, *tu quoque* (you do it too!), so familiar from sibling rivalry. At best, it is a polemical defense of necessity: everybody has to take a leap of faith at some point or other—lamely presupposing any leap is as legitimate as any other. As someone who has landed hard on many a cliff-bottom, I beg to differ.

I started by rejecting the attitudinally foreshortened view that faith is ignorance. But here we see that the apparently opposite equation of faith as belief no sooner gets the two sides talking, than dispute breaks out, a spiraling squabble about belief and verification, self-evidence and ultimate evidence. The first view cuts off debate prematurely; the second view foments it endlessly, which would be fine if it were not so rancorous, circular and vain. A debate is set up over what to believe in, *what to have faith in*, rather than about *what faith is*. The object of faith (the object *x* of the phrasal verb *have faith in x*) becomes the battlefield: which *x* may we believe in? Meanwhile all questions as to the nature and experience of faith, for those who report it, get overlooked, shunted to the background. Faith is ignored in a new way, a second way, not by summarily discounting it, but by overt yet irrelevant philosophical debates about its ultimate validity as a way of coming to know.

It is worth crossing over this ground again, to present this line of reasoning more carefully, to expose the error in thinking and find a way out of this idle debate. Admittedly, there is lexical evidence in favor of the equation of faith and belief, as a quick glance at dictionary definitions of *faith* will suggest. *Faith* is cognate with Latin *fide*, meaning trust, from which we get *fidelity*; and with the Greek *pistis*, which means belief and is a root of our word *epistemology* (in Plato, *pistis* is a deficient sort of knowledge, at best the "prevailing wisdom" inside the cave, and as such is often rendered as *opinion*). So a primary meaning of "faith" is trust or confidence in a person, thing or truth. The epistemic aspect is shrouded in an emotional blanket. The OED nicely distinguishes trust "in its subjective sense" (a feeling) from trust "in its objective sense," meaning the observance of one's word, the keeping of promises (fidelity), thus, allegiance to duty or person. This objective sense has some overlap with *loyalty*, which was discussed earlier in chapter 4. Even subjectively, faith is taken in an interpersonal, rather than a narrowly epistemological context; that is, it concerns knowledge by acquaintance rather than knowledge by abstract representation, knowledge of people rather than knowledge of propositions. In philosophy, to focus epistemologically, we typically suppress these interpersonal meanings of the word; this I note in passing lest I seem to do so in the sequel. But it is to be admitted that interpersonal dimensions of meaning may be richly present in religious contexts, and will be foremost for those who believe in a personal deity. This emotional wrapping is one reason *faith* is distorted if regarded as merely a matter of belief, where belief is reduced to its content.

Faith as trust is like hope: it bears a reference to the future. Sometimes we need to trust someone to do something for us, and yet have little more than hope it will get done. If we take the leap, as we must, then we believe on insufficient evidence, though it be best. Other times, we may repose in our emissary, and we trust with confidence. From the sketchy instances of interpersonal *faith* there is a smooth transition to the epistemological sense, when we believe something on insufficient evidence, perhaps because the alternatives are all less evident. From here it is but a small step to the narrowest of definitions, which I am combating, but which nevertheless finds its place in the dictionary, namely: *belief in something for which there is no proof*. So, as I say, the definition belongs in the dictionary; I am not arguing with a book. It is the collapsing of definitions in thought that I object to, in this case equating faith as *credence without evidence* with another meaning of "faith," also in the dictionary, namely, *belief in the truths of religion*, in God, the authenticity of revelation, specifically the (unspecified) beliefs effective of salvation (St. Peter's keys). The latter meaning is important in shifting from the believing to the thing believed, from the subjective state to the object of that state. This semantic nominalization is not merely objectification; a normative dimension is superadded: faith is that that which is *or ought* to be believed. The specific content of the beliefs necessary for salvation is, of course under dispute, but the *Oxford English Dictionary* (OED) tellingly notes that "there is general agreement in regarding [*faith*] as a conviction practically operative on the character and will, and thus opposed to the mere intellectual assent to religious truths (sometimes called speculative *faith*."[7] Thus the dictionary itself goes some way to making my point: we cannot argue against faith by treating it merely as a species of intellectual assent. Otherwise we shall find ourselves talking only to the faithless.

Nevertheless, as the definitions given so far indicate, even faith as credence can be distinguished by its object, by what it is we have faith in. From the point of view of semantics alone, it may be in God, in doctrine, in a code, but also in a person, an arrangement, or even an implement. Any form of trust or reliance is faith, if we wholly relax the requirements on the object.

We can interpret this variety of faiths, united by belief and distinguished by object, as two claims. First, we can identify the faith with the believing, and take the subjective act of believing to be essentially the same, regardless of object. This (in a way) is what I have been doing so far, in holding out hope for a generic, neutral definition of faith, acceptable to all parties to the dispute. I have also been claiming that this easy-going indifference, though it belongs where we find it in the dictionary, is misguided and unhelpful in the philosophic endeavor.

The second closely-related implicit claim is that religious faith is unique or special merely *due to the loftiness of its object*. Faith is a species of belief whose uniqueness is determined by the uniqueness of the object of faith, not by the nature of the act itself. This second claim is usually advanced as an intellectual defense of faith. It is one way to cleave to faith as belief, but at the same time avoid the rat's nest of issues skirted above. Note that I shall be proposing a more radical distinction between faith and belief, while the distinction now before us is decidedly less radical, being merely a distinction among objects. True faith, it says, is faith in the correct objects. Otherwise, faith is just belief by another name.

This position is not insane. It may seem boring. Mere credence in the regularity of nature is at best natural faith, an animal's or a physicist's faith. If I invest in a company by buying shares in it, I put my faith in the stock market and in that corporation. If I trust a con and get defrauded, one can say my faith has been broken. But nothing religious is going on here at all (on the contrary, in the last case, something *irreligious* has happened). What makes faith religious is the choice of object: one buys into God, or this or that particular divine doctrine; or one trusts one's eternal interests to a cosmic personality. What makes faith religious is the object of the phrasal verb *faith in*, in particular, the divinity of that in which one has faith. This is not Mammon, nor any thief. To switch the defense to offense, one might go further and say that science cannot even investigate this realm, since it only accepts as verification evidence of a very different sort and level.

This ploy may seem to be an advance, but it too makes a fatal mistake, and allows me rather to drive my wedge deeper. I am not arguing against the room it creates for freedom of faith, which I accept as a fundamental human liberty. Faith deserves a wide berth. What goes wrong, in my eyes, is that it persists in presuming that the movement in faith is identical to the movement of credence, *only the object differs*. What is going on when you believe you have two feet, or that the earth is round(ish), or that the sun is no god, or that there is a God, is the same gesture, the same assent, only in each case differently oriented, now toward nature, now beyond it. Only in one case is this assent an ascent, but that is incidental. Yet I say faith is not equivalent to any odd belief, nor yet is it a mere species of belief-looking-at-the-right-thing. I want to separate it entirely from belief, and place it in different epistemic company altogether. For looking up is not really the same as looking down, nor is it yet a matter of seeing what may be up there to be seen. Yet faith is like looking up: it is more like hope than belief. To reduce faith to belief is to eliminate its emotional register, in an act of epistemic purism.

If "faith" could only be defined as *not* mere credence, then the above philosophical spat could be dissolved in a single stroke. This time I heartily recommend such definitional dissolution, despite the semantic cost, which is a wedge between faith and belief. And this cost is not to be discounted, nor the distinction cheaply bought, since it wreaks havoc in conventional thinking, a havoc comparable to that caused by the artificial and temporary declaration at one intersection that for a time red shall mean go, and green stop. And yet—just as that dangerous and counterintuitive measure might be temporarily expedient, and enable traffic elsewhere in the grid to resume regular flow, so too this contrary and violent wedge might relieve the semantic congestion so obvious in the idle seesaw of this debate. So why not? Let's try it on for size.

There are many reasons to permit this reversal of mental traffic, epistemic benefits rather like light entering a darkened room. One low-hanging fruit is the death of the banal opposition of faith and doubt. Belief and doubt may be contraries, but faith and doubt are sometime bedfellows. I will not argue much for this here, as I have already stamped my verbal feet about it before.[8] Believers are no strangers to doubt. Faith may or may not survive doubt. The existence of doubt is not a refutation of faith. Faith is often more like struggle than belief.

Faith, to me, is more like surrender, less like a bid for knowledge. Yet it is profoundly related to truth; that relation *is* surrender. Faith is perhaps the nearest proximity to truth that does not claim it. Why should philosophy not love it, on etymological grounds alone? Since it is a personal matter, I will speak vaguely and indistinctly about my own experience, the only way I know how. I like to distinguish God as self or consciousness from the divine, that is, from a principle or law that may be neither a self nor conscious, but which is yet numinous or transcending or uncanny or otherwise godlike. An encounter with the latter need not call for or demand any belief at all. Faith can be seen as a (disciplined) openness toward experience of the divine, without the pretense of express belief in a divine self (a deity or god). Indeed, some beliefs offer only a deadening closure to all such future openness, and are therefore an obstacle to faith.

Have I succeeded? Have I torn apart your mental lexicon? Is it possible that faith in truth may proceed without belief? Is it not, in the end, the true believers who are the enemies of faith?

THE SACRED

It is difficult for philosophers to discuss the sacred without profaning it, at least if they are to speak *as philosophers*. But almost invariably they pay it this minimal respect, of *keeping it separate and apart* from philosophy. Of course, speaking *as a philosopher* is not necessarily advisable, and one is certainly entitled to drop the mask from time to time. But let us push the pretense further, and imagine philosophy had some positive obligation to speak *to* and *of* the sacred, to reason into it, if not reason it out entirely. For surely the strangeness of the sacred *as a philosophical subject* is that it wholly and most uncannily *defies* reason, befuddles it, and therefore rarely bemuses it. Why not see if we cannot be bemused by the sacred, and encounter it, if at all possible, through the form and mediation of a philosophy essay. Less likely things have happened.

Our word *sacred* is the past participle of Middle English *sacren*, to consecrate, or to render holy. Its Latin root *sacrare*, to set apart as holy, akin to *sancrire*, a verb meaning to make holy. There is as well the adjective *sacer* (meaning sacred), plus the nominalization *sacrum* (a sacred thing). The word *sacrifice* is perhaps its bloodiest living English cognate.

Another noteworthy set of meanings of the Latin verbal root is *to set apart* or *to allot*, hence *to curse*. The sacred is declared before it exists, it separates out the worthy and venerable from the profane and proscribed. The injunction of the sacred is that it must be maintained in its pristine purity, away from the defilements of the routine and everyday. This dualist antagonism (pure/impure; with-us/against-us) seems to be inherent in the notion of the sacred.

One can say that the sacred is what is regarded with reverence. But our reverence may also go missing or be misplaced. So what is sacred is what is *entitled* to veneration and to reverence, and what is associated with what is so entitled. The etymologies given above point in the direction of the holy. But what is that? In root, it means free from injury, whole, hale; by extension the holy is what is perfectly good, free from sin, and thus worthy of veneration, of being set apart. So the explanatory circle is complete and we are back where we started. This all but exhausts the philosophical help the dictionary can provide, except that *divine* is given as another synonym of *holy*. But I save this for later, since it subtly shifts the question away from the meaning of "sacred" and "holy" to the question of what is sacred and holy. I will focus on that question later.

To regard the cow as sacred is an Indian institution of great antiquity. It is connected with the milk that it offers, so essential and quotidian a food source, that does not involve killing (*ahimsa*).[9] But the word for cow can also mean light, and the "cows of dawn" represent the first light of dawn, which is a symbol of spiritual enlightenment. In the West, "Holy Cow!" is an innocent expression of child-like surprise; and the phrase "sacred cow" is used to denote something held to be above criticism, yet ripe for it. The phrase is a reproach. Here we see how what is held literally to be sacred becomes from another perspective childish, a cliché, a fetish, and no longer a symbol of the sacred, only of the irreproachable. I recall an offensive T-shirt (worn by a noted evolutionary philo-biologist at an academic conference) that read "sacred cows make great hamburgers." The sacred is also a target.

Philosophers in centuries past encountered Religion, and came away with their own pared-down package, the Philosopher's God of Rational Theology. This God in Theory exhibits a suitable array of perfections, such as omniscience, omnipotence, first cause, ultimate end, supreme being, infinitely infinite (as if any finite expression could capture that idea), and so on and so on. Notice that the sacred does not enter into it, except perhaps as an asymptote of wonder. It is as if the feeling of regard for the sacred is wholly another business than that with which philosophy occupies itself. And what else is the sacred, finally, than a feeling, an attitude, an orientation and spiritual deference, with a will more or less resolute to purify itself?

Encounter with the sacred is far more visceral than is reasoning about the ultimate parameters of existence. In an even more important contrast, philosophy is reputedly born of love, while the experience of the sacred is a species of fear, albeit a refined yet primeval fear, an awe; for example, that special fear and trembling felt before God or before anything else august or majestic. One fears a bear or a lion *for one's life*, but in the case of the sacred one fears *for the significance of one's life*. It is kin to the feeling that springs from a frank recognition of the smallness of our existence, the puniness of our most worldly concerns, and the vanity of all our vaunted wisdom. The right glimpse of the vast dark and endless night sky with its bewilderingly numerous glistening stars can startle us with a poignant reminder of our impotence and ignorance. Believers or not, we may—like Job in the face of the Unaccountable Almighty—rush to plant our foreheads in the dust. The sacred is what is apart from us, over and above us, above and beyond us, about which no true knowing is possible, and even daring to know is impermissible. How could philosophy be on friendly terms with the sacred thus defined?

Yet for all its strangeness, the sacred is strangely familiar. Certainly it is commonly and widely attested to. Those who claim to know it do so on the grounds of a most intimate and personal experience. It has been reported and studied by anthropologists in diverse cultures the world over. There is alleged to be something deeply and specifically human about this encounter with the sacred, thereby defining the human being not only by its rational faculties, but by certain spiritual possibilities as well. One's culture may lock one out of such experiences (as modern secular or non-religious cultures may be said to do); or it may *lock in* the interpretive parameters of one's experience of it. Still, that only circumscribes the social contingencies that may impinge on the experience of the sacred; it does not eliminate the sacred or reduce it to culture, still less to pathological subjectivity. The point is this: the sacred has as good a claim to reality as do dreams. The sacred is strange and familiar like dreams are strange and familiar. Indeed, dreams are a major venue for the encounter with the sacred. As a psychological phenomenon, inclusive of its various social dimensions, the sacred is present and something to be accounted for.

Perhaps Reason itself has something to learn by looking at this phenomenon, even while bracketing all questions of its ultimate validity. For we need to go beyond this question of the psychology of the sacred, and on to the ontology of it, the being and reality of the sacred. At least, this is the line I am drawing, for the purposes of this essay, between a mere recognition of a psychological reality, on the one hand, and philosophical pronouncements upon the substance of a topic. So let us begin again, with an eye to the question of nouns, not merely adjectives. Let us look—not at the question what is it like to *experience* the sacred, that raw divine fear just canvassed, but at that harder, more metaphysical question: what is (or ought to be regarded as) sacred?

As a philosopher, I am ashamed even to think I have a right, still less a duty, to speak to this lofty and sensitive issue. But undaunted I will tread onward, hoping not to step on any pious toes. For the sake of inquiring, the sacred is not to be dismissed as merely subjective, a relativist's whim. Nor is every impulsive claim to recognize it to be regarded as authentic. Yet I am not attempting the impossible, namely to produce a criterion by which to distinguish authentic from inauthentic experiences of the sacred. All I have suggested, so far, is that any test for authenticity is not wholly a matter of evaluation of the subjective experience, but must involve some consideration of the (wonted or alleged) object of the experience. It is with this modest end in mind that I turn to the question: What is it, finally, that *is* sacred; and not merely: what does it mean to be sacred? This is the hunt for the *sacrum*, not just the sacred.

The answer that leaps most obviously to mind is God, not indeed the denuded God of Rational Theology, the spirit of a living faith. What other fount of the sacred could there be? In so far as the sacred is what is holy, and the holy means the divine, then it would seem God is the obvious candidate as the being most worthy of pious veneration. But there are layers of philosophic subtlety here, so in the interests of exploring philosophic options, let's draw some fine lines. There is God; and there are the gods (or deities); and there is the divine, a law or principle, but a mere abstraction. Are they not holy in different ways? God as Absolute Spirit, as perfect goodness, has dibs on holiness. But are personifications ever perfectly good? Deities are personifications, depictions of the divine as an individual subjectivity with enduring traits and self-consciousness, having mental capacities like love or anger or jealousy or care or knowing. Can we have the same feeling-relations with a personage as we can with the Most High? Is encountering the holy-with-a-mask not totally different than encountering the holy-without-a-mask? But beyond God and gods, there is the merely god-like, the divine. No person, so not grasped by personification; absolute, perhaps, in that it is unconditional, but no Spirit. I am thinking of the Tao, the eternal way that cannot to told. The Tao is arguably sacred, but not God nor any deity, and is misconstrued if wantonly personified. The Way is a law or principle, not a person or an eminent majestic being. Texts too can be sacred, or divine, without being gods; but that is usually understood derivatively, as "contagion" from some original source. But the nameless Tao is the original source, so it does not derive its holiness from elsewhere. Indeed, if it is not an outright mistake, it is at least a faith-defining doctrine to equate the sacred with God, or even with any particular set of deities, and maybe with divinity as such. The sacred may be honored without being personified. The holy may be acknowledged even when God is not. To be godless does not entail one abandons the sacred. Atheists too are even accountable for the sacred, for the divine may be a what without being a who. (In the case of the Tao, we may have to say a What-Not; but the point remains.)

Far be it from me to settle which of these three candidates to be the *sacrum*, that is, the most proper object of the experience of the sacred. Options are my mandate. To end, let me give a brief survey of some philosophical and some anti-philosophical theories regarding the sacred and holy.

Consider first an overtly atheist—even hostile—account of the sacred. In *Human, All too Human*, Friedrich Wilhelm Nietzsche sketches the cultural origin of the sacred as the antiquity of the veneration of a tradition. Ancient morality (as opposed to the rules of selflessness enshrined in the modern ethics of Immanuel Kant) required piety in the form of obedience to "an age-old law or tradition," the purpose of which was "maintaining a *community*, a people."[10] Any old superstition will due to kick the thing off, then "each tradition grows more venerable the farther its origins lies in the past," a process that relies on *forgetting*. "Finally, the origin becomes sacred and awakens awe."[11] Here we have all the hallmarks of a scientific account of the sacred: superstition, obedience, ignorance, and fear. The theory strikes a blow against all four.

Modernity itself can be seen as the uprising of the secular and as the privatizing (de-public-ing) of the pretensions of the sacred. Sociologist and reluctant philosopher Emile Durkheim (1858–1917) advanced a theory of the sacred that rings some of the Nietzschean notes just sounded. But, on account of its unifying social function, Durkheim was anything but hostile to ritual. Indeed, Durkheim's distinction between the sacred and the profane (not the less extreme opposition between the sacred and the secular) must be understood not merely as a theory about what is essential to religion: it is far too profound to stop there. The flag is sacred. Even a scrap of the flag is sacred. No religion is involved here, but perhaps the key to religion is.[12]

The sacredness of the flag is due to it being a collective representation of the collective, of the society itself and the interests of the whole. Religion, for Durkheim, was the original form of this metaphorical collective self-representation. Thus religious institutions too are founded on collective representations of the general interest, and derive their authority and even a sort of objectivity therefrom.

On the basis, then, of the sacred-profane distinction, Durkheim forges not only a theory of religion, but a theory of society as such. The sacred is what is set apart by society to designate itself, in order that it may assert the collective interest over and above the unregulated private interests (the anomic profane). Without the sacred being set apart, society would be unable to marshal individual feeling toward social ends. "Religious force is the feeling the collectivity inspires in its members, but projected outside and objectified by the minds that feel it. It becomes objectified by being anchored in an object which then becomes sacred, but any object can play this role."[13] In spite of this arbitrariness, there remains some objectivity in Durkheim's account of the sacred, not because it represents the natural world (taken that way, it is a mere "tissue of lies"[14]); but because it is an accurate (though figurative) self-representation. By sharing such a representation, the individual with sacred thoughts is able to sacrifice themselves for the good of the whole society which the totem or sacred meaning represents.

In Durkheim we see in part the birth of sociology from philosophy. Arguably, we have not moved far beyond philosophy, despite trying. We can try to depart philosophy in a different direction to approach the sacred, but turning to theology. I wrap up this long and I am afraid still empty-handed essay with a brief reference to Rudolf Otto's tremendously fascinating account of the holy.[15]

To approach his subject, Otto lays aside philosophy and the attempt at rational understanding. Instead he wants to emphasize the feels. To do so, Otto puts aside (not to say *sets apart*) the *concept* of the holy, but not in order to impugn concepts or the rational understanding. The concept of the holy is not rejected (he calls it an *a priori* category); still less is it subtly undermined by an account of its origin in emotion, error and superstition. Unlike Nietzsche and Durkheim, Otto is a believer (not, however, a Christian supremacist). The *concept* is merely put aside in order to be gone beyond, so that real religion may be got to. The concept has a Hebrew name (*qādosh*), but "the Latin *sanctus*, and more accurately still, *sacer,* are the corresponding terms."[16] But Otto also coins the brilliant new term *numinous* for his purpose, modeled on the word *ominous*. Yet far from explicating the concept, or defining holiness the way a profane philosopher might, Otto tells us he is instead evoking religious feeling, the better to know the holy, since reason only goes so far. Speaking emotively, *the holy is the awful overpowering energy that fascinates*. The *mysterium tremendum* [great or profound mystery] scares and overpowers us with its urgent majesty, yet draws us ineluctably toward it. Our intellectual defenses down, we approach a-feared and aroused. Yet what we approach goes so far beyond our intellectual pigeon-holes of omniscient, omnipotent and omnibenevolent that we may only gape and wonder and love back. But unlike mystics we have no need otherwise to dispense with rationality or the consciousness of everyday.

In other words, contact with the sacred is an experience of Total Otherness (*ganz anders*), of transcendence, of forces or powers or meanings or realities beyond human ken. This is meant to be a more descriptive, more phenomenological account of that which we encounter when we feel the holy dread we call respect for the sacred. This sort of description tries to provide insight by gaining doctrinal neutrality; though Otto is a Christian, his account is by intention *not* restricted to Christianity, but offered instead as what is essential to any religion. The transcendent is wholly other but it has currency in all the world's traditions. As in Durkheim, that claim is highly questionable. For instance, Otto does not hesitate to find the holy in the Tao and in Buddhism. If the holy means perfectly good, it would apply, as the Buddha is said to have rooted out all sin; but this is precisely the ethical and rational sense (the "concept" of the holy) that Otto put aside to begin. Insofar as the experience of sacred or the holy involved dread of a great power (*majestas*), it seems singularly inapplicable to the Tao as divine principle, and to the Buddha in *Abhaya mudrā* ("Fear not!" hand gesture).

The power of Otto's account is felt most vividly in the idea that in the feeling of sacredness the self is in immediate contact with Absolute Otherness. By its contact it is known (and that in innumerable cultural forms). But as absolute other, it is unknowable. You can just taste the paradox.

I have inched toward the sacred, but it outpaces me in retreat. Is the sacred perhaps scared? I am typing as fast as I can, but the essay is over and I must admit defeat. Can't someone sprinkle some holy water or ashes over my slow-moving text, consecrate it a little? It deserves a good burial. I commend it to the grave, unfinished as it is.

Bless you too. Let us congregate in the hallowed name of Philosophy, and once more enact our convivial ritual. Let's get holy.

WORSHIP

Worship is the exultation of the bow. Whether on your knees, your face in the dust, or choking near the sacrificial flames; whether at the sanctified place and ordained time, or according to your own whimsical and extemporary ceremony; whether your idols are graven and detestable, or your master is invisible and invincible, worship delivers what William James called an "organic thrill" and promises a share in divine glory.[17] Some will tell you it is obligatory, others will say it is a human necessity. "All glory to God," they say in the doing, but thereby they also mean to gain in righteousness. And even the righteous will tell you (along with the disbelievers) that we need our worship more than God needs our worship.

In our age, public worship is practically an embarrassment. One does not discuss one's worship around the water-cooler or over the backyard fence. ("So, the other day, praying to God, I realized my cosmic insignificance. It was great!") Real men keep that kind of thing private. Worship is for softies. One is not supposed to have anything to say about it. I am confident, given my knowledge of these things, that I will say all the wrong things. Let that be your warning, and my advance plea for forgiveness.

For those late world-enders new to worship, I offer this precautionary advice, based on my cursory study of these matters. You will be glad to know that worship no longer requires human or animal sacrifice. For millennia now, blood has not worked to propitiate the gods, although it is still routinely spilled for political reasons (attended by all the routine religious rationalizations, of course).

People are much less picky these days about where you worship (as long as it is not in their face). It seems God's grandeur is no longer an architectural thing. Originally God gave location hints, and alters were built where divine interventions occurred. Gradually, God stopped showing up, and people built temples anywhere. Thereafter those sites became holy, and the temple needed to be kept pure. Construction followed obscure but divine rules, and every brick had to be in the right place for the ritual worship to succeed. Nowadays any old shed clapped together will do, or a tent, even a street corner. Radio and television made the airwaves, especially Sunday morning time slots, into virtual houses of worship. It turns out—your living room and Zoom account are location enough. Your body is the temple, the Hindu Scriptures agree.[18] And in Romans, "offer your bodies as living sacrifices."[19] So despite God's apparent retreat from the world, worship is diversifying and cropping up all over.

Another big improvement has come from innovations in what to worship. Moloch and Ba'al are out, as is Thunder and Fire; and all the gold and silver idols have long been melted down and spent. Power and gold continue to attract devotees and to win their worship, but that has by now become almost wholly secular. Hero-worship has faded, but in its place we have the glamor industry and an unsurpassable celebrity system. The only sacrifice still required for any of these pursuits is your sanity (which anyway is not very practical in the contemporary world). Even the duty to worship has been replaced by a broad normalization of the ideals of fame, ambition and lucre:

they are what everyone wants. So you no longer need to feel bad about selling your soul for them.

For a long time, all the most respectable objects of worship have been invisible, which leaves the adoring a lot of latitude for interpretation. Basically, nobody can really check what you are worshiping in there, so you can get away with revering almost anything, as long as you do not tell anyone. Here on the West Coast the only blasphemy is suggesting that maybe not just anything goes.

Indeed, excessive love of anything can be called worship. But worship by the pious is generally restricted to God, or abstract principles like Truth and Right. The intricate interdependencies of Nature, "whose subtle weaves in time make all the generations possible,"[20] also garner their share of adulation. Deuteronomy prohibits worship of the sun, the moon or the stars (on penalty of stoning),[21] but perhaps the earth itself and nature are making a comeback, grabbing back part of their ancient market share of worship. Nevertheless, however green the churches are becoming, there remain many who insist on revering the creator more highly than all that is creaturely, and who recommend reserving your most high love for the invisible spirit that moves the world, and not for the inscrutable tangle of Leviathan, the world-dragon.

When God appears to Job and his friends from a whirlwind, he asks what they think they know, and whether they can grasp the inestimable mystery that is the world.[22] In effect: "Were you there when the heavens were erected? Can you bridle Leviathan?" Job drops, prostrates, his forehead to the earth. The reasons for the world are not knowable to us. This is cause for wonder, and worship is to spirituality what wonder is to philosophy. Wonder is the awe of philosophy; worship is the awe of spirituality. The perplexity of the world compels wonder, but does it provoke worship? When God draws near, becomes familiar, the posture of worship is instinctively assumed, even by the most rational heathens. And it is no wonder! So I ask: does philosophy have its worship? Or is philosophy merely an idol-smasher? Or perhaps it is hair-splitting to draw distinctions within awe, as if awe were not all reason being silenced.

In a world of one-upmanship, worship is self-downmanship. Worship is submission. In Greek and Hebrew the word for worship originally signified service, in particular, the labor service a slave owes its master. Worship is a reminder of our humility. In the wager of worship, God holds the highest card. Worship is like self-decapitation: when your head has got you into trouble, why not lose it? Worship puts the self out of the way, relegates it to a lowly position, the better to appreciate the magnanimity of God. Worship fixes us in our place, insists we are one small part only. It regulates the self by putting itself in right relations with all that is sacred and holy.

Socrates was not fooling when he said his mission of philosophy was sacred, demanded of him by the gods. His ignorance was his worship: it was his bow to truth. Not my will, but thine be done—that is the mental gesture of worship. Not my opinions, but the real Truth: that painful sacrifice of the *appearance* of knowledge is what all honest skeptics must demand of themselves. Socrates sacrificed his knowledge to wisdom: he gave up everything he thought he knew to have a new chance with Truth, a new relationship. Henceforth, truth would lead the way, and he would follow (as he said) wherever the argument leads. Logic and reason itself become the altar, which then became stained with the blood of the ignorant, ultimately, with Socrates' own blood.

Do not worship from a distance. Step near. Enter Reason's temple. Present your living bodies to Philosophy.

COMPASSION

Compassion, in three words, is truth, love, and everything. Or at least, these are the pegs upon which I shall hang this essay.

Truth

At first it may seem that truth and compassion ought to be distinguished. Much seems to separate them. May I hand out some worn truisms? Truth is known to the mind, compassion to the heart. Truth is intellectual and thought about; compassion is emotional and felt. Truth imposes, it is recognized, even deferred to. Compassion only gives; it is projected and sent outward without hindrance. Truth excludes, for it separates out the false. Compassion includes, it extends to one and all.

These dualistic truisms are not only well-worn, they are also worn out. Banish them all! Truth and compassion may not be strictly identical, but they are kissing cousins, and inseparable.

First, truth flanks compassion like bread in a sandwich. Compassion may arise spontaneously, and one might even say it must, since compelled compassion is no compassion. But compassion is not a duty or ethical necessity; it is a virtue, a spiritual excellence, over and above the stern call of duty. But how can it arise at all without conditions or context? At the very least, there must be an object at whom the compassion is directed. One may have compassion for all beings together, but here we have many objects, not none. Compassion that is strictly nameless is only a useless wish, albeit pleasant in the feeling. Compassion arises from the recognition of suffering, or at least of the potential for improvement or advancement in the object. The recognition of suffering is the recognition of a truth, as is the recognition of imperfection. Compassion addresses itself to specific needs; its hands are never idle. Compassion always addresses a known misery, and knowledge implies truth.

Fine, you say, but is this sandwich not open-faced? What other bread is there? So there is truth before compassion, stimulating it. Is there truth after compassion, like a second slice? Indeed, compassion makes possible knowledge not otherwise attainable. Love of others reduces one's exaggerated concern about one's own problems, and this improved perspective is more in line with truth. Compassion for self yields self-knowledge not attainable to those who reserve a special aggression to self, in a heroic self-delusion. The truth of the equality of all is what underlies the applicability of compassion to all beings, but it is only visible to the self that knows its selflessness. One may even say, the more perfect or complete one's compassion, the more one sees the fundamental non-duality of our joint nature. Some truths must be felt, and that is only possible when compassion has softened one's hard edges.

The truth of relatedness inspires and underpins compassion, which alone develops the sensitivity to perceive the truth of relatedness. Truth and compassion form a virtuous cycle that spirals development ever higher. They are not bifurcated categories. They are not parallel silos of virtue, but an interacting double helix. By no means should the graceful, subtle and active distinction between them be confused with the static, dualistic, and physiologically antiquated metaphor of heart and mind. The latter is a cultural confusion no less pernicious for its advanced age and undimmed allure.

But a logical circle will not convince you, so I mention instead the vast realm of moral truth, much of which is unknowable without compassion, if only because compassion in part makes things true. On the pragmatic conception of truth, particular social realities that (like recycling) depend on many people doing a little rather than any one doing most. Moral truths are social truths that are maintained in the believing, and cease to be true when they have ceased to be believed. That does not make them arbitrary, but it does allow for a semblance of collective freedom, the basis of all legitimate togetherness. Compassion makes certain kinds of communities possible, composed of truths woven by social action. In short, some truths depend upon compassion, which wraps up both my sandwich and my argument. Onward to Love.

Love

Granted, at first blush, compassion seems more like love than truth, but herein lurks another welter of illusions. Let me begin by granting the equation, at least nominally. I have already substituted "love" for "compassion" once in my argument, and I reserve the poetic right to equate them, and make either do the work of the other. After all, loving couples help each other out; why should not the intimate verbal couple composed of these two words do so as well? I will therefore not attempt to drive any final semantic wedge between love and compassion, for they are working namesakes, and one must never sever asunder what god or semantics has put together.

That said, let me now proceed to divide rhetorically what I have nominally entwined. For there are yet worlds of difference in the connotations of these allied words. One falls in love, but never in compassion. Love is tempted to possession, compassion never is. Love is partial, and segregates out immediate loved-ones from all the rest for special favor. Compassion is impartial, abounding universally, extending near and far, to the loved and to the unloved, as much to the good as to all evildoers. Even spiritual love hates the sin (though it spares the sinner), whereas in compassion there is zero room for hate.

Love is heated, compassion is calm. Love feeds desire, compassion abides in equanimity. Love is passion, compassion is dispassion. Love bleeds from the heart, and is crushed if not requited. Compassion gently overflows and asks nothing in return. Love stops at the child, the boyfriend, the hubby, one's parents, and sometimes the relatives (provided they do not stay longer than a week). Compassion passes beyond the walls of home or city, beyond nation or team or even species. Compassion is a limitless abode. Love stops at the fated One. Compassion yields to the Many.

Compassion is loving-kindness: aspects of feeling and action are both present. Indeed, my rhetorical black-and-white, on nearer refraction, presents a rainbow, a myriad of things to do in the throes of compassion. In what follows, I rely in large measure on Maha Thera Narada's translation *A Manual of Abhidhamma*.[23]

Compassion is only one of four limitless abodes, limitless because they are attitudes that apply universally to all beings. This is a meditative state relating you energetically to the universe, not a nesting instinct or a comfort drive, not social grooming or family planning. This is no worldly abode, but a godly realm, a form of divine mind, a slice of sublime life. That is fancy talk to say it is a state of life, rather than a state of mind; it is a way of mental being, not just a mood or a passing emotion. Compassion is not a feeling but a flow of feelings—steady, exuding, filling all space.

But as such it does not exist alone. Three other illimitable abodes arise together and support each other. I have mentioned loving-kindness (or *metta*) which softens the heart. It is distinguishable from personal affection (from love, as I have called it, above), and indeed an enmity exists between them. For affection masquerades as compassion, and fakes it. However, *metta* also has a direct or diametrical opposite, namely, hatred, one of the roots of all evil. Hatred lashes out, protecting the illusory boundary around the self. Compassion reaches out, but in so doing weakens that same boundary. *Metta* culminates in identification of oneself with all beings. The gesture of *metta* is the disarming smile.

Another illimitable abode is called *karuna*, also a kind of compassion, but the kind that *makes the hearts of the good quiver when others are subject to suffering*. Quivering is not softness, so these two are distinct qualities, indeed different acts of the meditating mind. *Karuna* is the will to remove suffering and reduce harm. Sadness and grief are the inferior namesakes of this harm-reduction approach to compassion; in truth, they are enemies of compassion, and sap its strength. But the mirror image or direct moral opposite of *karuna* is cruelty of any kind. Perhaps the signature gesture of *karuna* would be the comforting embrace.

Mudita or infinite sympathetic joy, a third abode, is quite another form of compassion. If *karuna* removes harms, *mudita* celebrates blessings. Its gesture, I imagine to be a warm congratulatory handshake. Its diametrical opposite is jealousy, and its ersatz form is exhilaration, excitement. This compassion exults in the joys of others, admiring their virtues without taint of envy or selfish desire. This is neither soft nor quivering—so a third quality emerges, another gesture or act of compassion that does not detract at all from the other two, but adds to them.

The fourth factor in sublime mentality is, perhaps, not strictly a sort of compassion, but it is like a fuel to the other three limitless abodes. It is dispassion, equanimity, a mind balanced between desire and aversion. Its cheap imitation, a shoddy knock-off, is hedonic indifference. Equanimity is a positive state of mind, not a neutral state of mind. It is an active presence brought to bear on experience which has consequences in the form of increased sensitivity, an enhanced capacity to feel. Equanimity increases subtlety, as one assumes a finer and finer balance. When equanimity is present, its mirror image opposite cannot be. This is passion, including those passions just mentioned that directly oppose the three compassions. Equanimity is not compassion, but its presence counteracts hatred, grief, and envy, thus allowing the myriad of compassionate attitudes to flourish.

And Everything

Therefore equanimity, as the fuel of the compassions, is a immediate cause of compassion, a friend and accomplice of compassion, and in that sense it becomes compassionate, even if it is not a form of compassion per se. In a court of law it would make no difference. And this allows me my transition to my third peg, everything. Equanimity brings everything together. It overcomes the divisions implicit in the fevered mind, which seeks a false unity in attachment to things. Impartiality smiles at all opposites, embracing them all, accepting every experience. Equanimity faces life and death the same way. It sees pleasure and pain, but it never winks or cries. Everything is okay to equanimity, although most of it hurts like hell and is painful to watch. Even the dissolution of the self, and the compassionate identification with all beings, with its total destruction of the illusion of independent existence, merits only the calm curious gaze of equanimity. So you see my sneaky argument: equanimity is everything, and equanimity is compassion, so compassion is everything.

Compassion is truth—my first overstatement. Compassion is love—my second overstatement. Now the third—compassion is everything. I have not left this to hang on one tenuous argument, but I have hinted at it all along. Compassion extends to one and all, I said, compassion is universal. *Metta* culminates in identification with all beings. What melts the boundary between self and other unites all things. What transcends the narrow partisanship of me and mine, brings us together, and places me on the same level as all you others. Compassion is also everything in the way that leadership is everything: and compassion, I allowed, ought to lead to truth. What should it profit a man if he gain everything and lose compassion? Compassion is more than everything—it rules all else, the love that conquers all.

IMMORTALITY

He who binds to himself a joy
Does the winged life destroy;
But he who kisses the joy as it flies
Lives in eternity's sun rise.

—William Blake[24]

Said the spirit to its mortal frame: "You are not forever. Already you are breaking down, becoming clumsier, weaker. You are not long for this world, because you are from and of this world. I, however, am forever, but I am only visiting you for a little while. I have not minded being neglected and overlooked by you; I have been patient while you indulged in your life. I admit, just once I became dejected when you were asked to speak openly for me, and you remained silent. But that passed, as will you. Yet I will survive, and one day I will leave you. For me at that moment there will be some sadness, for it will be our final parting. Also I will lose my current perspective on time, which you provide, being so firmly positioned within it. (It has been interesting, though it does drag on a bit). There is a kind of forgetting that occurs when one resumes one's eternal posture. People worry about it, exaggerate the knowinglessness of death; due to their mortal uncertainty they discount the infinite, obliterating the splendor of the knowledge to which one also returns. Yet I will hate to see you go, shuffled off, in a heap, or a hole, reduced perhaps to ashes. They say the dead feel no pain, but it is their bodies they no longer feel. Mourners sometimes take comfort that the deceased is protected in death, but it is only the body that is protected after death;—*they* protect it, so that they can mourn over it and weep upon it. Eternally we are beyond suffering, but not beyond pain. And the immortal spirit is not protected *by* death, because it is beyond death, untouched by it, beyond protection too, and beyond all need of protection. Never forget, while you still have tears, that spirits too, can weep."

And the spirit continued: "You are not just any body, you are mine, and I have always loved you. You started the bitter feud of dualism, and you continue to wage it solo. Your biggest weapon against me is your neglect. Your life long you have paid little attention to me, while I have always loved you, stood beside you unwavering, always offered you my aid and counsel. In your darkest moments I was there. In your victorious heights I was there. In clear sight of danger you recklessly risked, I spoke firmly in your ear and you saved yourself and several others. Still I got no thanks. Most pathetic is the way you punish yourself with your love of poisons in order to keep me at arm's length. The least reflection shows you cannot harm me in this way. You harm only yourself, and thus become blind to my subtle love of you. If you could but rouse yourself in my memory, awaken again to the pure love of the eternal, feel my gentle murmuring in your heart, and requite me now with a fleeting kiss, I would bless your bodily existence again and return you to your natural senses. For we were made to be together, sweet body, together in this very moment. Refuse me no longer. Kiss my timeless lips."

But the disbelieving body was unmoved by the rapturous pleadings of its immortal spirit, and went on chewing its earthly cud. It faintly heard the passionate spirit-song, but only considered it good for its digestion. At length the spirit came very close and whispered, in a voice of great authority: "I *was* from the very beginning. I was here before you were physically possible, before life itself, before the earth. I sang for you for eons before your arrival. Now I am with you I want to help carry your burdens, but you are too proud of your edges and boundaries to recognize me. Only look to me, and you will see infinity. Leap into my well, and you will enjoy a bottomless glory. I am contained as a requisite aspect of each passing moment; through me you share in all creation. You can see my face in the birth and death of each instant, but not with those fleshpots you call eyes. I am your intersection with the divine and all things holy, but you have forgotten how to kneel, how to feel, how to heal yourself. Embrace me and be restored. Do not wait till the next great scare, or for the shock of age or approaching death, before you prostrate to me. I will be with you then, but thereafter I will be without you. So come to me now, come urgently, with all your current vigor. Deny no more our fated union, for the moment of love is upon us even now . . . *one kiss! . . .*"

And yet, in spite of the spirit's heated ministrations, the body resisted her advances and continued its digesting, ruminating like an old cow on the known, and keeping its preachy songbird suitor away by giving its tail a flit.

NOTES

1. There is an allusion here to the lyrics of Leonard Cohen, "The Stranger Song," *Songs of Leonard Cohen* (album) (New York: Columbia Records, 1967).

2. Of course, if faith is taken as a species of ignorance, as belief without evidence, then the doctrines of reincarnation and karma are indeed matters of faith; for it is hard to say that there is any more evidence for these theories than for the existence of pearly gates at the end of time. But I am rejecting that very conception of faith (see next essay in this chapter); for one cannot simply stipulate that faith is ignorance, if one is to play fair. My point is *not* that there exists adequate evidence for any of these doctrines, but that assent to them (faith in them) is in itself not a virtue. Nor is obedience or credulity. Not blind faith in, but insight into—or understanding of—karma and reincarnation (*samsara*) is what is required if one would reach the highest goal of liberation (*moksha*). Belief despite evidence confers no merit. At best, it is entry-level child's play.

3. In Sigmund Freud's theory, "the *superego* is an agency or institution in the mind," in *Civilization and Its Discontents* (1930), trans. Joan Riviere (New York: Dover, 1994), 63. He writes: "Civilization, therefore, obtains the mastery over the dangerous love of aggression in individuals by enfeebling and disarming it and *setting up an institution within their minds* to keep watch over it, like a garrison in a conquered city" (51–52; emphasis mine). To this one might well ask: what is a social institution, and what is it doing in the mind?

4. Compare: There is an accepted sense of the word "theory" that is synonymous with a sense of the word "hypothesis." Yet it is misleading to speak of the *hypothesis of natural selection*, as if that theory were not manifestly established, that one can, without inconsistency and even some understatement, call it a well-established hypothesis. There is something iffy about a hypothesis, going by the semantic feel of the latter term. But that semantic feel is no analytic truth; it is easily erased by prefixing the term with adjectives like "proven" or "confirmed." One cannot stipulate one's way to a philosophy, but people try.

5. On inductive logic, or what he calls "probable reasoning," see David Hume, *Enquiries Concerning Human Understanding and Concerning the Principles of Morals*, ed. from Posthumous ed. of 1977, L. A. Selby-Bigge, 3rd ed., ed. with rev. P. H. Nidditch (Oxford: Clarendon Press, 1978), sect. 4, 25; 6, 46–47. Also see Hume's *A Treatise of Human Nature* (1739–1740), ed. L. A. Selby-Bigge. 2nd ed., ed. P. H. Nidditch (Oxford: Clarendon Press, 1978), bk. 1, 3. Inductive arguments are non-demonstrative arguments, arguments that give evidence but not proof of their

conclusion. Since inductive arguments are empirical, they have often been a disappointment to philosophers.

6. Hume on the necessity of belief to get on with life, or "animal faith": "To consider the matter aright, reason is nothing but a wonderful and unintelligible instinct in our souls" (Hume, *Treatise*, bk. 1, 3, 16; see also bk. 1, 4,7). Despite offering a kind of mental health warning, against the "pensive melancholy" and "cold reception" that await those who engage in "abstract thought and profound researches," Hume argues for a balanced approach: "Be a philosopher; but, amidst all your philosophy, be still a man" (Hume, *Enquiries Concerning Human Understanding* [1748/1777], sect. 1, 4).

7. Throughout this paragraph, I again rely for many particulars on the *Oxford English Dictionary* (*OED*), Compact ed. (Oxford: Oxford University Press, 1982); but the key definitions mentioned are also in *Merriam-Webster Collegiate Dictionary*, 11th ed. (Springfield, MA: Merriam-Webster, 2003), the quotation is from the "theological" entry for *faith* (1.3) appears on 952.

8. Faith and doubt go together, so doubt per se is no refutation is faith. The fallacy is the clamoring for certainty, an aim best served by dropping it. Making do with ignorance is not really a choice, except for those who forego omniscience.

9. *Ahimsa* is non-violence; see the heading "Good," in chap. 5 of this book.

10. Friedrich Wilhelm Nietzsche, *Human, All Too Human: A Book for Free Spirits* (1878), trans. Marion Faber, with Stephen Lehmann (Lincoln: University of Nebraska Press, 1984), 66; emphasis in the original.

11. Friedrich Wilhelm Nietzsche, *Human, All Too Human*, 66.

12. Emile Durkheim, *The Elementary Forms of Religious Life* (1912), trans. Carol Cosman, abridged with intro. Mark S. Cladis (Oxford: Oxford University Press, 2001). The flag is discussed chap. 7, sect. 4, 169–74.

13. Durkheim, *Elementary Forms*, 174. "Collective representation of things often attribute to them properties that are not inherent in any form or to any extent. They can turn the most ordinary object into a sacred and very powerful being. And yet, though purely ideal, the powers conferred operate as though they were real; they determine man's conduct as imperatively as physical forces" (173).

14. Durkheim, *Elementary Forms*, 170.

15. Rudolf Otto, *The Idea of the Holy*, trans. John H. Harvey (Oxford: Oxford University Press, 1923).

16. Otto, *Idea of the Holy*, 6.

17. William James, *The Varieties of Religious Experience: A Study in Human Nature* (1901–1902) (New York: Collier, 1961), chap. 2, 40. Based on 1901–1902 lectures. "Religious awe is the same organic thrill which we feel in a forest at twilight, or in a mountain gorge; only this time it comes over us at the thought of our supernatural relations."

18. There is 1 Corinthians 3:16–17: "Know ye not that ye are the temple of God, and that the Spirit of God dwelleth in you?" (*Holy Bible*, Authorized King James Version [hereafter cited KJV], Collins World, n.d.), as well as 3:19–20. In context, a key biblical concern here is sexual ethics. But in the Indian context the phrase has a quite different significance. With allusions to the Vedic fire ritual, *Brahma Upaniṣad* 2 refers to the "god-filled fire that keeps guard inside the Brahman-city of human

body." See also *YogaSīkhā Upaniṣad* verse 4, in Paul Deusson's *Sixty Upaniṣads of the Veda*, trans. V. M. Bedekar and G. B. Palsule (Delhi: Motilal Banarsidass, 1980), pg. 2, 710. In the Upaniṣad context, with the identification of Atman and Brahman, self and god, and of god and the ritual implements, these latter in turn come to be identified as self. When internalized and introjected, the external implements, even the officiating priests and the actual fire, become extraneous, and the whole spiritual business moves within, where it always was. The external ritual drops away and one seeks to know God within without mediation. "The body is the temple" comes to mean that one can seek the truth within, without obligatory intercessors or officiating intermediaries. Also, conversely, the actual Hindu temple symbolizes the macrocosm as the body of God.

19. Romans 12:1, *The NIV Study Bible: New International Version*, general ed. Kenneth Barker (Grand Rapids MI: Zodervan, 1985) (hereaftere cited NIV).

20. From "Gold is Plenty," an unpublished poem by the author.

21. Deuteronomy 4:19 and 17:3–5 (KJV).

22. Job 38–42 (KJV).

23. Anuruddha, A *Manual of Abhidhamma*, ed. and trans. Maha Thera Nārada, 4th rev. ed. (Kuala Lumpur, Malaysia: Buddhist Missionary Society, 1979), see esp. 404–5.

24. William Blake, "Eternity," in *The Portable Blake*, ed. Alfred Kazin (New York: Penguin, 1978), 135.

Bibliography

Allinson, Tris, ed. *State of the World's Birds: Taking the Pulse of the Planet*. Cambridge, UK: BirdLife International, 2018. https://www.birdlife.org/sites/default/files/attachments/BL_ReportENG_V11_spreads.pdf (accessed September 11, 2021).

Anuruddha. A *Manual of Abhidhamma*. Edited and translated by Maha Thera Nārada. 4th Revised ed. Kuala Lumpur, Malaysia: Buddhist Missionary Society, 1979.

Aristotle. *Categories*. (3–24), Translated by J. L. Ackrill. In *Complete Works of Aristotle*, edited by Jonathan Barnes. Princeton, NJ: Princeton University Press, 1984.

———. *Complete Works of Aristotle. The Revised Oxford Translation*. 2 vols. Edited by Jonathan Barnes. Princeton, NJ: Princeton University Press, 1984.

———. *Metaphysics*. Translated by W. D. Ross. In *Complete Works of Aristotle* (1552–1728), edited by Jonathan Barnes. Princeton, NJ: Princeton University Press, 1984.

———. *Nicomachean Ethics*. Edited and Translated by H. Rackham. In *Aristotle in 23 Volumes*, Vol. 19. Cambridge, MA: Harvard University Press, 1934. http://data.perseus.org/citations/urn:cts:greekLit:tlg0086.tlg010.perseus-eng1:1.

———. *Nicomachean Ethics*. Translated by Terence Irwin. Indianapolis: Hackett, 1985.

———. *Nicomachean Ethics*. Translated by W. D. Ross, revised by J. O. Urmson. In *Complete Works of Aristotle* (1729–1867), edited by Jonathan Barnes. Princeton, NJ: Princeton University Press, 1984.

———. *Politics*, translated by Benjamin Jowett. In *Complete Works of Aristotle*, edited by Jonathan Barnes. Princeton, NJ: Princeton University Press, 1984.

Bacon, Francis. *Essays* (1625). Amherst, NY: Prometheus Books, 1995.

Bateson, Gregory. *Steps to an Ecology of Mind*. New York: Ballantine Books, 1972.

Berger, Peter L., and Thomas Luckmann. *The Social Construction of Reality: A Treatise in the Sociology of Knowledge*. New York: Doubleday, 1966.

Blackmore, Susan. *Consciousness: An Introduction*. 2nd ed. Oxford: Oxford University Press, 2012.

Blake, William. *The Portable Blake*. Edited by Alfred Kazin. New York: Penguin. 1978.

Bodhi, Bhikkhu, trans. *The Connected Discourse of the Buddha: A New Translation of the Samyutta Nikāya*. 2 vols. Boston: Wisdom Publications, 2000.

———, ed. *In the Buddha's Words: An Anthology of Discourses from the Pāli Canon*. Boston: Wisdom Publications, 2005.

Bodhi, Bhikkhu, and Bhikkhu Nanāmoli, trans. *The Middle Length Discourses of the Buddha: A New Translation of the Majjhima Nikāya*. 4th ed. Translated, edited, and revised by Bhikkhu Bodhi. Kandi, Sri Lanka: Buddhist Publication Society, 1995.

Brown, Stuart. *Leibniz*. Minneapolis: University of Minnesota Press, 1984.

Buber, Martin. *I and Thou* (1923). Translated by Walter Kaufmann. New York: Charles Scribner's, 1970.

Campbell, Joseph. *The Hero With a Thousand Faces*. 2nd ed. Princeton, NJ: Princeton University Press, 1968.

———. *Transformations of Myth Through Time*. Directed by Stuart Brown. In association with Public Affairs Television and Alvin H. Perlmutter of Apostrophe S. Video. 14 episodes, 1989.

Campbell, Joseph, with Bill Moyers. *The Power of Myth*. New York: Doubleday, 1988.

———. *The Power of Myth*. Aired on PBS in 1988. Mystic Fire Video/Wellspring. DVD. 6 hours. 2001.

Canadian High School Ethics Bowl. Last updated 2021, https://www.ethicsbowl.ca/ (accessed September 12, 2021).

Cannon, Walter B. *The Wisdom of the Body*. Revised and enlarged ed. New York: W. W. Norton, 1939.

Chan, Wing-tsit. *A Source Book in Chinese Philosophy*. Translated and compiled by Wing-tsit Chan. Princeton, NJ: Princeton University Press. 1963.

Chāndogya Upaniṣad. Translation by Swami Lokeswarananda. Calcutta: Ramakrishna Mission Institute of Culture, 1998.

Chomsky, Noam. "Noam Chomsky on Taxes." *Chomsky's Philosophy*. October 25, 2015. https://www.youtube.com/watch?v=oYuQRjLcGjY (accessed July 15, 2021).

———. *Understanding Power: The Indispensable Chomsky*. Edited by Peter R. Mitchell and John Schoeffel. New York: New Press, 2002.

Chuang Tzu [Zhuangzi]. *Basic Writings*. Translated by Burton Watson. New York: Columbia University Press, 1964.

Cleveland-Peck, Patricia. "I Drink, Therefore I Am." *Sunday Telegraph*, November 10, 1996.

Confucius. *The Analects*. Translated by D. C. Lau. New York: Penguin, 1998.

Covey, Stephen R. *The Seven Habits of Highly Effective People: Restoring the Character Ethic*. New York: Free Press, 1989.

Cramer, Phebe, ed. "Defensiveness and Defense Mechanisms." Special issue. *Journal of Personality* 66 no. 6 (December 1998): 879–1157. https://onlinelibrary.wiley.com/toc/14676494/1998/66/6 (accessed September 14, 2021).

Curd, Patricia, ed. *A PreSocratics Reader: Selected Fragments and Testimonia*. 2nd ed. Translated by Richard D. McKirahan and Patricia Curd. Indianapolis: Hackett, 2011.

Dalley, Stephanie, trans. *Myths from Mesopotamia: Creation, the Flood, Gilgamesh, and Others*. Revised ed. Oxford: Oxford University Press, 2000.

Damasio, Antonio. *Descartes' Error: Emotion, Reason, and the Human Brain.* New York: Avon, 1994. Reprint. New York: Penguin, 2005.

———. *Looking for Spinoza: Joy, Sorrow, and the Feeling Brain.* Orlando, FL: Harcourt, 2003.

———. *The Strange Order of Things: Life, Feeling, and the Making of Cultures.* New York: Pantheon, 2018.

de Paula, Luisa. Review of *Philosophy A-Z. Essays for Cafe Philosophy*, by Michael Picard. *Philosophical Practice: Journal of the APPA* 10, no. 2 (July 2015): 1608–11. https://appa.edu/product/philosophical-practice-volume-10-2-july-2015-printed-version/ (accessed September 11, 2021).

Descartes, René. *The Philosophical Writings of Descartes.* Volumes 1–2. Translated by John Cottingham, Robert Stoothoff, and Dugald Murdoch. Cambridge: Cambridge University Press, 1984–1985.

Deusson, Paul. *Sixty Upaniṣads of the Veda.* Volumes 1–2. Translated by V. M. Bedekar and G. B. Palsule. Dehli: Motilal Banarsidass, 1980. Original German editions 1897–1921.

Duchesne-Guillemin, Jacques. *The Hymns of Zarathustra: Being a Translation of the Gāthās Together With Introduction and Commentary.* Translated from French by Mrs. M. Henning. London: Murray, 1952.

Dunbar, R. I. M. [Robin]. *Grooming, Gossip, and the Evolution of Language.* Cambridge, MA: Harvard University Press, 1998.

———. "Group Size, Vocal Grooming and the Origins of Language." *Psychonomic Bulletin & Review* 24, no. 1 (February 2017): 209–12. https://doi.org/10.3758/s13423-016-1122-6.

Durkheim, Emile. *The Elementary Forms of Religious Life* (1912). Translated by Carol Cosman. Abridged with Introduction by Mark S. Cladis. Oxford: Oxford University Press, 2001.

Einstein, Albert. *Relativity: The Special and General Theory.* New York: Henry Holt, 1920. https://www.ibiblio.org/ebooks/Einstein/Einstein_Relativity.pdf (accessed October 8, 2021).

Erikson, Erik H. *Childhood and Society.* 2nd ed. New York: W. W. Norton, 1950.

Freud, Sigmund. *Beyond the Pleasure Principle* (1920). Translated by James Strachey. New York: Bantam Books, 1959.

———. *Civilization and Its Discontents* (1930). Translated by Joan Riviere. New York: Dover, 1994.

———. *The Ego and the Id* (1923). Standard ed. Translated by Joan Riviere. Revised and edited by James Strachey. New York: W. W. Norton, 1960.

———. *The Interpretation of Dreams* (1900). Translated by James Strachey. New York: Avon, 1965.

———. *Three Essays on the Theory of Sexuality* (1899). Translated and edited by James Strachey. New York: Avon, 1962.

———. *Totem and Taboo* (1913). Translated by James Strachey. London: Routledge, 2002.

Friedländer, Paul. *Plato: An Introduction.* Princeton, NJ: Princeton University Press/ Bollingen, 1973.

Gandhi, Mohendas K. [Mahatma]. *All Men Are Brothers.* Edited by Krishna Kripalani. Paris and New York: UNESCO, 1958.

———. *Voice of Truth.* Edited by Shriman Narayan. Ahmedabad: Navajivan Publishing, 1968.

Gaukroger, Stephen. *Descartes: An Intellectual Biography.* Oxford: Clarendon Press, 1995.

Gay, Volney P. *Freud on Sublimation: Reconsiderations.* Albany: State University of New York Press, 1992.

Gleick, James. *Chaos: Making a New Science.* New York: Penguin, 1987.

Gödel, Kurt. "An Example of a New Type of Cosmological Solutions of Einstein's Field Equations of Gravitation." *Reviews of Modern Physics* 21 no. 3 (1949): 447–50. https://doi.org/10.1103/RevModPhys.21.447.

Goenka, S. N. *The Discourse Summaries.* Bombay: Vipashyana Vishodhan Vinyas, 1987.

Goethe, Johann Wolfgang von. *Maxims and Reflections.* 2nd revised ed. Translated by Thomas Bailey Saunders. London: MacMillan, 1908.

Guthrie, W. K. C. *Socrates.* Cambridge: Cambridge University Press, 1971.

Heidegger, Martin. *Basic Writings: From Being and Time* (1927) *to The Task of Thinking* (1964). Revised and expanded ed., edited by David Farrell Krell. London: Harper Perennial, 2008.

———. *On the Way to Language.* Translated by Peter D. Hertz. San Francisco: Harper & Row, 1971.

Hesiod. *The Poems of Hesiod.* Translated by R. M. Frazer. Norman: University of Oklahoma Press, 1983.

Hobbes, Thomas. *Leviathan* (1651). Edited by C. B. Macpherson. London: Penguin, 1985.

Holy Bible. Authorized King James Version (KJV). Collins World, n.d.

Hume, David. *Enquiries Concerning Human Understanding and Concerning the Principles of Morals.* Edited from Posthumous ed. of 1977 by L. A. Selby-Bigge. 3rd ed. Edited with revisions by P. H. Nidditch. Oxford: Clarendon Press, 1978.

———. *An Enquiry Concerning the Principles of Morals* (1751)*: A Critical Edition.* Edited by Tom L. Beauchamp. Oxford: Oxford University Press, 1998.

———. *A Treatise of Human Nature* (1739–1740). Edited by L. A. Selby-Bigge. 2nd ed. Edited by P. H. Nidditch. Oxford: Clarendon Press, 1978.

James, William. "Does 'Consciousness' Exist?" (1904). In *The Writings of William James: A Comprehensive Edition* (1904), edited by John J. McDermott, 169–83. Chicago: University of Chicago Press, 1977.

———. *The Principles of Psychology* (1890). Authorized ed. 2 vols. New York: Dover. 1950.

———. *The Varieties of Religious Experience: A Study in Human Nature* (1901–1902). New York: Collier, 1961.

———. "The Will to Believe." In *The Writings of William James: A Comprehensive Edition* (1904), edited by John J. McDermott, 717–35. Chicago: University of Chicago Press, 1977.

———. *The Writings of William James: A Comprehensive Edition.* Edited by John J. McDermott. Chicago: University of Chicago Press, 1977.

Jamison, Stephanie W., and Joel P. Brereton, trans. *The Rigveda: The Earliest Religious Poetry of India.* 3 vols. Oxford: Oxford University Press, 2014.

Jones, William. "The Third Anniversary Discourse." Paper delivered February 2, 1786. "On the Hindus." *Asiatick Researches* 1, 415–31.

Joyce, James. *A Portrait of the Artist as a Young Man.* New York: B. W. Huebsch, 1916.

Jung, Carl G. *Archetypes and the Collective Unconscious.* In *The Collected Works of C. G. Jung*, 2nd ed., edited by Gerhard Adler and R. F. C. Hull, Volume 9, Part 1, 3–41. Princeton, NJ: Princeton University Press, 1968.

———. *Dreams.* Translated by R. F. C. Hull. Princeton, NJ: Princeton University Press, 1974.

———. *Synchronicity: An Acausal Connecting Principle* (1952). Translated by R. F. C. Hull. London: Routledge and Kegan Paul, 1972.

Jung, Carl G., and C. [Karl] Kerényi. *Essays on a Science of Mythology: The Myth of the Divine Child and the Mysteries of Eleusis.* Translated by R. F. C. Hull. Princeton, NJ: Princeton University Press, 1969.

Kant, Immanuel. *Critique of Pure Reason* (1781/1787). Translated by Norman Kemp Smith. New York: St. Martin's Press, 1929.

———. *Critique of Pure Reason* (1781/1787). Edited and translated by Paul Guyer and Allen W. Wood. Cambridge: Cambridge University Press, 1998.

———. *Grounding for the Metaphysics of Morals* (1785). 2nd ed. Translation by James W. Ellington. Indianapolis: Hackett, 1983.

———. *Logic* (1800). Translated by Robert S. Hartman and Wolfgang Schwarz. New York: Dover, 1974.

———. *Observations on the Feeling of the Beautiful and Sublime* (1764). Translated by John T. Goldthwait. Berkeley: University of California Press, 1960.

Keats, John. *Poetical Works.* Edited by H. W. Garrod. Oxford: Oxford University Press, 1987.

Kopp, Sheldon B. *If You Meet the Buddha on the Road, Kill Him!* New York: Bantam Books, 1972.

Krishnamurti, J. [Jiddu]. *Freedom from the Known.* Edited by Mary Lutyens. Chennai: Krishnamurti Foundation, 1969.

———. "Truth Is a Pathless Land." Speech dissolving the Order of the Star of the East, Ommen, Holland, August 3, 1929. https://jkrishnamurti.org/about-dissolution-speech (accessed August 8, 2021).

Laden, Anthony Simon. *Reasoning: A Social Picture.* Oxford: Oxford University Press, 2012.

Lao Tzu. *Tao Te Ching.* Translated by Arthur Waley. Hertfordshire, UK: Wordsworth, 1997.

Leibniz, Gottfried Wilhelm. *Discourse on Metaphysics* (1686). Reprint ed. Translated by George R. Montgomery. La Salla, IL: Open Court, 1973.

———. "Letter to Arnauld, April 30, 1687." In *Philosophical Writings*, edited by G. H. R. Parkinson, translated by Mary Morris and G. H. R. Parkinson, 65–71. London: J. M. Dent, 1973.

———. *New Essays on Human Understanding* (c. 1704). Translated and edited by Peter Remnant and Jonathan Bennett. Cambridge: Cambridge University Press, 1981.

Lewin, Kurt. *A Dynamic Theory of Personality: Selected papers.* Translated by Donald K. Adams and Karl E. Zener. New York: McGraw-Hill, 1935.

———. *Principles of Topological Psychology*. Translated by Fritz Heider and Grace M. Heider. New York: McGraw-Hill, 1936.

Lindsay, D. Stephen, Delroy L. Paulhus, and James S. Nairne. *Psychology: The Adaptive Mind.* 3rd Canadian ed. Toronto: Thomson Nelson, 2008.

Locke, John. "A Discourse of Miracles" (1702). In *The Reasonableness of Christianity*, edited by I. T. Ramsey, 78–87. Stanford, CA: Stanford University Press, 1958.

———. *An Essay Concerning Human Understanding* (1690). Edited by Peter H. Nidditch. Oxford: Clarendon Press, 1975.

———. *Second Treatise of Government.* Edited by C. B. Macpherson. Indianapolis: Hackett, 1980.

MacLellan, Lila. "The Scientist Who Coined 'Stress' Wished He Had Chosen a Different Word for It." *Quartz at Work*. June 29, 2018; last updated July 2, 2018. https://qz.com/work/1316277/ (accessed July 2, 2021).

Mandeville, Bernard. *The Fable of the Bees and Other Writings*. Abridged ed. Edited by E. J. Hundert. Indianapolis: Hackett, 1997.

Manitoba Association for Rights and Liberties. Last updated 2021. http://www.marl.mb.ca/ (accessed September 12, 2021).

Marinoff, Lou. *Essays on Philosophy, Praxis, and Culture: An Eclectic, Provocative, and Prescient Collection*. New York: Anthem Press, 2022.

Mascaro, J., trans. *The Upanishads.* London: Penguin Books, 1965.

McClain, Ernest G. *The Pythagorean Plato: Prelude to the Song Itself.* York Beach, ME: Nicolas-Hays, 1984.

McDonagh, Don. *Martha Graham: A Biography*. New York: Popular Library, 1975.

Mead, George H. *Mind, Self, and Society*. Edited by C. W. Morris. Chicago: University of Chicago Press, 1934.

Merriam-Webster Collegiate Dictionary. 11th ed. Springfield, MA: Merriam-Webster, 2003.

Milton, John. *Paradise Lost*. In *Complete Poems*, edited by Charles W. Eliot. Seventh Book. New York: P. F. Collier, 1909–1914. https://www.bartleby.com/4/407.html (accessed September 12, 2021).

Miura, Isshū, and Ruth Fuller Sasaki. *The Zen Koan: Its History and Use in Rinzai Zen*. New York: Harvest, 1963.

Müller, F. Max. *India: What Can It teach Us? A Course of Lectures Delivered before the University of Cambridge*. London: Longmans, Green, 1883.

———. *Lectures on the Origin and Growth of Religion as Illustrated by the Religions of India*. London: Longmans, Green, 1878.

Nadler, Steven. *The Best of All Possible Worlds: A Story of Philosophers, God, and Evil in the Age of Reason.* Princeton, NJ: Princeton University Press, 2010.

Nietzsche, Friedrich Wilhelm. *Daybreak: Thoughts on the Prejudices of Morality* (1881). Translated by R. J. Hollingdale. Cambridge: Cambridge University Press, 1982.

———. *Die fröhliche Wissenschaft* ("la gaya scienza"). München: Wilhelm Goldmann, 1887.

———. *Human, All Too Human: A Book for Free Spirits* (1878). Translated by Marion Faber, with Stephen Lehmann. Lincoln: University of Nebraska Press, 1984.

———. *On the Genealogy of Morals* (1887). Edited by Keith Ansell-Pearson. Translated by Carol Diethe. Cambridge: Cambridge University Press, 2007.

The NIV Study Bible: New International Version. General editor Kenneth Barker. Grand Rapids MI: Zodervan, 1985.

Olivelle, Patrick, trans. *Upaniṣads.* Oxford: Oxford University Press, 1996.

Otto, Rudolf. *The Idea of the Holy.* Translated by John W. Harvey. Oxford: Oxford University Press, 1923.

Oxford English Dictionary (*OED*). Compact ed., 22nd printing. Oxford: Oxford University Press, 1982.

Phillips, Christopher. *Socrates Café: A Fresh Taste of Philosophy.* New York: W. W. Norton, 2001.

———. "What Happens at Socrates Café," in *Cafe Conversations: Democracy and Dialogue in Public Spaces*, edited by Michael Picard. Vancouver, BC: Anvil Press, forthcoming.

Picard, Joseph Romeo William Michael. "Impredicativity and Turn of the Century Foundations of Mathematics: Presupposition in Poincaré and Russell." PhD diss., Massachusetts Institute of Technology, 1993. http://hdl.handle.net/1721.1/12498.

Picard, Michael. "Bewusstsein und Realität: Die Frage des Idealismus in der frühen indischen Philosophie." Unpublished invited lecture. Gesellschaft für Philosophische Praxis, Bergisch-Gladbach, Germany, August 16, 2019.

———. "But Is It Philosophy? Cafe Philosophy and the Social Coordination of Inquiry." In *Practicing Philosophy*, edited by Aleksander Fatić and Lydia Amir, 163–81. Newcastle upon Tyne, UK: Cambridge Scholars Publishing, 2015.

———, ed. *Cafe Conversations: Democracy and Dialogue in Public Spaces.* Vancouver, BC: Anvil Press, 2022.

———. "Integrity: A Philosophical Exploration." *Proceedings of the XXIII World Congress of Philosophy: Philosophy of Values*, Volume 68, 95–98. Athens: Greek Philosophical Society, 2018. https://doi.org/10.5840/wcp232018681518.

———. "Mythology." *Philosophers' Café* (SFU Continuing Studies, Living Thoughts) (Spring 2008): 2–3.

———. *Philosophy: Adventures in Thought and Reasoning* (2007). Revised ed. New York: Metro Books, 2012.

———. "Philosophy Sports as the Next Café Philosophy." In *Cafe Conversations: Democracy and Dialogue in Public Spaces*, edited by Michael Picard. Vancouver, BC: Anvil Press, 2022.

———. *This Is Not a Book: Adventures in Popular Philosophy*. London: Quid, 2007.

———. "Tug of Logic: A Competitive Board Game for Collaborative Reasoning." *University of British Columbia, Vancouver Campus*. May 31, 2019. https://ecps.educ.ubc.ca/tug-of-logic-a-competitive-board-game-for-collaborative-reasoning/ (accessed September 16, 2021).

Plato. *Collected Dialogues of Plato*. Edited by Edith Hamilton and Huntington Cairns. Translations by A. E. Taylor. New York: Pantheon Books, 1961.

———. *Complete Works*. Edited by John M. Cooper. Indianapolis: Hackett, 1997.

———. *Plato's Republic*. Translated by G. M. A. Grube. Indianapolis: Hackett, 1974.

Ricoeur, Paul. *Freud and Philosophy: An Essay of Interpretation*. New Haven, CT: Yale University Press, 1970.

Riess, Helen. *The Empathy Effect: Seven Neuroscience-Based Keys for Transforming the Way We Live, Love, Work, and Connect Across Differences*. Boulder, CO: Sounds True, 2018.

Roberts, Ff. "Stress and the General Adaptation Syndrome." *British Medical Journal* 2, no. 4670 (July 1950): 104–5.

Ross, G. MacDonald. *Leibniz*. Oxford: Oxford University Press, 1984.

Rousseau, Jean-Jacques. *Basic Political Writings*. 2nd ed. Translated by Donald A. Cress. Indianapolis: Hackett, 2011.

Salmon, Wesley C., ed. *Zeno's Paradoxes*. Indianapolis: Hackett, 2001.

Sargeant, Winthrop, trans. *The Bhagavad Gitā*. Edited by Christopher Key Chapple. Albany: State University of New York, 2009.

Sartre, Jean-Paul. *Existentialism Is a Humanism* (1946). Translated by Carol Macomber. New Haven, CT: Yale University Press, 2007.

Sautet, Marc. *Un café pour Socrate: Comment la philosophie peut nous aider à comprendre le monde d'aujourdh'hui*. Paris: Robert Laffont, 1995.

Schopenhauer, Arthur. *The World as Will and Representation*. Translated by E. F. J. Payne. 2 vols. New York: Dover, 1969.

Selye, Hans. *The Stress of Life*. New York: McGraw-Hill; 1956.

———. *Stress Without Distress*. Philadelphia: Lippincott, 1974.

Shackleton, Doris French. *Tommy Douglas*. Halifax, NS: McClelland and Stewart, 1975.

Shakespeare, William. *The Tragedy of Hamlet, Prince of Denmark: Text of 1603 and 1623*, 3rd. Series. Edited by Ann Thompson and Neil Taylor. London: Arden, Thomson Learing, 2006. http://shakespeare.mit.edu/hamlet/ (accessed September 14 , 2021).

Smith, Adam. *The Theory of Moral Sentiment*s (1759). Edited by D. D. Raphael and A. L. Macfie. Indianapolis: Liberty Classics, 1982.

———. *The Wealth of Nations* (1776). Books 1–3. Revised ed. London: Penguin, 1986.

Spinoza, Baruch. *The Ethics: Treatise on the Emendation of the Intellect and Selected Letters*. Translated by Samuel Shirley. Edited by Seymour Feldman. Indianapolis: Hackett, 1982.

Star, Darren. "The Cheating Curve." Directed by John David Coles. *Sex and the City*. July 11, 1999. no. 206. Season 2, Episode 6. New York: HBO, 1999.

Stern, Carrie. "Erick Hawkins." *Dance Teacher*. September 29, 2007. https://dance-teacher.com/erick-hawkins/ (accessed June 6, 2012).

Taylor, Charles. *The Malaise of Modernity*. Concord, ON: House of Anansi, 1994.

Taylor, Shelley E., Laura Cousino Klein, Brian P. Lewis, Tara L. Grunewald, Regan A. R. Gurung, and John A. Updegraff. "Biobehavioral Responses to Stress in Females: Tend-and-Befriend, Not Fight-or-Flight." *Psychological Review* 107, no. 3 (2000): 411–29. https://doi.org/10.1037/0033-295x.107.3.411.

Thomson, James F. "Tasks and Super-Tasks." *Analysis* 15, no. 1 (1954): 1–13. https://doi.org/10.1093/analys/15.1.1. Reprint. *Zeno's Paradoxes*, edited by Wesley C. Salmon, 89–102. Indianapolis: Hackett, 2001.

Thurman, Robert A. F., trans. *The Tibetan Book of the Dead*. New York: Bantam Books, 1994.

Truth and Reconciliation Commission of Canada. *Honouring the Truth, Reconciling for the Future: Summary of the Final Report of the Truth and Reconciliation Commission of Canada*. 2015. http://www.trc.ca (accessed August 13, 2021).

U.S. North American Bird Conservation Initiative (NABCI). *The State of the Birds 2019 Report*. Washington, DC: U.S. Department of Interior, 2019. https://www.stateofthebirds.org/2019/wp-content/uploads/2019/09/2019-State-of-the-Birds.pdf (accessed September 12, 2021).

Walshe, Maurice, trans. *The Long Discourses of the Buddha: A Translation of the Dīgha Nikāya*. Boston: Wisdom Publications, 1987.

Wittgenstein, Ludwig. *Culture and Value*. Edited by G. H. von Wright and Heikki Nyman. Translated by Peter Winch. Chicago: University of Chicago Press, 1980.

———. *Philosophical Investigations*. Translated by G. E. M. Anscombe. Oxford: Basil Blackwell, 1958.

Wosk, Yosek. "Simon Fraser University's Philosophers' Café: A Synoptic History." In *Cafe Conversations: Democracy and Dialogue in Public Spaces*, edited by Michael Picard. Vancouver, BC: Anvil, 2021.

Zehm, Günter Albrecht [Pankraz]. "Pankraz, Dr. Achenbach and das denkende Herz." *Die Welt* 38, February 15, 1982.

Zukav, Gary. *The Dancing Wu Li Masters: An Overview of the New Physics*. New York: Bantam Books, 1979.

Discography

Cohen, Leonard. "The Stranger Song." *Songs of Leonard Cohen* (album). New York: Columbia Records, 1967.

Fekaris, Dino, and Frederick J. Perren. "I Will Survive." *Love Tracks* (album), by Gloria Gaynor. London: Polydor, 1978.

Garcia, Jerry, and Robert Hunter. "Eyes of the World." *Wake of the Flood* (album). Sausalito, CA: Grateful Dead Records, 1973.

Lady Gaga, Natalie Hemby, Hillary Lindsey, and Aaron Raitiere. "I'll Never Love Again." *A Star Is Born* (album). Los Angeles: Sony Records, 2018.

Page, Jimmy, and Robert Plant. "Stairway to Heaven." *Led Zeppelin IV* (album). Los Angeles: Atlantic, 1971.

Presley, Elvis. *50,000,000 Elvis Fans Can't Be Wrong: Elvis' Gold Records, Vol. 2* (album). Hollywood, CA: RCA Victor, 1959.

Index

About the Author

Michael Picard teaches philosophy at Douglas College in Vancouver, BC, Canada. Picard holds an MSc and PhD in Philosophy from Massachusetts Institute of Technology, and is an APPA-certified philosophical counsellor. He founded and facilitated Café Philosophy in Victoria, BC, Canada, a series of public participatory philosophy events that ran weekly for over twelve years, later creating Philosophy Sports to improve the depth and dynamics of participatory philosophy. Author of the award-winning philosophy primer, *This is Not a Book* (Quid, 2007), he is currently preparing English translations of *Philosophical Practice* and *On Right in Wrong*, by Gerd Achenbach, German philosopher and pioneer of philosophical praxis. He has taught widely on the subjects of logic, psychology, cognitive science, leadership, and sustainability.